WATERCOLOR IN ARCHITECTURAL DESIGN

WATERCOLOR IN ARCHITECTURAL

ARCHITECTURAL

Ronald J. Kasprisin

DESIGN

VNR VAN NOSTRAND REINHOLD
New York

Library of Congress Catalog Card Number 89-34043
ISBN 0-442-22925-9

Printed in the United States of America

Designed by East End Graphic Arts

Van Nostrand Reinhold
115 Fifth Avenue
New York, New York 10003

Van Nostrand Reinhold International Company Limited
11 New Fetter Lane
London EC4P 4EE, England

Van Nostrand Reinhold
480 La Trobe Street
Melbourne, Victoria 3000, Australia

Nelson Canada
1120 Birchmount Road
Scarborough, Ontario, M1K 5G4, Canada

16 15 14 13 12 11 10 9 8 7 6 5 4 3 2 1

Library of Congress Cataloging in Publication Data

Kasprisin, Ronald J.
    Watercolor in Architectural design: a handbook
    for students and professionals/
    Ronald J. Kasprisin.
        p.   cm.
    Includes index.
    ISBN 0-442-22925-9
    1. Color in design.   2. Watercolor painting —
    Technique.
    I. Title.
    NK1548.K38   1989
    745-4 — dc20

To
Jennifer Kasprisin
My "wet-on-wet" Specialist

Contents

Foreword

Capturing the reality of the world around us has been the traditional use of watercolor as a medium. In this expansive volume, Ronald Kasprisin extends the boundaries of watercolor to its use as an effective means of visualization in the design process itself. The very act of sketching and painting with watercolors is a creative process, and its use in the design process is therefore appropriate and sympathetic.

Because the design process and the act of placing pigment suspended in a water medium onto a paper surface share certain dynamic qualities, it might be useful also to point out other similarities between the two. In both the creative process and the use of watercolors, the fluency and flexibility of approach are essential. In producing the values, colors, patterns, and textures that simulate the three-dimensional reality of what might be, the watercolorist must be selective in choosing the palette and controlling the direction of the process. Yet, even after planning the organizational composition of the image to be painted, the accidental nature of the watercolor process demands that one be able to take advantage of chance. The unique interaction of water, pigment, brush, and surface also requires that one must be able to tolerate the ambiguity of painting without being able to predict the outcome. Finally, the use of watercolors in the design process encourages the designer to see in new ways and to go beyond the world of white, gray, and black.

Although the focus of this handbook is the watercolor medium, perhaps the more important lesson it contains is the thoughtful and creative use of visualization, which is critical to any design process. Whether drawing with a pencil or painting with watercolors, we all are capable of imagining and visualizing design choices and therefore of having some control in the decisions that will affect our future.

Frank Ching

Preface

Watercolor in Architectural Design is a handbook describing the use of watercolor in the design professions. It is specifically addressed to architects, urban designers, and landscape architects but also serves as a resource for interior design and other design professions to which color communication is important.

This book discusses the importance of watercolor as a model for design, its application to the design professions, and the approaches and techniques available to the designer to achieve quality results. The book should be useful to both designers who require specific instructions on technique as well as those who are searching for an exciting art form through which they can represent their ideas and designs.

First, *Watercolor in Architectural Design* helps both students and professionals develop an understanding of the process of watercolor painting. Second, it teaches students and practitioners methods and techniques that they can use to become proficient in watercolor. And third, it explains the process of using watercolor in the actual act of design, not only making color decisions but also using each individual's own expression with watercolor as a means of exploring design shapes, images, and concepts.

Watercolor images combine form, pattern, color, and concepts into one graphic visualization, and I hope that this book will lead many designers—not only artists—to experiment more with watercolor as a communicative and design tool.

I wish to thank Molly and Jennifer Kasprisin for their interest and encouragement during the enjoyable but long process of writing this book, and I also wish to thank Francis D. K. Ching for making this project possible in the first place.

My special thanks go to James Godwin Scott, who taught me that painting is communicating the essence of a place for others to experience through the painter's eyes.

The artwork was photographed by Gregory Minaker and Joe Manfredini (Seattle). Unless otherwise noted, the watercolor and pen and ink illustrations are by Ron Kasprisin, architect and urban planner. Some of the watercolor illustrations were sketched first from photographs of architectural subjects. A list of photographers and architects is included in the References.

WATERCOLOR

A Medium for Communicating Design

Watercolor for Designers

Chapter

1

Communicating with Watercolor

This is a book about communicating with watercolor in the design professions. As a medium for design, watercolor has often been an intimidating medium for designers, because of its ever-changing characteristics and also because of its inability to be reproduced economically. This book will attempt to help the designer develop confidence using watercolor and will demonstrate its flexibility as a design tool, presentation technique, and art form. Rendering with watercolor is secondary to its use as a design tool and art form.

Perhaps more than any other medium, watercolor requires the user to design his or her painting with great care, because once the painting is begun, the dynamic characteristic of the medium requires fast,

decisive action. Watercolor also requires understanding how the parts relate to the whole in both application as well as design. Because the end result can rarely be reworked, as it can in acrylics and oils, the pieces must be related in design and coordinated in tone and intensity while the painting is being done.

Watercolor is the epitome of the overall design process with the painter translating an idea or subject into desired images with tools and materials and solving problems as he or she progresses. Watercolor is evolutionary, being mixed with both determinism and chance.

The designer enters into a symbiotic relationship with the medium, a creative partnership. Once the watercolor application has begun, the designer relinquishes control over the end result and becomes a part of the act, constantly making deci-

sions and solving problems as he or she responds and adapts to the actions or effects of the watercolor as it reacts with the paper and previously applied pigments. The key principle is that the means is the end, and the final result is distinctly different from the original intent. The end result is a combination of the designer's interpretation of the subject material, the watercolor medium's fluidity and energy, the designer's hand-tool skills, and the essence of the subject itself.

Professional designers often end up with the same image as the one they began with, untouched by the graphic communication process. This book contends that such designers should collaborate with their working medium (watercolor, pen and ink, colored pencils, computers, or whatever) and participate in an evolutionary process, that is, one that changes every

3

time a problem is identified and solved on paper, altering the actual design from the intended design. Unfortunately, many designers slip through this graphic exploration phase and produce results that are either clichés or mere intellectual exercises, simply because they neglected to play or participate with their medium in the design process. Again, this book demonstrates the potential of watercolor as a creative partner in this collaborative act we call design and tries to encourage more designers to become artists.

The Background of This Book

Watercolor in Architectural Design began a number of years ago as a reworking of Arthur Guptill's *Color in Sketching and Rendering*, last published in 1949 by Reinhold Publishing Corporation of New York.

Arthur Guptill drew on his knowledge and experience as an architect and an artist to depict the practical uses of watercolor in what was then termed *representative painting*. Today we refer to it as *realism*, a translation or rendering of what actually exists (or could exist) regarding the built environment. Guptill relied on his talks and lectures at the Pratt Institute and the Brooklyn Institute of Arts and Sciences to create a foundation course in sketching, using watercolor as the medium. He targeted his book to "the architect and such of his professional relatives as the landscape architect and the interior decorator." His book is perhaps the last such specific reference book on watercolors for professional designers and students of professional programs. Although there are a myriad of "how to" watercolor books on the market for artists, few since Arthur Guptill's have been written for the design professions.

Watercolor in Architectural Design begins where *Color in Sketching and Rendering* left off, that is, as an updated reference book for designers interested in preparing realistic renderings or illustrations of work after the design has been completed. In addition, once I started to explore the concepts of color as light and the design process inherent in the act of watercolor, I soon found that color was a dynamic design tool, an energy or force in motion, that should be an integral part of the design process from inception to completion, not an afterthought of applied color.

Designers and/or students do not need to be master artists in order to be accomplished in watercolor communication and thinking. More important is their desire to reach that level of proficiency at which they can communicate concepts and ideas, both realistic and semi-abstract, to both designers and observers. At this point as well, design illustration often becomes its own art form.

This book, therefore, has two objectives:

1. To give designers enough information about materials, equipment, techniques, and approaches to enable competent and effective communication and illustration.
2. To introduce designers to watercolor energy as a design tool, in the same manner that a pen, pencil, or marker is used to create shape, pattern, and proportion, except that watercolor is both "moving" pigment and light balancing the traditional black-and-white representation of building form through hue, tone, and intensity of light.

When an observer views an urban scene —composed of buildings, landscapes, and other artifacts—the first impression that registers in the eye and mind is light (as color) defining shapes. If the observer squints his or her eyes, the scene will become a series of light and dark shapes with midtone grays (warm and cool) and highlight hues (colors). Then, when the observer begins to focus on various shapes, the buildings' dimensions, massing, components, and proportions become evident. But the first image, translated into the brain as light and dark shapes, is light (color). If we can appreciate the impact of light (color) on all forms of the city, we can begin to develop a new sense of perspective for design, one that may expand the modernist and functional design directions of previous decades of design.

Pigment and Light

More than any other medium, watercolor has the unique ability to both absorb and reflect multiple light particle-waves, because of its distinguishing characteristic, transparency. The reason that watercolor is transparent is that it is a suspension of pigment particles in a water solution. When applied to white paper, the water–pigment solution, or *wash,* is of such a density as to permit light to pass through it, thereby striking the paper and being reflected back to the eye of the observer. Along the way, pigments either absorb the light particle-waves or reflect them, thus creating a color image. Watercolor becomes luminous and bright, literally enlightened when the light reflected from the white paper passes back through the layers of pigment in the wash. It is this excitement and this energy of watercolor that I wish to impress upon and to make useful to the designer.

Watercolor's Potential as a Design Tool

Human settlements, both large and small, are direct, three-dimensional reflections or physical translations of a society's dynamics, that is, its physical, behavioral, economic, and social energies or forces. These settlements' built form has become complicated, in part because of the complex overlay and interaction between individual and group, among the group's functional needs, and between those needs and the space available in which to obtain or provide the necessities of (urban) living. Most contemporary civilizations are situated in semichaotic urban complexes, created by inherited frameworks and new social and economic pressures, and in physical envelopes or enclosures that attempt to "package" these urban dynamic forces. The designer—whether architect, planner, landscape architect, or interior designer—is therefore confronted with the challenge of making sense out of the multiple layers (in time and space) of urban dynamics.

As designers, we have certain basic choices for what we do and how we do it. For example, we can choose to design urban enclosures based on corporate or institutional program efficiency and budget, to design them based on a need for peer-group and monetary recognition and achievement, or to design them to respond and react to the individual and collective dynamics contained in those enclosures. Or we can base our choices on the design itself. All of these motives are valid; most are interchangeable; but the product, the urban enclosure (and interior) is generally anonymous (corporate and institutional, regardless of peers' accolades on form and style), expedient (convenient, guided by economics), and/or disordered.

What does all this have to do with watercolor? Watercolor as a process parallels that of urban design, requiring the designer to simultaneously integrate multiple technical skills, which reinforces the discipline of design. Watercolor is the full spectrum of light, represented by shapes in patterns versus the "norm" of black and white represented by calligraphy. These characteristics can enrich the process of urban design through their application in design. Indeed, color, as represented in watercolor, is a dimension absent from both the urban process and the specific architectural product.

The need for designers to incorporate color in the design process has long been debated. Purists—in regard to structure and form—may argue for omitting color and instead emphasizing architectural systems. Others may believe that decoration —ornament and facade—override the expression of these systems. In both approaches, color as light is often minimized or ignored entirely as "coating," a superficial application of pigment.

Color as light creates reflective images on our senses. In the hands of a designer, these images can help define the product (individually and collectively, as in the urban scale) being designed, by being incorporated in the design process from its conceptualization. Because watercolor is both a design process and a representation of color as light, I cannot overemphasize its importance to the built form of human settlements. If our discussion of watercolor does nothing more than educate the designer—whether the systems are purist or decorative in regard to the dynamics of changing light (chroma and tone) on a building enclosure—then it will have succeeded. Our addition of hue to the existing use (albeit implied) of chroma and tone will awaken interest in color as a design element, as ever-changing light images.

In *Color in Townscape,* Duttman, Schmuck, and Uhl (1981) traced the rebirth of color in architecture and investigated the discussions at the turn of the century between colorists and noncolorists. These authors quoted Fritz Schumacker in his 1901 *Color in Architecture:*

> The entire aesthetic economy of a building should rightly include color as prime element from the outset; barring the most primitive designs, one cannot hope to enrich a construction that has been conceived without a thought to color by tacking it on afterwards. . . . The process of architectural design must itself be different if color effects are desired than if drab neutrality will suffice. (Duttman et al. 1981, p. 10)

Color in the urban setting can be provocative, for both the observers of the setting and the designers assessing the role and degree of its use. Does color in our cities act as a mere backdrop, or does it actually affect our working and living environment?

> If whatever is new, interesting, unusual has the power to provoke us, then color can have that power too. . . . The more provocative a stimulus is to our perception, the more it can set creative power free, excite the desire to take an active part in shaping our surroundings. Once imagination is stimulated to produce new and individual images, the chances are that some of them will be images of freedom. (Duttman et al. 1981, p. 27)

Explorations in Process

To bring the previous discussions into focus, let us discuss the advantages and disadvantages of watercolor as a design and communicative tool for designers.

Watercolor, like any serious design process, requires the following basic steps:

Phase 1   Preparation and setup of the materials needed to construct the watercolor.

Phase 2   Selection and awareness of the subject or content, by means of diagrams summarizing the composition, viewpoint, light and shadow, and tone.

Phase 3   Preparation of a sketch draft, represented by smaller sketch studies experimenting with hue, chroma, composition, focus, and the like.

Phase 4   Problem solving, in which materials, techniques, and concepts are mixed, tested, evaluated, modified, retested, and committed.

Phase 5   Layout of the final painting on quality materials.

Phase 6   Painting of the final image, the design itself.

Phase 7   Presentation of the finished product.

Obviously, every painting effort does not have to be as elaborate as this. As the designer's experience increases, these phases will become more automatic. than deliberate. But because this process does parallel the overall urban design process, it can be applied directly to architecture, landscape architecture, and interior design. For example, consider the following suggestions:

- When selecting your work materials, be sure to include a watercolor sketchbook for color diagrams and sketch studies.
- During the survey and inventory phase, when the site and area data are assembled and analyzed for problems, potential, and program elements, use small watercolor diagrams to represent the data. Unusual site features or program requirements can be doodled in your sketchbook, alongside your field trip notes. Your doodles can then be photographed and put on slides for impressive presentations to clients and/or citizen groups. The result of this doodling should be "force" or "determinants" diagrams that impress on your mind (and your clients') the key issues of the site.

Color also will add a surprising dimension to the diagrams that you previously completed in black and white during this stage.

- Another use for watercolors in design is during the concept development stage of a design, in which formality should be abandoned and replaced with looseness and spontaneity. Use watercolor blocks or larger sketch pads for more focused work. Beginners may use watercolor for massing and large color shapes and patterns, adding detail with colored pencil, felt pens, pencil, or technical pens (a very effective beginning). At this stage, watercolor can stimulate the designer in three ways: First, color (like pen and ink shadows on a building site plan) provides an interesting and stimulating art form in the guise of technical design. Second, for the designer, color creates a sense of realism or context, whether in plan diagrams or three-dimensional sketches. And third, watercolor helps form evolutionary directions for the use of color in shapes and patterns within the design itself.
- Watercolor can also be used to study tone with a minimal interest in hue. For example, one color can be used to provide washes for ink or pencil drawings as background, shadows, light and dark highlights, and the like, all representing the play of light on building surfaces.
- The "temperature" of materials—warm and cool in appearance—can be effectively portrayed by watercolor and is most helpful in selecting materials and colors.
- There are two differences in the application of watercolor, as opposed to that of oils, colored pencils, and acrylics: First, watercolor is not as predictable or controllable as are the other media. Even in the hands of an experienced artist, its very nature (pigment in water solution) is flowing, merging, and generally kinetic —"accidents" are commonplace and often welcome. Second, watercolor is luminous and transparent, acting as "see-through" layers that allow the designer much flexibility in experimenting with materials, shapes, patterns, and textures.
- Watercolor is a valuable tool when selecting the color forms and color schemes for final design products, as well as the final graphic representation of those products. The designer can choose among the precision of realism, the mood and conceptualization of semi-abstraction, or the imagery of abstraction.

Even in an urban setting, color is still spontaneous, provocative, and alluring. If more designers investigated, through the medium of watercolor, the use of color in their design process, human settlements would benefit from a more conscious but still provocative, still accidental, and yet connected application of color and space. Our cities mirror our behavior and attitudes, but by and large we have built them without "seeing" them. But as vital extensions of ourselves, cities deserve the expression of vigor and energy we so enthusiastically lavish on ourselves.

Not everyone will agree with the importance placed on color in design in this book, and for them, this book should be considered a reference for watercolor rendering. But for others who wish to incorporate color into urban, architectural, landscape, or interior design, I hope that this book will have fulfilled its goal of providing inspiration, examples, and techniques.

References

Bechtel, Robert B. 1977. *Enclosing Behavior*. Stroudsburg, Pa.: Dowden, Hutchinson, & Ross.

Duttman, Martina, Schmuck, Friedrich, and Uhl, Johannes. 1981. *Color in Townscape*. San Francisco: Freeman.

Guptill, Arthur L. 1949. *Color in Sketching and Rendering*. New York: Reinhold.

A Definition of Color

What Is Color?

The scientific concept of color is still being debated, whether light (the source of color) is composed of waves or of particles. But for architects, planners, landscape designers, or interior designers, color does not really need to be defined, except to say that although the definition is conceptual, the concrete rules of application still seem to work. Indeed, the principles governing the application of color have been—long and widely—accepted and used.

An interesting comparison between the Newtonian and quantum physics' conception of light and color was made by Gary Zukav in his overview of the new physics, *The Dancing Wu Li Masters* (1979). In this new physics, light represents energy, and it affects the observer of light in ways that

transcend simple refraction. To the artist-designer, color is a component of light; that is, it is the effect of wavelengths (or particles or both) of light viewed in a combined manner (white) or as separated into different hues (colors) after being influenced by atmospheric and material compositions. To metaphysicists, light is the prime source of all energy in the universe. Because color is light, reflected or refracted, light as a primary energy is transmitted to the world through color.

Color is to watercolor as ink is to an etching: Each has a power of expression. Color, however, has the added dimension created by its interaction with light. Unfortunately, the seeming complexity of this dimension—its choice and use—discourages many designers and artists from using its full expression in watercolor.

PRINCIPLES

Light creates color. Thus without light, color would not exist. Contrary to popular belief, green grass in the dark is not green —it is colorless! (Mayer 1985, Wilcox 1983). As light is diminished, color is also diminished, not merely masked.

Each color is thought to be a separate wavelength (or particles grouped in a wave), usually perceived together as the color white or daylight. No color predominates in this combined state, yet each has its own wave characteristics. If the colors or waves are separated—for example, through a prism's angles—the various color waves can be distinguished. Those waves that have the shortest wavelengths (the distance between the centers of each wave) and that vibrate the most will bend the most. Thus, as each wave is separated from the white light, its own color or hue can be distinguished as it strikes a white surface. The primary and secondary colors of the light spectrum, from the longest to the shortest wavelength, are red, orange, yellow, green, blue, and violet.

Separating light, as with a prism's angles, is not the only means of distinguishing colors. More commonly, color becomes visible when it strikes a surface, because it is reflected in varying combinations of waves by the molecular composition of the surface. For example, black surfaces absorb the most light waves, whereas white surfaces reflect almost all light or color waves; yellow surfaces absorb all color waves except yellow; and so on. A black surface actually heats up, because it stores (absorbs) so much light. The reflections of combinations of different wavelengths also form various combinations of color (Mayer 1985, Wilcox 1983).

An example of white light being visibly divided into its component colors is the rainbow diagram (Mayer 1985, Wilcox 1983). Light entering one drop (or sphere) of rain is separated into its color components. As the raindrop falls (because of gravity) and the sun stays in its relative fixed position, the angle of reflected light changes and thus changes the perceived color of the raindrop as it falls. The observer on the ground sees only a band of color created by the constantly replenished and constantly falling raindrops. The color remains fixed in each band for a given pe-

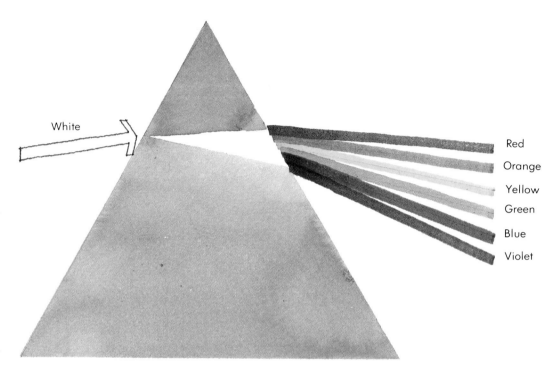

White

Red
Orange
Yellow
Green
Blue
Violet

Color Separation

riod of time, owing to the fixed position of the sun and the consistency of the rain (or mist) in the air. Only those colors reflected at certain angles relative to the observer on the ground are visible.

DAYTIME EFFECTS ON COLOR

The time of day affects the colors of the world and everything in it. At sunrise and sunset, the longer wavelengths reach our eyes first, after being dispersed by particles in the atmosphere. The yellows and reds are dominant. As midday approaches, the shorter wavelengths reach the earth, with the blue and violets being refracted by the atmospheric particles. The blues mix with the white light to form the blue to pale blue skies we associate with our planet. By midday the light overhead tends to be

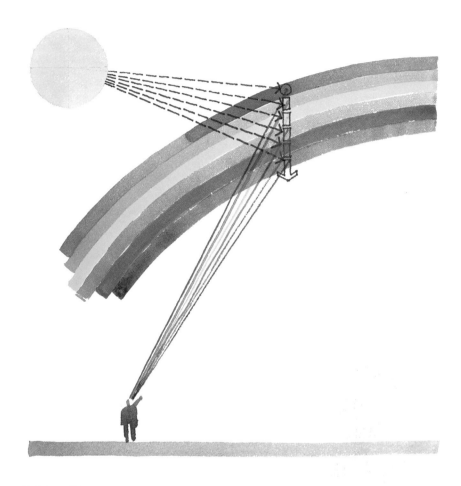

Rainbow Diagram

similar to a giant mixing bowl in which the particle mass bounces and refracts the light waves at many different angles, creating a neutral color image.

GUIDELINE 3

Owing to the time of day, type of cloud cover, and atmospheric particles, not all objects in space (buildings, landscapes, and the like) have one consistent color but are constantly changing hue. Their "local" color is like a chameleon reacting to environmental factors.

GUIDELINE 4

A List of Daytime Color Patterns

Early morning	yellows to reds
Midmorning	
Midday	light blue to white
Midafternoon	
Late evening	yellows to reds

Properties

The word *color* is a language "envelope" that contains the many aspects of our visualization of different characteristics of light. Color as a concept is composed of

Hues: A label for separate light waves.

Chroma: An intensity of hue, such as strong to weak.

white or very light, because the refracted angle is less oblique. If the atmospheric particles were of a different size, we could very well have a red, yellow, or green sky!

GUIDELINE 1

Midday has the most white light, so that on a cloudless day the colors reflected from earth's surfaces are closest to their true value.

GUIDELINE 2

Clouds refract light and disperse all the wavelengths of color and then reform them to create white-to-gray colors, depending on the density of the clouds. Clouds are

Tone: A value, regardless of hue, representing light to dark.

HUES

The Primary Hues (Color)

A *primary hue* cannot be created from mixing other hues or colors in the spectrum. But two groups of primary hues will, when mixed, produce almost every other hue. These two groups are red, yellow, and blue, used primarily by artists and called the *subtractive primaries,* and red, green, and blue, referred to as the *additive primaries.* The additive group is used primarily in color lighting and is based on the Young–Helmholtz theory of color vision (Sidelinger 1985). According to this theory, red and blue mix to make magenta; blue and green make cyan; and green and red make yellow—all lighter secondary hues. In regard to the application of watercolor, the subtractive primaries, red, yellow, and blue, will be the main emphasis of this book. As most designers know, red and blue make purple; blue and yellow make green; and yellow and red make orange—all darker secondary hues.

The subtractive mixing of colors refers to the combining of two or more substances such as pigments or ink that reflect light. When the three subtractive primaries are mixed in equal proportions, only one-third of the light energy entering the surface of the pigment or ink is reflected, with the remainder being absorbed. Dark gray is the result (Sidelinger 1985).

GUIDELINE 5

A primary hue cannot be made from mixing other hues from the color spectrum.

GUIDELINE 6

When two or more primaries are mixed together, they can produce almost every other hue in the spectrum.

GUIDELINE 7

Paint reflects certain hues or color waves and absorbs others. This absorption causes the colors (as light) to decrease in brightness.

GUIDELINE 8

When the three primary colors are mixed together in equal proportions, gray is the result.

GUIDELINE 9

Two primary hues mixed together produce secondary hues; two secondary hues mixed together produce tertiary hues; and so on.

RELATIONSHIPS

The Color Wheel

A color wheel is an arrangement of hues or colors in the order in which they appear in the spectrum. They are divided into *warm* and *cool* colors as well as *primary, secondary,* and *tertiary* colors. In addition, the wheel contains complementary, or opposite hues, although this is often con-

fusing to artist-designers. *Complementary colors* are any two colors of the spectrum that, when combined, produce a neutral hue. On both the Manual Color Circle and the Munsell Color Circle, the mixtures of opposite hues often referred to as complementary hues produce a neutral gray.

GUIDELINE 10

When opposite or complementary hues are mixed together, they produce various gray colors.

Opposite Hues

The most common subtractive opposite hues are

Red and green

Yellow and purple

Blue and orange

Red-purple and yellow-green

Yellow-orange and blue-purple

Blue-green and red-orange

Again, any set of opposite hues, equal in tone and chroma, will form grays, or more precisely, neutral grays. These opposite grays are warmer and more intense than are grays created from black and white, which lose their intensities when tinted with white or shaded with black. Thus black and white is preferably not used to produce gray (Sidelinger 1985).

Color Wheel

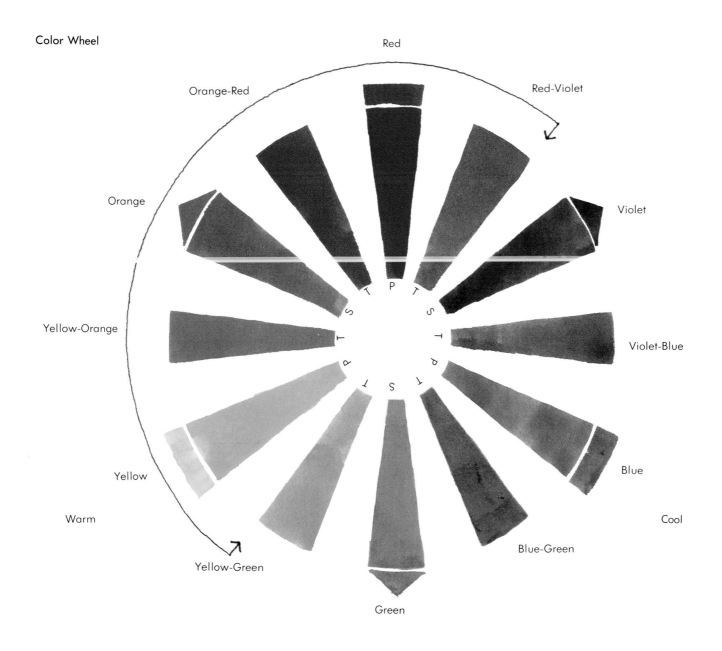

Red

Red-Violet

Orange-Red

Orange

Violet

Yellow-Orange

Violet-Blue

Yellow

Blue

Warm

Cool

Yellow-Green

Blue-Green

Green

When placed side by side in equal amounts, opposite hues contrast sharply; thus the term *opposite* is preferred to *complementary*.

GUIDELINE 11

The closer that two colors come to an opposite relationship in the same temperature (e.g., warm to warm or cool to cool), the more contrast they will achieve.

GUIDELINE 12

If opposite hues are mixed in uneven amounts, they will produce neutrals that lean to the dominant color. Colored neutrals are very effective as shadows and background.

In regard to light and shadow reflected from various building materials, colored neutrals are useful to make surfaces stand out from their light source or to delineate masses and shapes in distant backgrounds.

One effective way to achieve contrast with opposite hues is to use a small proportion of an opposite hue on a larger field of its *neutralized opposite*. In other words, one opposite can be neutralized by another, with the nondominant hue in a smaller proportion (and unneutralized) on the field of the dominant neutralized hue. Overmixing will create "muddy" effects. The reverse combination will also work.

The contrasts between opposites can be muted if they are lightened by means of tinting or darkening. In each case, the contrast of the two opposite colors, regardless of tone, is softened in intensity.

Finally, opposite hues or colors can achieve *harmony* if the darker-tone color is added to the lighter-tone color in graduated segments. This segmentation will produce an incremental addition of parts to achieve an appealing whole.

Munsell Color Tree

Albert H. Munsell's color notation system, which he developed in 1905, is used as a color reference by the United States National Bureau of Standards. The Munsell system is a set of charts arranged three dimensionally into the Munsell Color Tree. The trunk of the tree is a neutral gray, and all of the colors are arranged in circles around the trunk, like leaves on a tree. The Munsell tree shows five principal hues, five intermediate hues, and ten secondary hues.

The five principal hues are

Red

Yellow

Green

Blue

Purple

The five intermediate hues are

Yellow-red

Green-yellow

Blue-green

Purple-blue

Red-purple

The ten secondary hues are

Red-yellow-red

Yellow-red-yellow

Yellow-green-yellow

Green-yellow-green

Green-blue-green

Blue-blue-green

Blue-purple-blue

Purple-purple-blue

Purple-red-purple

Red-purple-red

In the Munsell system, the values (tones) of each hue are determined by comparing each hue against the neutral gray trunk. The lighter-valued hues are at the top, and the darker-valued hues are at the bottom. The nine value levels on the Munsell tree are arranged from N1 at the bottom (pure black) to N9 at the top (pure white). The chroma, or intensity, of a color is arranged in fourteen steps of intensity from the neutral trunk outward, weak to strong.

Temperatures of Colors

Colors can be classified on a color wheel according to their temperature, that is, their warmth or coolness. The warm colors are in the red, orange, and yellow range, and the cools are in the green, blue, and violet range. The following guidelines are to help designers select temperature in colors (Sidelinger 1985).

GUIDELINE 13

Warm colors always contain red or yellow and can generally be classified as

Red-purple

Red

Red-orange

Orange

Yellow-orange

Yellow

White

Cool colors always contain green or blue and can generally be classified as

Blue

Blue-green

Green

Yellow-green

Purple

Blue-purple

All these classifications are relative and so may change depending on the combi-

nations used. For example, a cool yellow-green used with a cool blue would be the warmer of the two colors and so, because of the yellow, could be classified as a warm color. In other words, the preceding rules can be broken.

GUIDELINE 14

Warm (and/or light-tone) colors and black

- Advance toward the observer.
- Have eccentric motion (i.e., radiate and/or expand).
- Can be distinguished from other warm colors.
- Seem larger than cool colors do.
- Seem lighter in weight than cool colors do.
- Seem sunny, opaque, stimulating, earthy, near, and dry.

Cool (and/or dark-tone) colors and black

- Recede from the observer.
- Have concentric motion (i.e., implode, contract).
- Integrate with other cool colors.
- Seem smaller than cool colors do.
- Seem smaller than warm colors do.
- Seem heavier in weight than warm colors do.
- Seem shadowy, transparent, sedate, rare, airy, and wet. (Sidelinger 1985)

GUIDELINE 15

Movement in painting can be created by changing from cool colors on one side of the work to warm colors on the other side, or cool colors in the lower portion of the work to warm colors in the upper portion.

GUIDELINE 16

Warm colors may be cooled by adding a small amount of blue-green or black (not preferred). And cool colors may be warmed by adding a small amount of red-orange or white (not preferred).

One should rely on black and white as little as possible, as they do not provide the intensity of the colors desired. Rather, white and black change both the tone and the intensity of the colors more than they do their temperature.

GUIDELINE 17

Smaller objects or spaces will seem larger and lighter if they are painted with warm (and/or light) colors. And larger objects or spaces will seem smaller and heavier if they are painted with cool (and/or dark) colors.

Proportions

Determining the proportions of colors to mix is often difficult for infrequent watercolor users. Competence comes with practice and more practice. However, the guidelines established by Albert Munsell, Goethe, and others were compiled by Sidelinger in his *Color Manual* (1985). The proportions are measured in numbers of areas rather than the volume of each hue, but the artist can use the same approximate proportions to estimate volumes.

The Goethe System, or the "Harmonious Scale of Areas of Primaries and Secondaries," is based on a balance of the proportions of opposite hues. In this system, a rate number is assigned to each color or hue. This number is the base quantity of area or volume that can be used (proportionately) to mix colors. Theoretically, in order to balance the proportions of two opposite or complementary colors, the rate numbers are simply reversed to determine the appropriate quantities. For example, to create a complementary gray (a balanced mixture) by using orange and blue (opposites), their mixture is balanced by reversing the orange-8 and blue-4 ratings to orange-4 and blue-8, or orange-1 and blue-2, or double the blue, proportionately. The proportions can be measured in drops or parts of paint and inches of area. Remember, however, as Sidelinger (1985) points out, these proportions are valid only for primary and secondary colors.

The Goethe system's proportions are as follows:

Yellow	9
Orange	8
Red	6
Purple	3
Blue	4
Green	6

The *Munsell system* is used to balance more complex colors, by multiplying the chroma number by the value number of the Munsell Color Notation for each color. This system is even more complicated than the Goethe system and becomes mathematically cumbersome for the designer.

GUIDELINE 18

For multicolored proportions, strong contrasting hues (colors), values (tones), and chromas (intensities) should be used in smaller areas and shapes, and weak contrasting hues, values, and chromas should be used in larger areas and shapes.

Grays and Neutrals

Neutrals are created when a third primary is added to a mixture of two other primaries or when two opposites (complements) are mixed together. The three-primary mixture lessens the saturation of the hues and so approaches gray. When mixed equally in chroma, dark gray will result because only one-third of the light (waves) reaches the surface. By varying the proportions, a wide range of true neutral grays is possible. Colored neutrals can be obtained by mixing two opposite (complementary) hues, varying the color range according to the proportions used (see Chapter 3).

GUIDELINE 19

Combine subtle grays with accents or highlights of an opposite color.

GUIDELINE 20

Create "positive" shapes using warm or cool gray backgrounds.

GUIDELINE 21

Use colored neutrals for shadows that harmonize with the "local" color.

Grays are perhaps the most important mixtures to understand and use, and the choice of pigments will determine their warmth or coolness.

References

Mayer, Ralph. 1985. *The Artist's Handbook of Materials and Techniques,* 4th ed. New York: Viking.

Sidelinger, Stephen J. 1985. *Color Manual.* Englewood Cliffs, N.J.: Prentice-Hall.

Wilcox, Michael. 1983. *The Dancing Wu Li Masters.* New York: Watson-Guptill.

Zukav, Gary. 1979. *The Dancing Wu Li Masters.* New York: Morrow.

FUNDAMENTALS

The Elements of Watercolor Use

Watercolor is composed of (1) transparent pigments that allow light to pass through to the paper; (2) lights and darks, which are referred to as *tone* or *value*; (3) warm and cool colors, such as red versus blue, which are referred to as *temperature*; (4) design, in which *shapes* are organized into patterns and compositions to portray images; and (5) *color* or *hue*, which is the name assigned to the various reflected light patterns produced in painting by mixing basic primary colors.

Each artist uses these elements in painting differently. Some artists emphasize design, shape, and color over tone, whereas others are strong tonalists, using light and dark contrasts with more grays to convey their ideas and subordinating one element in favor of others. If designers who are not familiar with watercolors nonetheless understand the role and sequence of their use, they can improve their work accordingly or at least avoid making unnecessary errors.

A Prelude to Painting

When painting with watercolors, numerous tasks and processes must be carried out simultaneously, which may be difficult for the painter until practice encourages the right side of the brain to take the lead. (There is a debate regarding the validity of the right and left brain theory, but suffice it to say that a natural flow takes over once enough experience is logged.)

GUIDELINE 1: PRACTICE

Using watercolors requires practicing techniques and methods in order to coordinate the many spontaneous decisions that painters must make. Painters should therefore be prepared to spend time working on basic techniques in order to become accustomed to the various materials, equipment, and pigments.

GUIDELINE 2: PATIENCE

Each painting (sketch or full-sized sheet) is an experiment in methods and techniques and should not be judged or compared with the work of others. In addition, all watercolor efforts should be completed, regardless of the painter's opinion of the work. The act of completion is an exercise in problem solving, and each completed painting will reward the painter with many lessons learned (and improve the painter's ability to transform a doubtful start into a successful graphic communication). Most paintings go through an "ugly" stage, at which they look hopeless, but it is at this point that the painter should resolve to complete the work—the results will be most surprising.

GUIDELINE 3: MATERIALS AND EQUIPMENT

Although materials should be used economically, good paper, brushes, and pigments will indeed help produce a better final work.

The Process of Painting

When painting with watercolors, the painter must consider numerous factors simultaneously when applying the paint. These factors include

- Tone, that is, light and dark values. Restrict yourself to four values: one light, two midtone, and one dark.
- Temperature, or the warmth or coolness of a color or hue. There should be a dominance of one temperature.
- Shape (and patterns of shapes), that is, the design of the painting, apart from its named subject matter. Represent shape and pattern with variety, interlocking shapes, and directional movement.

- Color, including composition, classifications, transparency, opacity, staining, complements, and mixing. Bright, high key colors are better placed as smaller sizes within a larger warm or cool colorful gray backdrop.

TONE (LIGHT AND DARK)

Tone describes the light or dark value of a painting, usually by using a nine-interval tone scale (see Chapter 5) as the maximum realistic division of lights from darks. But for more practical use, many artists use a five- and even a three-interval scale for painting. The four scales of one light, two midtones, and one dark will help in producing a strongly differentiated value system, especially when the light to dark contrast is emphasized at the focal area.

Tone is assessed and incorporated into a painting regardless of color. It is used to direct the viewer's eye to areas or centers of interest by using light, medium, and dark values of paint, represented by positive and/or negative shapes. For example, a white building shape may be strengthened as the center of interest by placing a dark tree shape in the background, thereby creating a high-contrast value between the white (light) and the dark—apart from the color.

GUIDELINE 4: TONE DEFINITION

Tone represents the light, medium, and dark values of any painting.

GUIDELINE 5: TONE DESIGN

A painting's tone pattern is designed by using white, grays, and black; or even just one color (plus white paper), by increasing or decreasing with water the dilution of the pigment.

GUIDELINE 6: TONE USE:

Tone is used to indicate which shapes in a painting are important, supportive, and subordinate, by means of light, medium, and dark values.

COLOR TEMPERATURE

Colors can generally be classified as *cool* or *warm*, ranging from violet, blue violet, blue, blue-green, and green as the cools and yellow-green, yellow, orange-yellow, orange, red-orange, and red as the warms.

Temperature also can act as a complement, by contrasting a cool shape with a warm shadow or a warm shape with a cool shadow. Temperature is discussed in more depth in "Color Mixing."

GUIDELINE 7: TEMPERATURES OF EARTH AND SKY

The colors of the earth (and reflected from it) tend to be warm, whereas the colors of the sky (and reflected from it) tend to be cool.

GUIDELINE 8: TEMPERATURE DOMINANCE

A painting should be dominated by either a warm or a cool temperature.

GUIDELINE 9: TEMPERATURE CONTRAST

The greatest contrasts between two colors occur between opposite temperature *complements,* for example, red (warm) versus green (cool) and orange (warm) versus blue (cool).

GUIDELINE 10: TEMPERATURE PLACEMENT

Cool colors cause shapes to recede and so are usually placed in background shapes, whereas warm colors bring shapes forward and so are used in foregrounds.

SHAPE

Shape is the basic design element of watercolor; that is, it establishes the spaces for color application. Besides area, shapes have edges or perimeters, which help relate one shape to another. Edges can be *hard, soft, interlocking,* or *lost and found.* A hard edge is a line separating one shape from another; a soft edge is a blending of one shape into another; interlocking edges are shape fragments from each contiguous shape extending into the other shape; and lost and found edges are a variety of hard and soft. The area of a shape has size, tone, color, and detail (texture and calligraphy). In the design of a painting, the overall

pattern of shapes defines what geometry is important, supportive, or subordinate, just as tone does. The placement of shapes then directs the viewer's eye to points of interest within the painting. (Shape is discussed in more detail in Chapter 5.)

GUIDELINE 11: SHAPES WITH NO NAME

Once a painting's theme has been established (for example, an office building or an entry courtyard), and the important supportive and subordinate shapes have been determined, the arrangement of those shapes is designed as shapes with no names, that is, as pure abstractions that in themselves make an attractive design (Schink 1988). The shape organization, pattern, color, tone, and temperature become the design. The object being painted no longer has a verbal name but an image in a graphic language.

GUIDELINE 12: VARIETY

Shapes should be varied for interest and stimulation, and elements should not be repeated unnecessarily.

GUIDELINE 13: SHAPE EDGES

Shapes are often represented by their edges, which indicate round versus square, hard versus soft, and smooth versus rough, and are related to adjacent shapes through contrast, blending, interlocking, and the like. Edges are the act of relating one shape to another, not the end of one shape and the beginning of the next.

COLOR COMPOSITION

Watercolor paints are made from extremely fine textured (ground) pigments that are placed in water-soluble, gum-binding material (Mayer 1985). The watercolor pigments are suspended in the water solution as finely ground particles. The particles do not dissolve, as they are insoluble. If a material does dissolve in the water solution, thereby creating a color, it is called a *dye.*

GUIDELINE 14: PIGMENT COMPOSITION

The pigments for watercolors are the same as they are for oils—it is the material to which they are bonded or in which they are diluted that distinguishes them.

COLOR CLASSIFICATION

Transparent watercolors are classified according to their origin: *organic* and *inorganic.* In recent years, they have also been classified as *natural* or *synthetic.*

GUIDELINE 15: CLASSIFICATIONS

Organic watercolors may be

Vegetable: Gamboge, a gum resin from a tropical Asian tree; indigo, a plant of the legume family; or madder, a vine and its roots.

Animal: Cochineal, dried bodies of female cochineal insects.

Synthetic.

Inorganic pigments (minerals) may be

Native earths: ochre, raw umber, raw sienna.

Calcined (changed to powder by heat) *native earths:* burnt umber, burnt sienna.

Minerals: cadmiums, cobalts, and oxides (Leland 1985, Mayer 1985).

TRANSPARENCY, OPACITY, AND STAINING

As we shall demonstrate in Part 3, transparency in watercolor can be classified as either *highly transparent, semitransparent,* or *opaque.* When mixing other colors from the primaries, highly transparent watercolors are preferred because the mixed colors will retain their transparency; that is, they will still allow white (paper) to be reflected back to the viewer. Semitransparent colors need to be diluted to retain their transparency. When opaque colors are mixed with other colors, they not surprisingly create opaque mixtures, which prevent the passage of light to and from the paper. But even though the opaques are not transparent, many do possess brilliance and intensity and so are important additions to many palettes.

Staining pigments penetrate the fibers of paper and thus color it permanently.

GUIDELINE 16:   TRANSPARENT COLORS

Transparent colors are naturally transparent, allowing the light to penetrate the white (paper) and be reflected.

GUIDELINE 17:   TRANSPARENT COLORS FOR MIXING

Transparent watercolors mix well with all pigments, particularly other transparents, and they are excellent for mixing to create secondary and tertiary colors. Learn to mix other colors from the basic primary triad combinations.

GUIDELINE 18:   SEMITRANSPARENT COLORS

Semitransparent watercolors require more dilution to become transparent.

GUIDELINE 19:   OPAQUE COLORS

Opaque watercolors block light from being reflected back to the eye from the paper and make opaque all mixtures of which they are a part.

GUIDELINE 20:   OPAQUE COLORS FOR MIXING

Opaque pigments are best used by themselves, without mixing. They also are effective when merged, as on wet paper, side by side with another pigment.

In order to test for yourself the transparency factor of each color you use, conduct the following exercise (Leland 1985):

Using a half-inch-wide flat brush, paint a vertical strip of black India ink on watercolor paper. Once the ink is thoroughly dry, paint each watercolor in a half-inch-wide band across the black strip. Examine the horizontal bands. The transparent watercolors make no mark on the black strip. The semitransparent and opaque colors, on the other hand, do leave a telltale mark on the strip. This transparency test is very useful in determining which colors to use in mixtures.

COLOR COMPLEMENTS (OPPOSITES)

The basic color wheel or color circle arranges each hue opposite its complement. The wheel or circle also groups colors by their temperature, warm or cool. Opposite colors complement each other or together complete what is otherwise incomplete; that is, they are stronger together than they are individually. For example, a brick (orange) building is complemented well by a street shadow (blue), providing opposite complements and a warm–cool temperature complement. (The section on color mixing offers guidelines for using color complements.)

Designers and painters should be familiar with the basic color circle, as well as the opposite relationships. Compatible color circles include

Selecting Compatible Pigments

Opaque	Transparent	Semitransparent
(U) cerulean blue	ultramarine blue	(U) raw sienna
cadmium lemon	Winsor blue	Winsor yellow
cadmium yellow	(U) indigo blue	Winsor red
(U) yellow ochre	Antwerp blue	Grumbacher red
(U) Naples yellow	cobalt blue	alizarin crimson
cadmium red light	viridian	(U) brown madder alizarin
cadmium red	Hooker's green dark	permanent rose
(U) Indian red	Winsor green	rose madder genuine
(U) light red	new gamboge	(U) burnt sienna
	aureolin	(U) burnt umber
		(U) Payne's gray, ivory, black, or neutral tint

(U = unsaturated)

Subdivisions of Compatible Pigments

Opaque unsaturated	Bright unsaturated	Old Masters' unsaturated
cerulean blue	indigo	Payne's gray, ivory, black, or neutral tint
yellow ochre	raw sienna	yellow ochre
Naples yellow	brown madder alizarin	raw sienna
Indian red		burnt sienna
light red		burnt umber

Delicate-transparent-saturated	Intense-transparent-saturated	Remainder: opaque and transparent-saturated
Antwerp blue	Winsor blue	ultramarine blue
cobalt blue	Winsor yellow	cadmium lemon
viridian	Winsor red	cadmium yellow
aureolin	Winsor green	cadmium red light
permanent rose	Grumbacher red	cadmium red
rose madder genuine	alizarin crimson	Hooker's green dark
		new gamboge

Source: Nita Leland, *Exploring Color* (Cincinnati: North Light Books, 1985), Fig. VII-4, p. 84.

These triads can be varied if the colors are taken from the same saturated or unsaturated grouping.

The Standard Triad (traditional red, yellow, and blue spectrum

 Cadmium Red

 New Gamboge

 French Ultramarine Blue

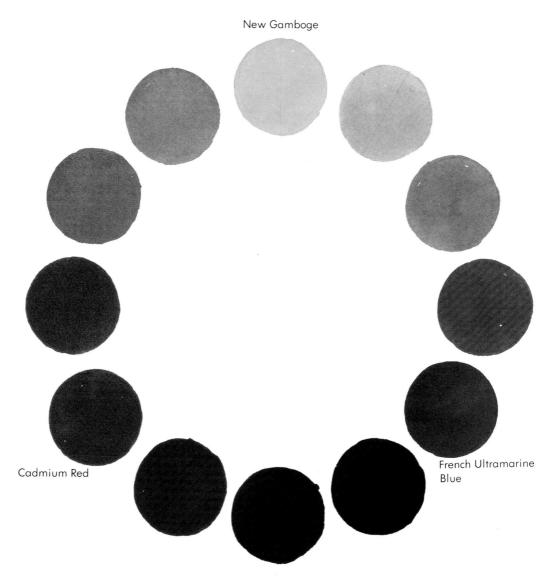

New Gamboge

Cadmium Red

French Ultramarine Blue

The Standard Triad Palette

The Transparent Triad (gentle and transparent)

Rose Madder Genuine

Aureolin Yellow

Cobalt Blue

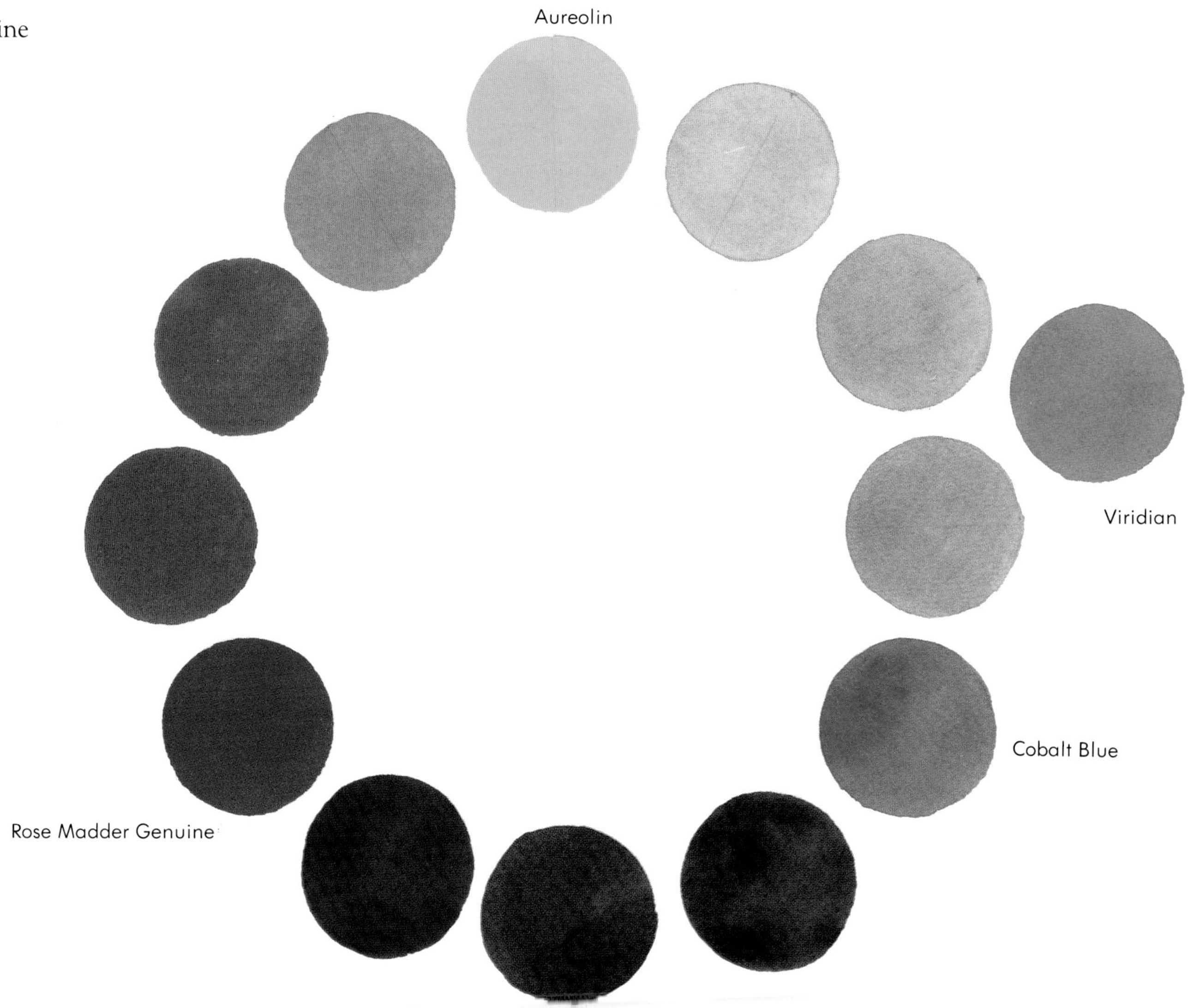

Aureolin

Viridian

Cobalt Blue

Rose Madder Genuine

The Transparent Triad Palette

The Intense Triad (strong)

Winsor Red

Winsor Yellow

Winsor Blue

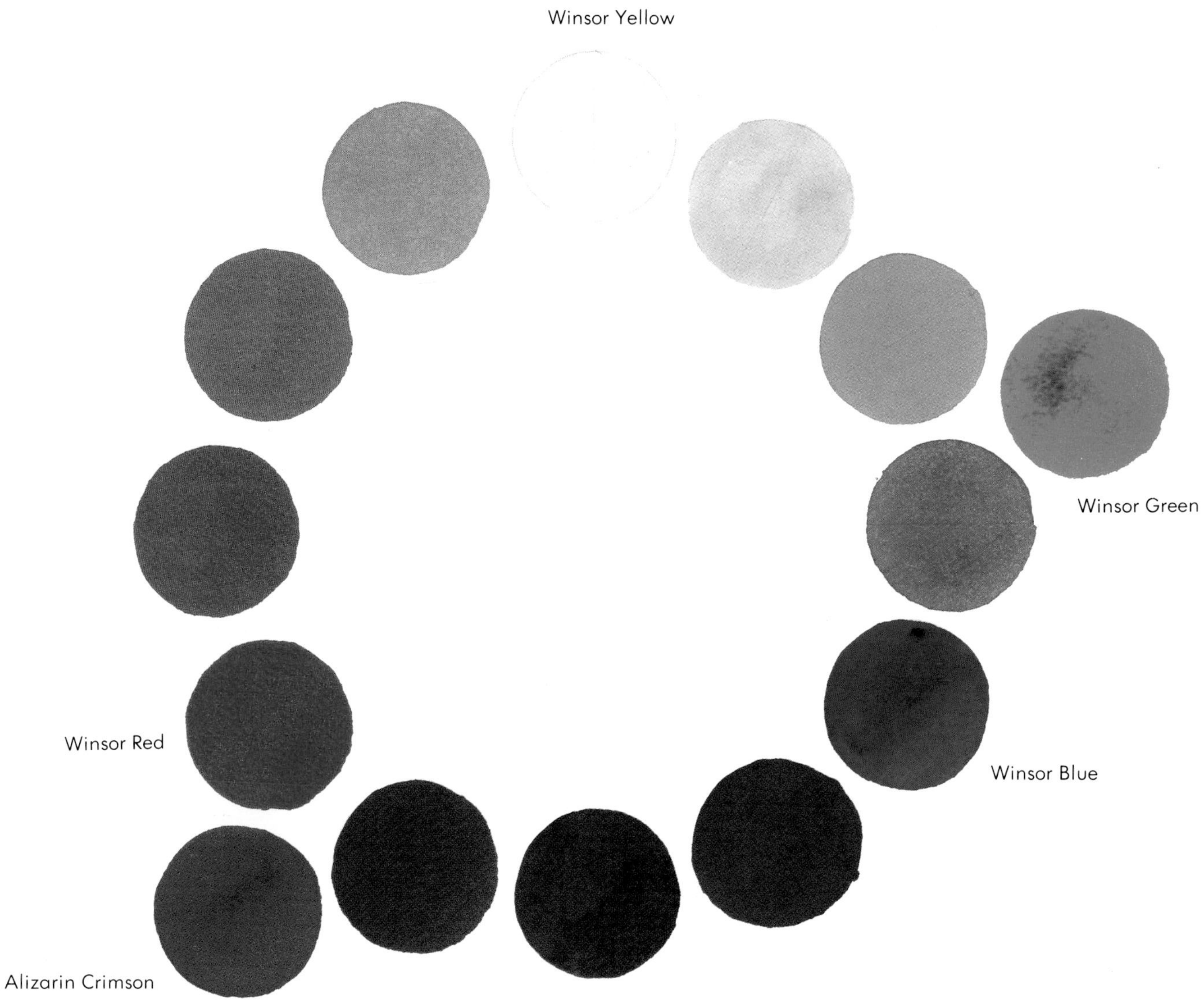

Winsor Yellow

Winsor Green

Winsor Blue

Winsor Red

Alizarin Crimson

The Intense Triad Palette

The Opaque Triad (dense, earthy)

Indian Red

Yellow Ochre

Cerulean Blue

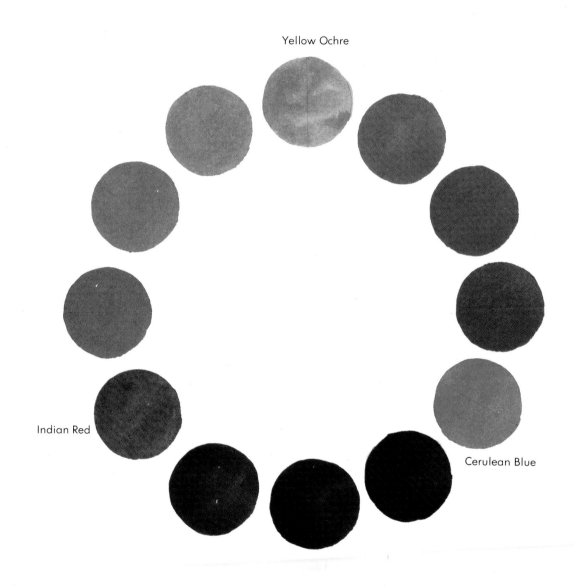

The Opaque Triad Palette

Old Masters' Triad (what many of the Old Masters had available to them)

Burnt Sienna

Yellow Ochre

Payne's Gray

The Bright Unsaturated Triad (rich, bright)

Brown Madder Alizarin

Raw Sienna

Indigo

GUIDELINE 21:   COLOR CIRCLES

Construct each color circle based on its triad of colors and use it for your reference. The act of constructing the circle for yourself is far more valuable than is memorizing the colors within each color circle. Colors vary according to the proportions used in the mixtures and the different brands of pigment.

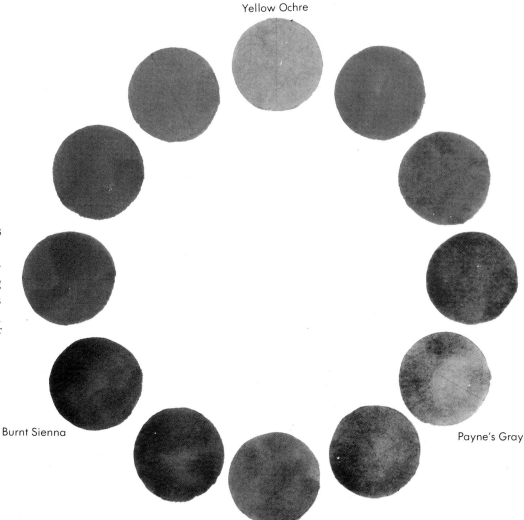

Yellow Ochre

Burnt Sienna

Payne's Gray

The Old Masters's Triad Palette. The Old Masters used Davy's Gray instead of Payne's Gray. They used this palette mainly because many of the contemporary colors did not exist or were not permanent.

MIXING COLORS

The information on triads and compatible color circles gives the designer enough information to begin mixing colors.

GUIDELINE 22: CHOOSING COLORS

Mix your colors from one of the triads rather than using premixed colors straight from the tubes, expanding your palette with stains and selected opaques as desired. This is good experience in determining the appropriate use of color.

Using Complements in Mixtures

GUIDELINE 23: MIXING COMPLEMENTS

The complement of a primary color is a mixture of the two remaining primaries. For example: (1) The complement of red is green, produced by mixing blue and yellow. (2) The complement of blue is orange, produced by mixing yellow and red. (3) The complement of yellow is violet, produced by mixing red and blue.

Mixing Grays from Complements

The grays that can be mixed on the palette from other pigments are far more varied and appropriate than are the tube grays.

GUIDELINE 24: CREATING GRAYS FROM PRIMARIES AND COMPLEMENTS

When a primary is mixed with its complement, a gray is the result. For example,

Grays from Unequal Triad Mixtures

Blue-Gray   Purple-Gray   Rose-Gray

After mixing a neutral gray made up of all three primary colors, add an unequal amount of one primary to achieve a warm or cool gray with a dominant primary color. For added interest, contrast that dominant color with its primary.

red mixed with green (its complement), blue mixed with orange (its complement), and yellow mixed with violet (its complement) all produce grays, each with its own warmth or coolness.

Grays are vital to any painting or illustration, as they provide the background for brilliant colors, vibrancy, and highlights.

GUIDELINE 25: LUMINOUS GRAYS

To mix grays that are luminous and not neutral, that is, that have a distinctive warm or cool temperature, combine unequal amounts of pigments, making one color dominant over the others. It is best to use transparent, not opaque, pigments.

GUIDELINE 26: HIGHLIGHT GRAYS

As a contrast to a gray, use the complement to the dominant color of the gray for a highlight or focal area.

More Grays from Unequal Triad Mixtures

Brown-Gray   Yellow-Gray   Green-Gray

Grays from Primaries and Complements. Mix grays by combining primary color with its complement, for example, blue with orange, to make a blue-gray.

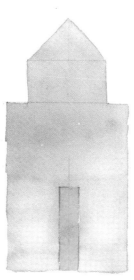

Blue-gray from orange complement

Purple-gray from yellow complement

Rose-gray from green complement

Mixing Vibrant Colors

Mixing vibrant colors requires an understanding of the pigments contained in each color. Use a color circle to determine whether a color is warm or cool and whether it borrows color from its neighboring colors. The following example (Dobie 1986) uses the color circle in this way:

- To mix a violet hue, select a blue pigment (with red in it) and a red pigment (with blue in it). According to the color wheel, you may combine French Ultramarine Blue (a warm blue because of the red in it) with Alizarin Crimson (a cool red because of the blue in it). The result is a bright violet.
- If you mix Winsor Blue (a cool blue with yellow in it) with Cadmium Red (a warm red with yellow in it), a dull violet-gray will result, because yellow is the complement of violet.

GUIDELINE 27: VIBRANT COLORS

- Select the desired color.
- Determine its complementary (opposite) color.
- Select two primaries to mix that do not contain this complement in any of their mixtures.
- Avoid using opaque pigments if possible.

For example:

- Select the desired color, such as vibrant green.

- Determine its complement: red.
- Choose two primaries that are not composed of the complement: Aureolin Yellow (leaning toward blue) and Winsor Blue (leaning toward yellow). Although Winsor Blue is a stain, it is also transparent (see Dobie 1986).

Another example:

- Select the desired color, such as vibrant orange.
- Determine its complement: blue
- Choose two primaries that are not composed of the complement: Cadmium Yellow (leaning toward red) and Cadmium Red (leaning toward yellow).

Mixing Greens

Greens predominate on most architectural and landscape architectural representations. To represent natural greens requires an understanding of the mixture of pigments needed to create both warm and cool greens. Although transparent greens such as Viridian are available, they are not "natural" in color.

In regard to mixing colors, Jeanne Dobie (1986) recommends using, for greens, one of the following four foundation pigments or mixtures:

Viridian + Aureolin Yellow

Winsor Green + Aureolin Yellow

Viridian

Winsor Green

These four greens will produce either cool or warm natural greens.

GUIDELINE 28: TRANSPARENT GREENS

Luminosity and transparency can be maintained by using transparent pigments for mixtures.

GUIDELINE 29: ADDING RED TO GREEN

When adding red (usually opaque) to green, use as little red as possible, as red and green are complements.

GUIDELINE 30: ADDING RED TO YELLOW AND GREEN

When adding red to yellow and green, mix the yellow and green together first, and then add the red in very small amounts until the desired effect is achieved.

GUIDELINE 31: WARM GREENS

Adding yellows to greens plus red produces warmer natural greens.

GUIDELINE 32: COOL GREENS

Adding reds to pure greens (Viridian and Winsor Green) produces cooler natural greens.

GUIDELINE 33: MIXTURE LIMITS

Limit the mixture of pigments to three colors.

GUIDELINE 34: USE OF GREENS

Use the brightest, most intense greens as the center of interest, and gray-greens away from the center of interest.

Aureolin plus Viridian plus Rose Madder Genuine

Aureolin plus Viridian plus Cadmium Red

Viridian plus Rose Madder Genuine

Viridian plus Aureolin

Viridian plus Cadmium Red

Viridian plus Alizarin Crimson

Mixing Greens

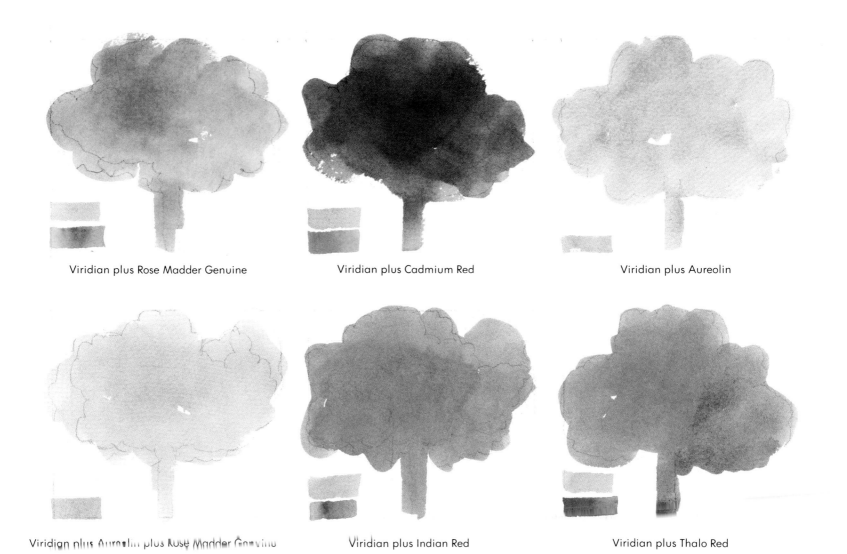

Viridian plus Rose Madder Genuine

Viridian plus Cadmium Red

Viridian plus Aureolin

Viridian plus Aureolin plus Rose Madder Genuine

Viridian plus Indian Red

Viridian plus Thalo Red

Mixing More Greens

Mixing Darks

Although "dark" implies the absence of "light," in nature and in urban settings there is no absolute dark. Shadows, recesses, and other dark representations still are affected by light, local color, and the reflections of adjacent materials. Consequently, darks can be rich, luscious, and even brilliant if the correct colors are combined.

One of the most common complaints of professionals dabbling in watercolors is the flatness and opaqueness of the darks in their work. Overwork and the color mixture are usually the culprits. To prevent this problem, first, avoid premade darks such as black. Few surfaces are truly black but are closer to blue, purple, and dark greens. Second, use darks not only as shadows and recesses but also as backdrops for lights. Third, when applying darks, make them dark enough on the first try.

GUIDELINE 35: COLORFUL DARKS

Darks should be colorful darks, not simply dark contrasts.

GUIDELINE 36: DARK COMPLEMENTS

To contrast a light color, choose a dark that is the complement of that light color.

GUIDELINE 37: STAINING DARKS

Staining colors make intense darks but should be used with care, as they are indelible.

Winsor Blue plus Indian Red

Winsor Blue plus Alizarin Crimson

Winsor Blue plus Cadmium Red

Winsor Blue plus Alizarin Crimson (equal amounts)

Blue-Base Darks

Using blues and greens as the basis for dark mixtures yields rich colors. Although blacks are useful in some applications, mixtures of blue and green, and green and red "color" the dark, giving it depth plus luminosity.

The following diagrams depict mixtures using Winsor Blue, Ultramarine Blue, and Winsor Green. Winsor Blue and Winsor Green are transparent staining colors, and Ultramarine Blue is a more opaque color. In each diagram, a red is added to "naturalize" (Dobie 1986) the base color, giving it a richer, deeper aspect.

GUIDELINE 38: BLUE-BASE DARKS

Winsor Blue or French Ultramarine Blue can be mixed with Indian Red, Cadmium Red, or Alizarin Crimson to create medium darks, either cool or warm in temperature. Each of these darks can be made darker by mixing the blue and red mixtures in near equal amounts and adding less water.

GUIDELINE 39: GREEN-BASE DARKS

Winsor Green can be mixed with Winsor Red, Cadmium Red, Alizarin Red, or Indian Red to create darks. When near equal amounts of red and green are mixed, near black is the result.

Equal Mixtures

Winsor Green plus Winsor Red   Winsor Green plus Cadmium Red   Winsor Green plus Alizarin Crimson   Winsor Green plus Indian red

Green-Base Darks

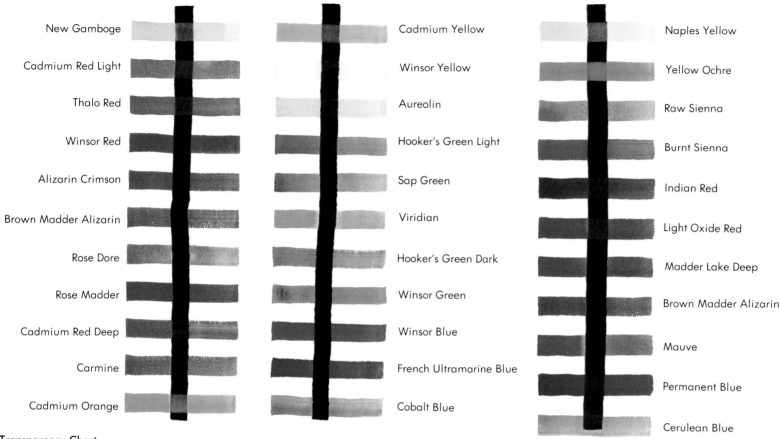

New Gamboge	Cadmium Yellow	Naples Yellow
Cadmium Red Light	Winsor Yellow	Yellow Ochre
Thalo Red	Aureolin	Raw Sienna
Winsor Red	Hooker's Green Light	Burnt Sienna
Alizarin Crimson	Sap Green	Indian Red
Brown Madder Alizarin	Viridian	Light Oxide Red
Rose Dore	Hooker's Green Dark	Madder Lake Deep
Rose Madder	Winsor Green	Brown Madder Alizarin
Cadmium Red Deep	Winsor Blue	Mauve
Carmine	French Ultramarine Blue	Permanent Blue
Cadmium Orange	Cobalt Blue	Cerulean Blue

Transparency Chart

Standard palette

Transparent palette

Intense palette

Opaque palette

"Old Masters" palette

Bright unsaturated palette

Each color circle is based on a *triad* of colors, a group of three colors from which all other colors in the color circle are derived, usually combinations of red, yellow, and blue. The following list of compatible triads consists of opaque, semitransparent, and transparent pigments, which are also subdivided into unsaturated and saturated pigments. (*Unsaturated* pigments are modified by neutral tones, whereas *saturated* pigments are pure, unmixed.) It is not necessary to memorize this list; rather, use it as a reference for creating compatible color circles.

Combinations of triads that form the basis for the color circles are listed next.

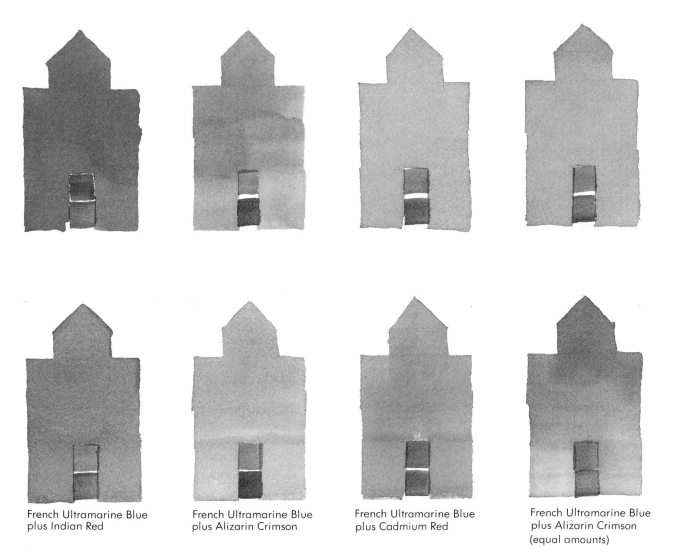

French Ultramarine Blue
plus Indian Red

French Ultramarine Blue
plus Alizarin Crimson

French Ultramarine Blue
plus Cadmium Red

French Ultramarine Blue
plus Alizarin Crimson
(equal amounts)

Staining Darks (Blue)

THE WETNESS EFFECT IN COLOR APPLICATIONS

The three basic approaches to watercolor application are wet on wet, wet on dry, and dry on dry, which are discussed in detail in Part 3. *Wet on wet* is the application of pigment in a water solution to wet paper; *wet on dry* is the same application to dry paper; and *dry on dry* is the application of pigment (straight from the tube or mixed with small amounts of water) to dry paper. Important to understand for all three approaches is the wetness factor or principle.

GUIDELINE 40: THE WETNESS PRINCIPLE

A water solution (with or without suspended pigment) will flow from a more saturated vehicle to a less saturated vehicle.

Example 1: A brush charged with a pigment in a water solution will not release any of its charge (except through gravity) onto a paper saturated with the same amount of water at the point of application.

Example 2: A brush charged with a pigment in a water solution will rapidly release its charge onto a wet paper that is substantially less saturated than is the charged brush.

Example 3: The same brush charge will release most of its water onto dry paper, but the charged solution will puddle on the paper rather than spread because of the dry surface. Furthermore, watercolor paper is "sized" or coated, making it less absorbent than unsized paper is.

GUIDELINE 41: THE DAMP SPONGE

When working with water colors, use a dampened sponge (natural or synthetic) to regulate wetness. The sponge should be kept damp, but drier than the charged brush. The charged brush can be touched to the damp-but-drier sponge to remove any excess solution before the brush is touched to the paper. This permits the painter to control better the amount of pigment in solution that is applied to the painting. A dry sponge thus will not work because there is no solution to act as a carrier within the pores of the sponge. Although the dry sponge will certainly absorb some water, there is not enough water solution in a charged brush to "activate" or charge the sponge.

GUIDELINE 42: WET ON WET

Pigment in solution applied to wet watercolor will spread quickly or slowly, depending on the degree of the paper's water saturation. The wetter the paper is, the more quickly the pigment in solution will spread. Conversely, the drier the paper is, the more slowly the pigment in solution will spread. Many artists use the *wetness sheen* as an indicator of drying speed: When the wet sheen disappears, they add their pigment in solution for a "controlled" spread.

References

Dobie, Jeanne. 1986. *Making Color Sing.* New York: Watson-Guptill.

Leland, Nita. 1985. *Exploring Color.* Cincinnati: North Light Books.

Mayer, Ralph. 1985. *The Artist's Handbook of Materials and Techniques.* 4th ed. New York: Viking.

Schink, Christopher. 1988. Watercolor Workshop, Issaquah, Wash.

Basic Materials

Basic Modes of Painting

For designers, there are two basic modes of painting, which require special equipment: sketching or fieldwork and studio painting. This chapter suggests the materials necessary to achieve successful but economical results in each mode. As painters progress in interest and methods of application, they can add more specialized and better-quality materials. "Recreational" watercolor painting is a popular activity, and there are a myriad of tools and supplies to choose from; but select only what you really need.

SKETCHING

Sketching in the studio or the field should be a simple and mobile process.

Therefore, all your equipment should be compact, light, and easy to use. The recommended materials include

- A small sketchbook and/or watercolor block, such as

    a 6″ x 9″ all-purpose sketchbook for pencil or pen studies, capable also of accommodating light washes.

    an 8½″ x 11″ or smaller sketchbook with a combination of watercolor paper and nonwatercolor paper for studies (see Lynch).

    a 5″ x 7″ watercolor block.
- One half-inch or one one-inch flat brush.
- One round brush, No. 8 or smaller.
- A small folding palette (3½″ x 8″, folded) or a self-contained travel kit that can fit into a pocket or a knapsack.

- A water container (thermos, large glass, or plastic bottle) with a lid.
- A water container for washes and brush charging (small plastic dishes). If you are not using plastic products, small glass jars are excellent.
- Protective clothing.
- A folding seat, for outdoor work.

Other equipment for fieldwork or sketching includes masking fluid, masking tape, soap and/or kneaded erasers, and a soft pencil. Some artists include a magnifying glass that causes the image to recede from view, as a means of evaluating their work's progress. Although this is useful, it is good practice for the painter periodically to step back physically at least four to six feet from the work to evaluate it. To accommodate larger works in the field, such as half- or full-size imperial sheets, a number of mounts and stretching techniques are available: (1) Stretch a sheet of watercolor paper on a piece of plywood, using staples, or on a mounting board with adjustable edges. Or (2) use clamps to fix the watercolor paper to the board; use at least 140-lb paper.

Finally, a tripod is strongly recommended for outdoor work. Tripods range from those that do no more than hold the painting to those that also store paints, brushes, and a water container. The water container can be hung from the bottom of a tripod by the container's handle, or it can be clipped to the tripod with clamps. In any event, keep it simple because you will have to carry all of it.

STUDIO WORK

Studio work affords the artist more time, space, and experimentation. However, it still is important to keep your supplies simple. The basic materials for studio painting include

Paper
- A supply of 140-lb watercolor paper; use half an imperial sheet as the minimum sheet size (an imperial sheet is 22" x 30"). 300-lb paper is excellent, costs more than 140-lb, and needs only to be clamped to a rigid board.
- A sketchbook for tone and temperature studies.

Brushes
- One one-inch flat.
- One two-inch flat for large washes and prewetting.
- One round, preferably a No. 4, 6, or 8.

Board
- A quarter-inch or half-inch sheet of plywood, cut at least 2 inches larger on all sides than the paper size being mounted, so that it is suitable for use with clamps or staples.
- Masonite and plexiglass as a substitute for plywood, particularly when tape or clamps are used instead of staples.

Mounting Materials and Equipment
- Stapler and staples.
- Clamps.
- Self-mounting board with adjustable metal edges.

Water Containers
- Glass or plastic jars of varying sizes.

Palette
- A choice of plastic, china, or enameled metal palettes. Having more than one palette allows different triads to be used for color mixing. Paints can be kept moist on a palette by placing a damp cloth over it when it is not being used. Arrange the colors in the palette by their relationship on the color circle. It is not necessary to clean the palette completely after every use. When you use it again, simply wipe off the surface layer with a damp sponge or cloth, and reuse the pigment underneath. However, do not be stingy with pigment. Add enough to the palette to be effective.

Pigments
- Begin with three pigments, one of the triads, and mix all of the secondaries and tertiaries from the triad. Avoid using white or black to change tone.

Masking Materials
- Masking fluid.
- Masking tape.

Miscellaneous Necessities
- Exacto knife or its equivalent.
- Sponge(s); natural is preferred.
- Drafting brush.
- Mixing saucers.
- Kneaded and/or soap eraser.
- Tripod (for both field and studio work).

Miscellaneous Amenities
- Equipment such as a slide projector and light table.
- Hair dryer (to speed the drying process).

Chapter 12 describes in detail these necessities and amenities, as viewed by many artists and manufacturers. But do not limit yourself to the basic materials and equipment outlined in this chapter. Experiment, and be comfortable. And there is no style or required dress, nor should there be.

Reference

Lynch, Tom. Tom Lynch Watercolors, P.O. Box 1418, Arlington Heights, Ill. 60006.

EXECUTION

Qualities, Elements, and Design Principles

Qualities are those features that make something what it "is." In painting, they are what distinguishes watercolor from oil painting or pastels, beyond the similarities of color and pigment. Many of the qualities described in this chapter pertain to the interaction of light with the medium and to the fluidity or dynamic forces it exhibits.

A watercolor's *elements* are its quantifiable aspects, which give shape, direction, and dimension to the subject being communicated. They are its design elements.

Finally, the rules or methods of application that guide the painter in using the design elements to achieve the qualities of watercolor are its *design principles*.

Watercolor Qualities

TRANSPARENCY

Transparency is the property or quality of watercolor that permits rays of light to enter it and be reflected back. Transparency is the underlying distinguishing characteristic of watercolor.

LUMINOSITY

Luminosity is a quality of watercolor caused by the painting's transparency, which permits the white of the paper to be seen, even in dark applications, through the layers of pigment, thereby maintaining the paper's integrity and influence. Luminosity is an important quality, which separates transparent watercolors from other media. Luminosity is distinguished from transparency by the former's glowing characteristic; that is, a painting can be both transparent and luminous, reflecting light with a special "enlightened" quality.

If designers acknowledge the concept of luminosity while painting, they can layer and glaze effectively by maintaining transparency—allowing the light to pass through each layer and be reflected back by the white surface (in varying hues). Experience will show that the use of black and/

or too many layers of muddy, overmixed colors will eliminate luminosity and transparency and make the work opaque, dull, and lifeless.

FUSION

Fusion is the combining of one color with another, a blending usually performed to effect a graduation in tone. This can be accomplished by placing two colors side by side on either dry or wet paper and allowing their edges to flow together. A distinctive characteristic of the fusion effect is that each color retains its original properties while mixing with the other.

IMMEDIACY

Immediacy is the directness of a portrayed image, the statement of a mood without the intervention of other media or go-betweens (Webb 1983).

INTIMACY

Common to most paint media, *intimacy* is the artist's personal expression for the viewer to see, the artist's interpretation of content and use of materials to express that content.

Beach House (10″ x 12″). Beach House is composed primarily of fusions. As a painting or rendering, it is incomplete regarding detail, but the concept is expressed in design, tone, and line by means of a series of fusions.

RHYTHM

Rhythm is the trace of the artist's tools on a painting that reveals the actual act of producing a watercolor. Stroke marks, direction, or pattern of work all contribute to a painting's rhythm.

SERENDIPITY

Watercolor has a unique ability among the color media to produce, accidentally, positive interactions and/or results, owing to its fluidity. This is *serendipity* and, once recognized, can be used to the designer's benefit rather than chagrin. The ability of the medium to flow, mix, and change beyond the designer's direct control results in a pattern or gestalt that is different from the designer's original intention.

Exercises are available that try to strengthen the right brain's influence on the act of watercoloring, thereby providing a setting for accidental or unplanned watercolor expressions. One example of such an exercise is to apply three to five colors in sequence to wet paper and agitate or move the paper in random patterns. Once the watercolor has dried (or has at least ceased spreading), the painter looks for hidden shapes, images, or patterns that can be expanded deliberately and then provides detail and highlights to reinforce the image. The best rule to follow is to be prepared to work with the medium rather than to attempt to control its actions.

ENERGY

The sum total of a watercolor's qualities, such as transparency, luminosity, and fusion, coupled with its fluidity and serendipity, give the watercolor an *energy* unique to its composition and interaction with light.

Watercolor Elements

One interpretation of the design of a watercolor is that it is the act of assembling elements in a pattern using a preconceived strategy. Another interpretation is that it is the act of communication based on an understanding of the qualities, elements, and principles of the medium. In either interpretation, quality design is the act of dealing with the expected as well as the unexpected changes that will (or may) occur when the pigment in the water solution is touched to the paper.

SHAPE

A *shape* is a visible form with particular qualities or properties that distinguish it from other visible forms. Shape is anything that has width and height and is curved, angular, or rectangular. With rare exceptions, shapes form the basic building blocks of any graphic illustration.

Shapes in a rendering, sketch, or other graphic communication should have variety. In painting, shapes are hardly ever symmetrical but should contain

- A variety of straight forms, curves, and angles.
- One dimension that is longer than the others.
- A gradation of width.
- Interlocking configurations with other shapes.
- A variety of edge conditions (soft, hard, or rough).
- "Inside" or "outside" shapes.
- Abstract shapes (defining buildings and other focus shapes).
- "Positive" and "negative" shapes.

A *positive shape* is a dominant shape produced by its strong values, its physical design, or the treatment of its background. A *negative shape* is the absence of a dominant shape.

Shape can be the primary focus (an object, a plane, or whatever), or it can be abstracted massings of land, sky, water, or buildings as the background. It can also be represented in the relationship of the painted to the unpainted surface.

The determination of what shapes will make up the painting, the placement of those shapes, and the tones (light and dark) used to represent them are some of the basic design steps in assembling a watercolor and contribute to the painting's overall pattern.

GUIDELINE 1

First, the overall shapes that are relevant to the communication of the context or

Lighthouse (10″ x 14″). The *Lighthouse* sketch is composed of straight lines, curves, and angles,
forming an interesting shape that penetrates the negative sky space.

concept are identified, and then the shapes that are unnecessary are eliminated from the drawing.

GUIDELINE 2

The positive shapes that will dominate should be emphasized.

GUIDELINE 3

Support shapes that highlight or draw attention to the dominant shapes should be selected. They can be negative shapes that are directional, intermediary, anticipating, or the like.

GUIDELINE 4

Negative shapes can be used to establish a setting for the focus or dominant shape. The negative shape will most likely be midtone, and therefore the actual shape (size, placement, direction) becomes exceedingly important.

GUIDELINE 5

White shapes are a common, useful tool for emphasis and form the basic focal shape of most paintings. A white shape can be either negative or positive. If the dominant shape(s) is painted in dark values (tone) and a strong intensity (chroma), the white shape can be used as a negative setting. If the white shape is used as an intense focal object, then that shape is positive. In most instances, white shapes are used as positive shapes.

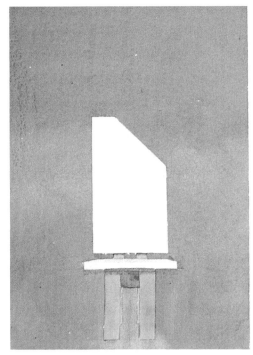

Moss Chair (10″ x 14″)

GUIDELINE 6

White shapes can be used as accents and highlights, and if they are, they should be kept small.

GUIDELINE 7

Negative shapes can be expressed as background silhouettes.

SIZE

Size refers to the largeness or smallness of the elements, including shape, line, and the like. Shapes either are larger or smaller than the others or are the same size.

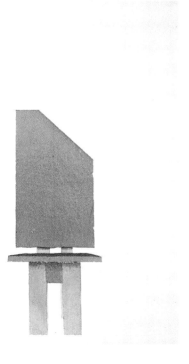

Size also refers to objects in the foreground, midground, or background or to the distance between objects.

GUIDELINE 8

The sizes of objects should be varied so as to create interest.

GUIDELINE 9

Sizes should emphasize strong rather than weak relationships; that is, a dominant shape should be substantially, rather than only slightly, larger than the rest of the shapes.

LINE

Lines are narrow symbols that can be straight and continuous, straight but broken, curved and continuous, or curved but broken. Line suggests enclosure, edge (non-enclosure), direction, movement, and contour. The width of lines is narrow in proportion to their length but may be wide visually (one-half to two inches or more), depending on their length.

A line's character—of both a straight line and a curved line—can be a hard straight edge, or it can be nervous, ragged, or consistently squiggly.

Lines should also contrast; that is, one should be much larger than the others.

DIRECTION

Direction is defined as either the point or orientation toward which one faces or the orientation of a particular movement (as

Line (10″ x 14″). Line work, or calligraphy, denotes length, width, motion, and pattern. The effectiveness of line work is not limited to the narrow symbol so typical of cursive writing. A line also does not need to be uniform in width to be a line, nor does it need to be solid straight. When using line work, experiment with giving the line "character," a feature that distinguishes it from other lines. In this example, both a graphos pen and a flat watercolor brush were used to portray different line types. The cross-hatch example demonstrates two kinds of lines, the overall pattern and the unit lines composing the pattern.

along a line). Direction in a painting should have dominance in one of the principal orientations: horizontal, vertical, or oblique.

The subject should determine the direction of the painting (Webb 1983). For example, a tall, narrow building dictates a vertical direction; a low, long building complex dictates a horizontal direction; and a worm's eye view of a tall building or the tilted mast of a sailboat may dictate an oblique direction.

Baltimore Aquarium (10″ x 14″). This massing sketch exemplifies the energy put into an illustration by means of the shapes' diagonal direction. This energy is also reinforced in the "lift-out" area in the sky shape, pushing the eye to the right and up.

GUIDELINE 10

Vertical direction suggests growth and dignity; horizontal direction suggests repose; and oblique direction is an "energizer," representing movement across other directions (Webb 1983).

GUIDELINE 11

When determining what paper shape to paint on, designers should avoid square paper, because it lacks variation. Horizontal images fit better on horizontal paper, and vertical images fit well on either horizontal or vertical formats.

HUE, CHROMA, AND TONE

Hue is the particular wavelength that is reflected back to the viewer's eye; that is, it is a particular color. *Chroma* is the intensity of that color (weak, neutral, strong). And *tone* is the value of the paint, regardless of color, and is represented by a light-to-dark-scale interval.

As a design tool, hue, chroma, and tone are as important as are shape, pattern, structure, and the like. Indeed, by manipulating one or all three in a painting, its effect and image can be substantially changed. Similarly, designers can learn to change a physical design by using all these elements. In sum, whereas color or hue and its intensity or chroma can alter a painting's image, its tone is the underlying fabric or glue.

Tone Classification

Tone can be classified as local, chiaroscuro, or arbitrary.

Local tone is the tone of an object independent of its illumination. Although everything we can see must have, by extension, a source of illumination, some tones are more closely related to the object than to its illumination. For example, certain building materials have a distinctive tone, regardless of their illumination. Or the identities of some materials are altered by their illumination. Likewise, colors can also be changed by their illumination.

Chiaroscuro is light and shade, or the expression of volume using the light and dark intervals of tone. Finally, *arbitrary* tone is the designer's choice of those lights and darks that can best highlight, communicate, or otherwise express a concept or enhance a design.

Tone Placement

The placement of tone determines the pattern of light, medium, and dark tones and represents their fundamental design use. The tonal pattern is the relation of one tone to another or numerous tones to other groupings to form a pattern. Tone enables shapes to be observed in either the background or the foreground.

Tone Scale

Tone is the value on a scale that is applied to shapes, patterns, and the like; it is the relative lightness or darkness of a color.

The three keys or intervals most often used to describe tone are high or light, medium, and low or dark.

For easy reference, tone can be divided into nine intervals, ranging from black (dark tone) to white (light tone). On some tone interval charts, the highest (white) tone value is the ninth, whereas on others, the highest (black) tone value is the ninth. Therefore, this book will use the words *light* (white) and *dark* (black), rather than numbers, to represent the tone range.

Few artists work with all nine tone intervals on one painting. Instead, they usually divide the range into three groups: light range, middle range, and dark range. In the preceding figure, the range has (1) as the lightest (white) and (9) as the darkest (black). The three groups are the light range, 1 through 3; the middle range, 3 through 7; and the dark range, 7 through 9. For example, a light-tone painting could use tone intervals 1 and 2 for the light range, 3 and 4 for the middle range, and 7 and 8 for the dark range. A dark-tone painting could use 3 for the light range, 6 and 7 for the middle range, and 8 and 9 for the dark range.

You should identify these groups in your tone or value sketch before you begin painting. To do this, prepare a series of tone sketches. By "squinting," you can identify and abstract the shapes or patterns that represent the major tone ranges. This will enable you to plan a painting by designing it around shapes and patterns that are tone ranges, requiring you to abstract

Dark

Light

Tone Scale (10″ x 14″)

or simplify the actual scene into a design that communicates the image without unnecessary clutter.

Light key suggests high illumination and luminosity, represented by white (paper) as the lightest or highest value. *Middle key* is the glue or backbone, the carrier or setting for the more dramatic lights and darks. Watercolorists often say that a painting is made or broken in the mid-key values. *Dark key* suggests the lack or diminishment of light, such as objects in silhouette or shade (away from the light source).

GUIDELINE 12

The tone scale is divided into nine values, ranging from light (white) to dark (black), generally grouped into the light range (the three lighter increments), the middle range (the three middle increments), and the dark range (the three darker increments).

GUIDELINE 13

The loss of the midtone creates undue competition among colors.

Tone Shapes and Patterns

Tone patterns are important to watercolor. Typical patterns of tone can be generalized into "ground" diagrams: foreground, midground, and background shapes. Even though there are nine observable tone intervals on the scale, we shall concentrate on the two ends and the middle of that scale: the light, mid-, and dark tones. There are six basic combinations of tones using foreground, midground, and background, with light, mid-, and dark tones.

Tone Pattern One

foreground—light tone

midground—midtone

background—dark tone

Tone Pattern Two

foreground—midtone

midground—dark tone

background—light tone

Tone Pattern Three

foreground—dark tone

midground—light tone

background—midtone

Tone Pattern Four

foreground—light tone

midground—dark tone

background—midtone

Tone Pattern Five

foreground—midtone

midground—light tone

background—dark tone

Tone Pattern Six

foreground—dark tone

midground—midtone

background—light tone

Further combinations can be achieved through superimposition (laying over) and quilting (dispersing many smaller shapes). For example, a light shape may be superimposed on a dark foreground, and a patchwork or "pointless" effect can be created with many smaller shapes of varying tone. Such combinations are secondary tone patterns composed of shapes that are

Tone Pattern One

Tone Pattern Two

Tone Pattern Three

Tone Pattern Five

Tone Pattern Four

Tone Pattern Six

added to the basic three grounds. Finally, by adding still more subgrounds with other shapes, the tonal pattern can be expanded into a realistic model for watercolor illustration.

Midtone Field Patterns

Another set of patterns useful in organizing tones is the midtone field, in which the midtone is the largest field on which lights and darks are superimposed. These patterns are particularly useful to designers. The midtone field can be composed of multiple shapes, colors, textures, and patterns, but the tone remains the same.

There are two basic midtone field patterns: dark on midtone (see Pattern 1) and light on midtone (see Pattern 2). In Pattern 3, a light-tone shape is superimposed on Pattern 1, the dark shape. In Pattern 4, a dark-tone shape is superimposed on Pattern 2, the light-tone shape.

Naturally, in actual painting, the values or tones will spread over a greater range than these diagrams depict. However, the painting should be a "fast read" in tone, that is, not confusing, with several parts all competing for attention.

GUIDELINE 14

A *fast-read* tone pattern is one whose light, mid-, and dark tones can be read clearly and easily from fifteen to twenty feet away.

GUIDELINE 15

In midtone field patterns, the midtone is

Midtone Field Patterns

Dark on Midtone (Pattern 1)

Light on Midtone (Pattern 2)

always the largest tone in size, although it can be composed of numerous shapes.

GUIDELINE 16

The light and dark shapes should differ from each other in size.

GUIDELINE 17

For maximum contrast, the light and dark shapes should be connected by means of touching, overlap, or silhouette.

GUIDELINE 18

Shape is more important to the dark and light tones than it is to the midtones. A light-tone shape will be in the forefront of the observer's perception, whereas a dark-tone shape will most likely be supportive or part of the background.

Watercolor is an act of design as well as communication. As a part of the design process, the watercolor's shapes, tone or value, and color or hue must be planned. Tone is the "driver" or "motivator" of the painting and influences the observer's perception of the topical shapes (the shapes that reveal the principal subject or topic). The design decisions should be made before the painting is begun, as then the designer's energy should be devoted to creative problem solving.

GUIDELINE 19

The design of a watercolor should include the preparation of (1) a tone sketch and (2) a tone-pattern draft.

Superimposed Tones

Light on Dark (Pattern 3)

Dark on Light (Pattern 4)

Tone Sketch

To make a tone sketch, prepare a small sketch (5″ x 7″ or smaller) of the subject to be painted. Use a soft pencil or a medium-point marker (i.e., Pentel sign pen, Flair, and the like) to plan the tone or value patterns. Generalize the shapes so that you do not complicate the drawing with too many pieces. Isolate those subjects or areas that are important to be read. Remember that the fast-read test applies as much to sketches as it does to the final painting. By generalizing the shapes and tone patterns, you will actually be planning and designing the painting. In addition, you will be rehearsing your overall approach to the painting.

The following figures show tonal sketches of a building entry way. In the first figure, the light tone is in the foreground, and the dark tone is in the background, with a light to midtone midground. The sketch is a fast diagram using a Pentel sign pen. The next figure is similar, with a more extensive midtone in the midground. The third figure depicts a light foreground, a large field midtone in the background and near foreground, and a dominant dark tone in the near background. This pattern focuses the eye on the two contrasting lights and darks. The fourth figure portrays a large light area on a midtone background with only a small midground dark tone to establish the focus.

The last two figures experiment with dark tones in the foreground and midtones and lights as supporting tones. In all sketches, experimentation is the motive for using the three basic tones.

The direction of light influences the placement of tones in these sketches: The midground contains light tones and midtones, whose placement depends on the location of the source of light. Dark shadow areas are actually dark-darks.

You do not need to make six sketches each time you paint, though they are a quick way of studying tone patterns. One or two quick studies may be all that is necessary to set up a painting.

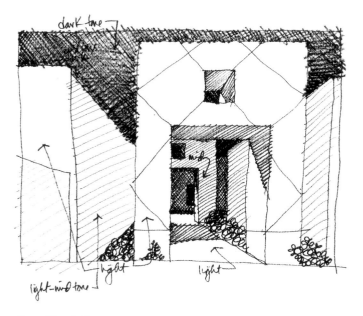

Tone Sketch One

Tone Sketch Two

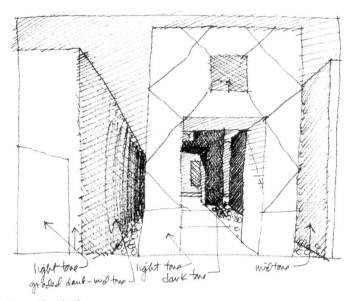

light tone
graded dark – mid tone   light tone
dark tone   mid tone

Tone Sketch Three

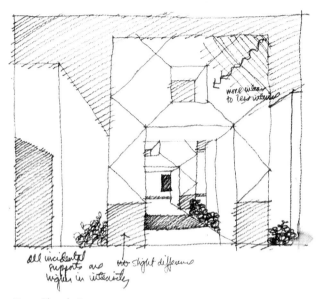

more values
to less values

all incidental
supports are   no slight differences
lighter in intensity

Tone Sketch Four

dark tone

Tone Sketch Five

dark tone
mid tone

Tone Sketch Six

Tone Draft (7½" x 10")

Portal One (10" x 14")

Tone–Shape Draft

As in any design problem, a draft illustration should be prepared before the final watercolor illustration. Using one, at most three, colors, prepare a draft illustration from the tone sketches. The draft should experiment with contrasts between light and dark tones, intensity, and tone placement and gradation.

The draft was prepared on a 10" x 14" Whatman Water Color Paper Block of 140-lb cold-pressed paper.

Portal One and Two represent a finished painting that resulted from a study in tone. The darks and lights are alternated in each painting. In order to build up the desired tone and to accomplish a lighting effect, graded washes of multiple colors were ap-

Portal Two (10″ x 14″)

plied to most of the shapes. Masking tape was used to achieve straight edges on the vertical and horizontal edges.

Planning Your Painting's Tone

A designer or painter can either "talk" a design or actually make it. But only by working through the process will problems be solved, design advances be made, and experience be gained. The following guidelines can be used to plan the painting.

Step 1. Prepare an outline sketch that depicts the overall design (shapes, patterns, and their relationships). Use a contour drawing or simple massing diagram. Limit this sketch to a 3″ x 5″ graphic. At a minimum, delineate the positive and negative shapes and identify them for dominance and/or support (Reid 1985).

Step 2. Identify the ground. Sometimes it is helpful to identify the midground first, and then the foreground and the background. Decide how best to highlight your subject by its placement in the painting.

Step 3. Using a marker or soft pencil, quickly shade each tone option (light, mid, and dark) for each ground. You can mix and match, placing dark tones in one, two, or all three grounds. With experience, you will be able to mix tones in numerous grounds and relate them by means of clustering, patterns, and other techniques. Abstract the objects that are supporting the focal object so as not to clutter the tone pattern.

PATTERN

Pattern is an arrangement or distribution of forms in regular or discernible movements or models that reveals a design configuration. In watercolor, pattern is composed of shapes, lines, tones, and hues. Patterns and movements can be portrayed in the following ways:

- Randomly (only in appearance, as nothing is truly random).
- Regularly (symmetrical, orderly).
- Repetitively (similar symbols and shapes but not necessarily in the same sizes).
- Alternating (changing back and forth between two or more shapes, tones, or whatever, but not necessarily at regular intervals).

For example, using shapes A and B, a regular alternate pattern would be ABABA-BAB, whereas an irregular pattern would be ABBBABAA.

According to Frank Webb (1983), pattern (design) elements are *nouns:*

Shapes	Textures	Colors	Tones
Sizes	Lines	Directions	

And pattern (design) movements are *verbs:*

Unify	Alternate	Repeat
Contrast	Gradate	Balance
Dominate	Harmonize	

Cloe Gallery (11″ x 15″)

The patterns depicted on the facade of the Cloe Gallery, London, are symmetrical geometric shapes. The upper window is composed of four half-circle shapes, and the lower window is made up of four triangular shapes. The repetition of each geometry (four times each in this instance) is connected to the other repeated geometry by means of a third pattern system: the stone blocks represented by both the joints and the light-toned stone color, which actually creates one effect with two patterns. A final pattern is contained in the two shadows on the half-circle window. This midtone pattern softens the darkness of the window area and subtly offsets the stark symmetry of the facade design.

By using white shapes set in a grid, the architectural facade of the NBBJ Penthouse in Seattle stands out as the dominant focus. A set of positive and negative interior shadow shapes set at angles to the white grid form the background for that grid while animating the painting with a varied pattern. The third pattern is directional, using deck board joints to highlight the white grid facade. This example uses shape, direction, and tone to create a design pattern.

GUIDELINE 20

In detailed settings, try to find simple patterns. When painting urban settings with several buildings or landscapes with complex foliage, organizing elements into simplified patterns will make the painting both readable and effective.

NBBJ Penthouse (11″ x 15″)

LIGHT

Light is the source of color and as such governs the outcome of a painting, determining whether it is flat and lifeless (the absence of light considerations) or has vigor and life. The color change in a building's surface from the bright, direct noonday sun to the late-evening purples and grays affects the perceived architecture in different ways. Architectural features disappear or stand out in high contrast, depending on the amount of light and its angle as it strikes the building. Surface textures appear and disappear, creating an animated texture and pattern. Similarly, the light's impact on landscape elements creates dark purples and grays in the early morning, changing to high-chroma yellow-greens, and blues and reds as the midday sun pierces the foliage and reflects off the flowers and grasses.

GUIDELINE 21

Determine the light source and its location.

GUIDELINE 22

Establish the light, middle, and dark tones with a preliminary sketch. As a rule of thumb, work with one light tone, two midtones, and one dark tone. This will simplify and strengthen the painting's contrasting tones.

GUIDELINE 23

Establish the highlights created by the light source, and preserve them in light tones or white paper.

Reflectivity

Color as light tends to be reflected from one object to another in a mirrorlike fashion. Even a dark object—if the painting maintains its transparency—will reflect colored light from nearby objects, mixing the reflected hues with its own hues. The achievement of this effect is rather simple, by using multiple-color graded washes or multiple-color mergings on wet paper. The reflected hue is applied close to the adjacent reflecting surface and then merged into the local color.

Edge Light

Edges can "catch" light as a highlight and can be an effective link between a midtone background and a dark-tone foreground. Edge light is often represented by a white line running along the edge of the shape. The white edge closest to the background is often a hard edge, whereas the white edge closest to the foreground shape is softer.

Recession

Light can be used to set back, or recess, shapes and forms. Shapes in the foreground or on the light-source side are lighter and more intense. Shapes in the distance or on the nonlight side are darker and less intense, creating a recessed or set-back image.

Bright direct lighting reduces details because the contrast is lost. The closer that an object is to a bright-light source, the less detail that it will reveal.

TEXTURE

Texture is an arrangement of surface materials. This arrangement can create either a smooth or a rough surface, and it requires the sense of sight and/or touch to identify it. Texture is important to watercolor because it provides a surface for light interaction.

Texture can give a painting "life" or "realism" because texture is an intimate, even sensual, bond between sight and touch. Texture can be smooth (hard or soft) or rough (hard or soft).

The texture of many objects in a watercolor is represented by their edges. For example, a wave of water can be white (paper) with a touch of blue on the interior, but the texture is really not represented until the edge condition is portrayed against a darker sky. Similarly, a building's surface texture can be defined by its edge contrasted against the sky (or another building) which is either lighter or darker.

Design Principles

Using the elements (nouns) previously discussed, designers must "design," or arrange each element in relation to the others in a way that communicates a message, image, or view to the observer. The following terms and descriptions refer to ways to use the elements of watercolor to portray meaningful designs. They are based on dis-

cussions by Frank Webb (1983), Tony Couch (1987), Charles Reid (1985), Jim Scott (1987), and other artists.

BALANCE

Balance refers to the resultant effect of the placement of shapes and other elements in a painting. Balance is the point of equilibrium, whether symmetrical or asymmetrical, at which everything is in proportion.

Tone (light and dark) can influence the balance of a painting. For example, because a dark shape appears stronger, a smaller dark object will balance a larger light object. Balance can be measured: light against dark, small dark shape against large light shape, and so on. The achievement of balance should be decided during the design process before the painting commences.

HARMONY

Harmony is the fitting of several parts into an agreeable or satisfying whole. It may be more intuitive than scientific. In any case, the designer's "eye" is the best final judge.

Stone Face (12″ x 22″). *Stone Face* was painted on hot-pressed paper, giving a different effect to the brush strokes. Brush calligraphy and spattering with a toothbrush added texture to the sunlit portions of the face.

Harmony in watercolor usually applies to color, the state in which adjacent colors are in harmony and opposite colors clash in contrast. Sizes, shapes, lines, and patterns in harmony "fit"; they do not conflict with or oppose one another.

GRADATION

Gradation is defined as a gradual, incremental change, such as the slight change from one tone interval to the next or from light to dark. Sizes can be graded from large to small; lines can be graded from long to short or wide to narrow. The main thing to remember is that the change is incremental or gradual.

The term gradation is often used in discussing tone and intensity. A tone can be changed over at least nine intervals or increments. A sky wash, for example, from the dark of outer space at the top of the painting to the light hazy horizon demonstrates a graded wash—one of the most common of all watercolor methods.

Graded tones and intensities of color can be used within objects to indicate light interactions with surface materials, from a light-white reflection graded to darker local colors. The reflections on a high-rise office tower's glass or metal surface can range from the bright white of the sun's direct rays to the darker local color of the material at the building face's edge.

Finally, gradation is both a design principle and a technique of application. Many examples of gradation will be demonstrated in later chapters.

UNIFICATION

Unification is the bringing together of all elements into one workable whole. Unification is a gestalt, "a unified physical, psychological or symbolic configuration which has properties that are more than the sum of the parts" (Webb 1983, p. 66). This unification is far more than piecing parts together and distinguishes an art work from a technical rendering.

DOMINANCE

Dominate is a verb meaning "to control by superior power or influence." In painting, hue intensity, tone, and shape all can dominate a work. The dominance of hue is an area often troublesome for beginners because the hue or color is given too much influence and the other elements of design are less respected.

Dominance can be subtle, or it can be outspoken and emphatic. Determining the form of a painting's dominance depends on the mood and image that the painter wishes to express. Dominance also implies subordination. To be in balance and unified, a painting must have both dominant elements and others that support, back up, or in other ways are subordinate (yet related) to the dominant elements.

AWARENESS

Awareness is the ultimate state of understanding, the point at which rules and guidelines are no longer needed (or heeded). It comes with practice, exploration, and experimentation, not rigidity or technical accuracy. Awareness is understanding that the subject (the observed), the artist-designer (the observer), and the method of observation (the act of painting) all are part of one process.

References

Couch, Tony. 1987. *Watercolor: You Can Do It.* Cincinnati: North Light Books.

Reid, Charles. 1985. *Pulling Your Paintings Together.* New York: Watson-Guptill.

Scott, James Godwin. 1987. "Luminous Old Building." Vancouver Island Workshop. Swartwout Publications Tape 587-6.

Webb, Frank. 1983. *Watercolor Energies.* Cincinnati: North Light Books.

Basic Application Techniques

The Approach

The designer's reason to communicate through graphics should determine his or her approach to the application of watercolors. It can be the exploration of massing and values using tonal studies; it can be a color study of materials; it can be the illustration of a completed design project; or it can be the expression of an image or the awareness of a certain building design or setting. Each objective can have a different time frame for the work or a different level of detail required, thereby influencing the approach that the artist chooses. There are three basic watercolor methods or approaches useful to the designer:

Wet on dry (the direct method).

Wet on wet (the wet method).

Dry on dry (the dry method).

Glazing and calligraphy are also described.

WET ON DRY (THE DIRECT METHOD)

The pigment, in a water solution, is applied to dry paper. Standard techniques include

- Painting with a wet brush, wet enough to provide a wet-working edge (the pool of water-suspended pigment that forms the "edge" between applied paint and dry paper).
- Working the wet edges over the paper once the solution has been applied, relating the wet edge to adjacent edges through techniques such as lost and found positive and negative shapes and lift-out methods.
- Working one section at a time, from top to bottom, bottom to top, and/or shape to shape.
- Prewetting certain smaller shapes.

Effects include

- Shapes contrasted with other shapes.
- Combinations of hard and soft edges.
- Shapes interlocking with other shapes.

WET ON WET (THE WET METHOD)

The pigment, usually in a water solution, is applied to a wet surface (saturated to slightly damp).

Standard techniques include

- Prewetting the entire surface (or major portions) before applying the paint.
- Applying pigment, straight or in solution, to the wet surface.
- Fusing or merging one application with another on the wet paper.
- Controlling washes and edges on the wet but drying paper to achieve varied effects.
- Prewetting thoroughly dried applications to repeat wet-on-wet procedures.

Effects include

- Soft transitions from shape to shape.
- Fuzzy or soft edges.
- Graded washes of single and/or multiple hues.
- Hard and soft edges achieved by controlling the drying rate of wet surfaces before applying paint.
- Mergings or fusions of hues.

DRY ON DRY (THE DRY METHOD)

The pigment, without or with very little water solution, is applied directly to dry paper.

Standard techniques include

- Applying pigment in a tiny amount of water to dry paper.
- Applying pigment without water in varying amounts to dry paper.

Effects include

- Textured patterns consisting of pigment and white paper combinations.
- Feathered edges, with the pigment brushed from more shape to less shape.
- Hard edges, for which a second application is laid over and/or adjacent to the first application, which has dried.
- Flatness, with little or no variation in tone or hue.

Obviously, there are exceptions to and variations of all of these techniques and effects. However, as a beginning, it is important to understand the principal differences among them so that when the rules are later broken, the reasons are understood and the designer will have more control over the final result. The second set of approaches includes glazing, calligraphy, and mixed media.

GLAZING

Glazing is overpainting the same area or shape with a highly transparent, weak-chroma (intensity) pigment highly diluted with water, though not with a large amount of this weak pigment and water solution. This approach uses both wet-on-dry and wet-on-wet techniques. Each application is allowed to dry thoroughly before the next glaze is applied.

Standard techniques include

- Applying diluted wash over another previously applied (dried) light wash in the same shape.
- Overlapping diluted washes from light to dark tones, using multiple overwashes.
- Overlapping shapes.

Effects include

- High transparency with a generally light tone to a midtone.
- High luminosity created by allowing light particle-waves to be reflected back to the eye despite multiple overpaintings.
- Positive and negative background shapes, all of which have light tones to midtones.

CALLIGRAPHY

Calligraphy refers to the use of line as a shape applied either dry or wet in a variety of chroma (intensity) or tones.

Standard techniques include

- Application of line(s) as highlights, as either edges or details and usually done in the last stages of a painting.

Effects include

- Detailing of objects in a literal sense (as opposed to shapes defined by background).
- Edge highlights.
- Representation of thin artifacts such as telephone wires and cables.

The Direct Method: Wet on Dry

PREPARATION

Studio Work

- Determine the viewpoint and angle of perspective by means of preliminary sketches.
- Make a tone sketch of the subject.
- Make a color-tone study (color diagram).
- Lay out a pencil image on a watercolor block or stretched paper (avoid using clamps in the studio unless the paper is 300 lb). Work with a half-imperial sheet size as a minimum or, better, a full imperial sheet size.
- Clean the palette with clear water, wiping residual pigments from previously used colors.
- Select palette colors and brushes.
- Premix any large quantities of washes.
- Moisten sponge.

Fieldwork

- Assemble the necessary equipment (easel, stool, water containers, and case for paints, brushes, and other tools).
- Follow the same steps as for studio work.

SEQUENCE

In direct or wet-on-dry painting, painters can achieve better control by painting the contiguous shapes first so that the fast-drying edges can be worked before they dry. This is not a hard-and-fast rule, but until designers gain sufficient experience, it is a wise one to follow. If an edge is to be left exposed, that is, next to an unpainted area, soften the edge by lift-out, interlocking, or lost and found techniques.

As with wet-on-wet painting, the direct method offers much flexibility, and so the following are meant only as guidelines:

- Decide on white (paper) areas to be left as white. Do not use Chinese White for white, as it is opaque. Cover up details or focal points using masking tape, tape and paper masking, masking fluid, or a combination of all. Masking can be done at any point in the painting sequence as long as the previous washes are thoroughly dry.
- Determine the source and placement of light from tone sketch(s), which should include a study of light and shade, reflectivity, local color, recession, and the like.
- Determine edge conditions between major shapes and/or tonal divisions, such as lost and found, interlocking, blending, or hard and soft edges. Small, thumbnail sketches can help in this step.
- Apply light tones beginning with the top of the sheet (or the bottom if the reverse sequence suits the subject and tone distribution) and working downward, shape by contiguous shape, stopping at an appropriate edge. Use the initial light tones to set overall color and temperature schemes and color and tone patterns. As you move from shape to shape, keep your edges wet in order to merge or lose and find them.
- Continue the light-tone applications of other shapes in the foreground, midground, or background.
- While applying the light tones, establish, if possible, the locations of the gray midtones, both warm and cool. This may be done by overpainting the lighter applications if they are thoroughly dry.
- Define negative shapes by applying midtone to darker-tone backgrounds (or foregrounds where appropriate) around or next to the lighter-tone shapes.
- To apply midtones in a unified, shape-to-shape manner, overpaint or glaze two or more contiguous shapes with a light wash to establish a warm or cool midtone unity to the painting.
- Establish sub-elements such as window openings, shadows, and textures that were earlier left white or light toned. Each sub-element should follow a sequence from light-tone to dark-tone application, detailing lighting characteristics, shape, reflections, and other distinguishing characteristics. Establish warms and cools with midtone to mid-dark tones by contrasting them, as with a warm shadow on a cool background and a cool shadow on a warm background.
- Add dark tones to create shadows, recessed shapes, and background glazes. The darks should be strong colorful darks placed to draw attention to the focal

areas, usually light. They should be applied dark enough the first time to reduce "fussiness" and overworked opaqueness.

- Add highlights such as a spot of strong chroma (intensity) color or line–shape calligraphy (sparingly if at all). Do not depend solely on texture and dark detailing to pull the painting together.

Many techniques are used to advance the painting from step to step:

- Keeping working edges wet by adding new brush charges to them.
- Lifting out excess moisture and intensity of hue or darkness of tone by wiping the affected wet area with a drier brush, rag, or sponge. This is called *lifting-out* and is a valuable technique. Don't be afraid to put pigment in a heavy water solution onto the paper—it is better to put on too much and be able to lift it out than not to put on enough and to try to add a charge to a drying wash.
- Always thinking of your edges: If you want to work on another area, define the edge of the first area before it dries (interlocking, lost and found, hard and soft, or whatever), but never leave a hard edge within a shape unless the shapes or forms require that edge (see Chapter 7).
- Overpainting previous applications, once they have dried thoroughly, to deepen the intensity of a color, to increase the luminosity of a shape, to alter the hue or color of a shape, or to add background shapes through glazing. For ex-

ample, if after the initial light and midtones have been applied (and dried), you wish to deepen the tone of a particular shape, simply overpaint that shape with a light-tone to midtone color (either the same or a different color).

- Finally, the direct method requires a more practical skill in laying washes. Without the security of wet paper, washes must be worked quickly and consistently, always anticipating the edge treatments.

GUIDELINE 1

Use very charged brushes for wet-on-dry techniques so that there will be ample pigment to work with on the dry or semidry paper. Larger brushes are better than smaller brushes for ninety-five percent of the painting, with small brushes best suited for final detail.

GUIDELINE 2

In direct method painting—because the applications will dry faster—be careful not to overpaint previously painted areas until they are dry. If you do, use a paper towel and scrub the paint, backrun, or blossom off and allow to dry. Then repaint.

GUIDELINE 3

Immediately after applying wet pigment solutions, use lift-out techniques with a brush or sponge to lighten, soften, and define shapes. Remove wetness from your brush by shaking (slatting), wiping (towel or cloths), or touching it to a damp but

drier sponge so that the brush is less damp than the paint you wish to remove from the paper.

GUIDELINE 4

Instead of using a pencil drawing as a base, use very light tones of the desired color scheme to sketch in major shapes on the paper. Although these will be painted over, they will help set the stage for color compatibility and will add underlayment shapes for variety.

GUIDELINE 5

Colors will always dry at least thirty percent lighter than they appear in their wet form on the paper. When applying darks, test them on scrap paper.

GUIDELINE 6

Paint in a sequential pattern where appropriate, from shape to contiguous shape and dried layer to dried layer.

The Wet Method: Wet on Wet

PREPARATION

Studio Work

- Determine the viewpoint and angle of perspective by means of sketches.
- Make a tone sketch of the subject.
- Make a color-tone study.

- Use stretch paper on a board or a watercolor block. Clamps are suitable for 300-lb paper.
- Layout a pencil image in shapes and patterns. A light table can also be used before the paper is mounted.
- Clean the palette with clear water, wiping residual pigments from previously used colors on the palette.
- Select palette colors and brushes.
- Premix any large washes.

Fieldwork

- Follow the same steps as for studio work.
- In addition, it is difficult and therefore not recommended to use clamps in the field (except for 300-lb or heavier paper) if the intent is to wet the paper thoroughly, as the paper will buckle, creating puddles.

SEQUENCE

Wet-on-wet painting permits artists to expand the number of their starting points on a painting. All or portions of the paper may be wet immediately before application. Depending on the artist's speed, the sequence is not limited to contiguous shapes, owing to the wet edges. Wet-on-wet offers variety in defining edges, including hard edges.

- Set up any masking that is desired, by using tape, tape and paper, masking fluid, or any combination of these.

- Determine which white (paper) areas are to remain. Many artists begin by leaving thirty percent of the paper white.
- Wet the paper in the desired areas or shapes.
- Allow the paper to dry slightly, with the degree based on your ability to control the applied washes. That is, a very wet paper (shiny) will flood with pigment applied with a wet brush, and slightly damp paper will slowly spread pigment applied with a wet brush. Experimentation and practice will determine the level of control with which you are comfortable.
- Working with light tones first, apply them wherever they are located, regardless of contiguous shapes.
- While the paper is still wet, merge or blend colors and tones by overlapping previous applications of paint. Do not wait too long or backruns will occur in previously painted areas. Apply only light tones in one phase, letting them dry, and then wet the area again to apply midtones and dark tones. Or blend light to dark, as appropriate, while the paper is still wet from the first soaking. Normally limit yourself to two midtones.
- Create hard edges by extending the wash into a dry paper area and letting it dry, or use masking. In addition, after one wash has dried thoroughly, you can use a second wetting and a second wash to create shapes on top of other washes with hard and soft edges.
- Plan the dark tones carefully so that no area will need to be overworked; that is,

make the dark tones as dark as you want them, in the first application.
- Paint focal areas or subjects after the backgrounds have been established, working from light to dark.

As in the direct method, the techniques of lift-out, defining edges, masking, and glazing all apply here as well.

Another step when using wet on wet is to paint the midtones first, leaving the lights as white and adding the darks later when the paper is partially dry. This will allow more definition of shapes. You can add light nonwhite tones to white shapes last to unify them but be careful not to lose the stark white (paper) shapes.

GUIDELINE 7

Once an area or shape has been painted and has begun to dry, stay away from it. Because it is less wet than your charged brush or freshly painted area, it will act as a sponge and draw moisture to it. After it has thoroughly dried, the wet-on-wet technique may be applied again (in effect as a glaze).

GUIDELINE 8

For dramatic effects, using a flat brush, dab each corner with a different color, and allow the colors to mix on the wet paper.

GUIDELINE 9

If the paper and the brush are about equally saturated, only the pigment will be transferred to the paper.

GUIDELINE 10

Wet-on-wet is particularly useful in laying down underlayments of fuzzy shapes, colors, and patterns. These provide subtle variety and interest after additional layers of paint are added.

The Dry Method: Dry on Dry

PREPARATION

Studio Work

- Determine the viewpoint and angle of perspective by means of sketches.
- Make a tone sketch of the subject.
- Make a color-tone study.
- Use stretch paper on a board, clamp paper on a board, or a watercolor block (owing to the dryness of the application, clamping the paper to a board is adequate, even for 140-lb. paper or lighter).
- Lay out a pencil image in shapes and patterns.
- Clean the palette with clear water and a soft rag or towel to remove old residue.
- Select palette colors and brushes.

Fieldwork

- Follow the same steps as for studio work.

SEQUENCE

- Mask desired areas. Tape is acceptable because the applications are not charged with much water and so should not run under the edge of the tape.
- Apply larger background washes using the direct or wet method. Light-tone washes are usually applied as a base color. Define shapes and temperature at this point.
- By "stippling" with a sponge or brush (usually a bristle brush), apply the first background colors such as the trees and distant buildings. Several colors may be applied with one application by dipping the instrument into more than one color. Because the application is dry, it is possible to use textured, stiff, and/or rough instruments. The instrument can be wet but is usually not charged with water.
- If only one color is applied in the first application, a second (or more of the same) color can be applied over the first for accent and depth (e.g., shadows), much as is done in oil painting.
- Create texture by adding a heavy load of noncharged pigment to the paper, rinsing the brush, and then adding a layer of another color and mixing the two together (an oil painting brush or bristle brush is useful for this technique).
- Lift out heavy applications of pure or slightly soluble pigment with a sponge and clear water.
- Create lighter values or tones by applying a highly diluted solution with a damp brush or sponge.

The use of texture is more important to the dry brush method than to the direct or wet methods, owing to the heavier application of pigment. In addition, the tones are usually darker, as the pigments are less diluted, and the dry brush method produces a far less luminous result than do the other methods.

Many dry method watercolorists use multiple layers of washes applied dryly (with just enough water to dilute the color to the desired tone). To achieve texture, dry brush detail is used extensively to reproduce surface blemishes, grains (as in wood), and details such as grass or weeds).

The drier the application of pigment is, the more control the designer will have over the end result, and the more the observer's focus will be on the detail. When using the dry method in conjunction with wet on dry or wet on wet, usually apply it last, after the tone and hue schemes have been established. All three methods are interchangeable.

Special Techniques

This chapter describes the many techniques available to the designer of applying watercolor. They should be regarded as subelements of the three general approaches of wet on wet, wet on dry, and dry.

Washes and Gradation

A *wash* is a mixture of any watercolor pigment and water, in varying amounts (Guptill 1949). There are two types of washes.

A *flat wash* is a uniform monochromatic wash with a constant tone throughout. It can be a clear, monochromatic single wash or layed flat washes or overwashes.

A *graded wash* is one that changes in hue and/or tone in small, incremental steps. Unlike flat washes, graded washes have many subvariations regarding their application, which include

Monochromatic graded-tone wash.

Graded multiple-color wash.

Streaky wash (monochromatic or polychromatic).

Vigorous wash.

Curved wash.

Overlapped wash.

French wash.

FLAT WASHES

Preparation

- Prepare the watercolor paper (mounting, stretching).
- Mask out areas to be avoided or to be left white.
- Premix a solution of pigment and water in a saucer, experimenting to reach the appropriate tone.
- Decide whether to use a wet-on-dry or a wet-on-wet method (wet the paper before applying the wash).
- Tilt the working surface to an angle of five to ten degrees so that the bottom edge (the leading edge of the wash) will

puddle, drawing the excess wash downward into that edge.

- Have ready a mop brush, damp sponge, paper towel, and/or blotter to control excess wash.
- Select medium-to-large brushes. Do not use small detail brushes, as you will need a brush that will hold a fair amount of water and pigment.

Sequence

- Wet the brush by swishing it in clear water. Remove the excess water by "slatting"—sharply snapping the brush toward the floor—or by touching the wet brush to absorbent material.
- Add the wash to the wet brush from the mixing saucer.
- To control the charge in the brush, touch the charged brush to a damp sponge to remove some of the charge before you begin the wash.
- Begin by applying the wash to the upper portion of the shape to be painted, moving the brush back and forth in horizontal movements from one edge of the shape to another edge of the shape, always moving the puddle (which should form at the lower edge) with the brush. If the puddle dries up, quickly recharge the brush with water, "slat," recharge it with premixed wash, and apply the new wash to where you left off. It is helpful to tilt the working surface enough to create a puddle; otherwise, a streaked or lined appearance may result. Ideally, the brush

Flat Wash

should be charged initially with enough wash to carry it through the entire shape (or to a convenient stopping point) without recharging— thus the need for a large-enough brush. The edge "puddle" between brush chargings should never be allowed to dry, or a line or edge will form, thereby destroying the clear wash. Speed is important, as even a wet edge will "backflood" if allowed to become damp and a wet charge is added to it.

With some experience, the brush will be able to move the puddle or the leading edge of the wash easily across the paper until the puddle is spent. It is easier to apply a wash to wet paper than to dry paper. For dry paper, the brush charge should be very wet, and the designer will need to work faster than with wet paper. If you get into trouble, do not try to work over the wet wash as it is drying. Either soften the leading edge with clear water and let it dry so that you can blend in another wash later, or let the edge dry completely and lift out the hard edge at a later time.

- Absorb the excess puddle with a blotter, damp-dry brush, sponge, or paper towel.

Absorb as much of the puddle as necessary, checking to see that it does not reform.

GUIDELINE 1

- Apply a flat wash with one brush charging, if possible. Do not be timid with the wash charge—a mop brush or blotter can easily absorb the remaining puddle if it is not needed.

GUIDELINE 2

The larger the wash shape or area is, the bigger the wash puddle and the bigger the brush will need to be.

GUIDELINE 3

The brush pressure should be light, using the tip and not the side of the brush. The water on the paper (the puddle) will literally wash from the brush as it (the puddle) begins to dry out. The brush merely transfers, without pressure, the wash from brush to paper, as if it were a pipeline holding the liquid until needed. This is one of the best examples of watercolor fluidity—the watercolor moves with only a little assistance from the painter.

GUIDELINE 4

Always work a wash along its edge until the end; *never* work back into it or paint over it while it is damp. A common flaw of many washes is the effort to repair a previously laid wash before it has dried, causing "fanning" or backwash marks. To repair an

Layered Flat Wash

area, it is better to let the wash dry thoroughly and then wash over it, or lift it out and re-wash the area.

GUIDELINE 5

Unstretched paper may buckle, creating valleys for the pigment to collect in and thus causing darker pigment pockets and marring a clear flat wash.

GUIDELINE 6

When moving the puddle back and forth in horizontal strokes, overlap the previous stroke by half a width or less in order to

reduce or eliminate light horizontal bands. Horizontal stroke options include left to right or back and forth, that is, left to right and then right to left, and then repeat.

LAYERED FLAT WASHES

Preparation

- Allow the first flat clear wash to dry thoroughly.
- Mask out any shapes not designated for the next wash.

Sequence

- Follow the same steps as for flat washes.
- Avoid lingering over the previous wet washes.
- Use the layered washes to define positive and negative shapes, background patterns, and the like.

The dark shape in the figure is the second wash application.

GRADED WASHES

A *monochromatic graded wash* is composed of one color or hue but is varied in tone from light to dark or dark to light. Although black and white may be used to change the tone (shade and tint), I discourage that practice, preferring instead to use varying amounts of the same hue.

Monochromatic Graded Wash

Preparation

- Prepare the watercolor paper (mounting, stretching).
- Mask out areas to be left white.
- Premix a solution of pigment and water, darkening the tone as desired. Because the wash will have a graded tone, from dark or midtone to light, the wash solution should appear darker than the desired end result, as it will dry lighter. Test the solution for tone on a piece of scrap paper. Some artists prefer to mix a number of saucers of wash, each measur-

ably different in tone. This provides more control over the graded washes as they are applied to the paper.

- Decide on a wet-on-dry or a wet-on-wet application, and if desired, prewet the shape to be painted. Practice with both methods.
- Tilt the working surface to an angle of five to ten degrees in order to create a puddle or leading edge at the bottom edge of the wash.
- Have ready a mop brush, damp sponge, paper towel, and/or blotter to control excess wash.

Sequence

- Wet the brush by swishing it in clear water, and remove the excess water by "slatting" or by touching the brush to a damp sponge (drier than the brush).
- Add wash to the wet brush from the mixing saucer or palette.
- Begin by applying the wash to the upper portion of the shape to be painted, forming a puddle or leading edge. Using horizontal strokes (left to right or back and forth), gradually dilute the wash tone from dark to light by going back to the

pail of clear water and diluting the wash mix by a smaller increment at each brush charging as you move the puddle edge down the paper. Repeat this dilution until you reach the edge of the shape.

A variation of this method is to dilute the premixed wash in the saucer for each increment. It will take practice to achieve enough of a gradation for any of these methods. In many cases, a weak, graded tone wash can be overwashed again and again—but only after each application has dried—to achieve the desired gradation.

GUIDELINE 7

Graded washes, from light to dark and dark to light, are achieved by diluting the pigment wash in small increments, using horizontal brush strokes.

GRADED MULTIPLE-COLOR WASHES

Graded multiple-color washes are either flat or graded washes that use two or more colors. They are useful washes to learn, as they may be applied to create many forms, including skies, terrain, and building facades.

Preparation

- Follow the same steps as for flat washes.
- If the areas to be painted are large, premix two (or more) washes in saucers, one for each color. If the areas or shapes are small, mix the wash solution on the palette.

Sequence

- Begin the first wash in the same manner as for a graded wash, lightening the first wash in small amounts at each increment and adding a small amount of the second wash until the first wash is phased out completely and the second wash dominates. This technique of "blending" is essentially overlapping two graded washes.
- As long as the puddle edge is wet, add, if necessary, small increments of the second color, changing color but not tone.

Multiple-Color Wash. In this wet-on-wet application, there are two ways to create a multiple-color wash: The first is to apply the first color in decreasing tones, and then to add the second color in light-to-dark tones to the first wet wash. The second technique is to apply the first wash from dark to light, revise the drawing, and paint the second wash from dark (at the buttons) to light at the merge point with the first wash. Note that the clear back run on the left side of the wash is caused by the clear water running from the taped edge back into the wash.

STREAKY WASHES

Preparation

- Wet the shape or area with clear water.
- While the paper is still very wet (with sheen), apply a heavily charged brushful of pigment to the area where the darkest tone is desired.
- Tilt the board in the direction of the wet areas so that the dark pigment will run into the remaining clear wet area, to create streaks.
- To stop the process, simply lay the board flat and allow the wash to dry. This is an effective way to create rocks and highly varied terrain.
- After the streaks have been established and are still wet, work other colors and/ or tones into the edges of the streaks to create shapes and patterns.

VIGOROUS WASHES

A *vigorous wash* is essentially a variation of the streaky wash except that the paper is allowed to lose its sheen and the board is not tilted. The dark pigment is heavily applied to the wet paper, usually as a background, and allowed to bleed into the clear wet areas. The result is a high contrast of dark to light with a soft transitional edge.

CURVED WASHES

A *curved wash* is used to show curved or rounded objects and can be achieved with one or two colors.

Streaky Wash. This wash is actually a combination of streaky and merged washes, that is, "fusions" of different pigments made to merge on wet paper.

Preparation

- Follow the same steps as for flat washes.
- No premixing is necessary unless the painted area is very large.

Sequence (One Color)

- Wet the area or shape with clear water.
- For curved linear shapes, run the brush loaded with pigment along one side of

the wet area, causing the color to blend into the clear wet area and to modulate from dark to light.

- For rounded areas, wet the entire sphere and run the pigment along the outside perimeter, coming to a point at each end of the curved (half-moon) application. The pigment edge will bleed into the clear wet surface.
- The reverse application is also effective: First apply the pigment to dry paper, and second, apply a clear wet stroke alongside (and slightly overlapping) the wet or moist pigment application, in order to entice the pigment to merge with the clear water.

In the preceding sketch, the right face of the building curves back, away from the direct light source. A swath of clear water was applied over the dry underlayment, and a blue-green (sky and building colors) was washed in along the far right edge, bleeding to the left into the clear wash.

Curved wash

OVERLAPPED WASHES

Overlapped washes are simply two overlapping, separate graded washes; the second wash is applied after the first wash has dried thoroughly. They are helpful for building up controlled washes depicting reflectivity (one material's local color reflected onto another's surface) and delicate shadow work.

FRENCH WASHES

French washes are a drafting aid to help establish incremental tones by means of a series of flat, not graded, washes. Their objective is to look like a graded wash, but their application is designed for intricate, delicate shapes that are difficult to paint with a graded wash.

Sequence
- With faint pencil lines, establish decreasingly narrower horizontal bands, each smaller than the one above.
- Apply flat washes to each band, altering the tone (lighter or darker) within each band, thereby creating a graded wash.
- Gently erase the pencil lines.

When applying washes to complex shapes, position the board in the most convenient manner. For example, when painting around a complex shape, do not hesitate to turn the board around and to

French Wash

begin working from the bottom to the top of the painting in a top-to-bottom motion. Indeed, rotating the board as the wash progresses is much easier than rotating yourself.

For wet and fast washes, new easel designs such as Mobil Easels allow for fast tilting and rotation without requiring the designer to move. Make certain, however, that any easel you consider buying does not limit you to only certain techniques.

Edges

BLENDING EDGES

To *blend edges* is to merge them without establishing a demarcation line or hard edge. Blending is accomplished by

- Applying two colors side by side on wet paper, causing them to bleed into each other.
- Applying a graded tone of one color into a graded tone of another color (wet on wet or wet on dry).
- Applying a graded tone of one color over another dry graded tone of another color.

SOFT EDGES

Soft edges are created by brushing pigment (pure or in solution) into a clear wet area, causing the pigment solution to spread into the wet area. Variations of this include

- Applying the pigment or pigment in solution to a wet area of paper.
- Applying the first pigment or pigment solution to dry paper (dry on dry or wet on dry) and subsequently running a brush charged with clear water along the edge of the pigment while the pigment is still wet, causing the pigment to spread into the wet stroke. This enables the painter to have more control over the pigment application and still create a soft blurred edge.

Soft edges can also be made by high-tone (value) contrasts between shapes: By contrasting a light toned shape—such as a tree mass against a dark forest background—the edges can be highlighted by the contrast of light and dark rather than the actual edge. In this example, the two colors can be merged slightly with a damp (not saturated) wet-on-wet application.

HARD EDGES

A *hard edge* is a solid boundary with a discernible, sharp termination. Edges support or define shapes. Hard edges can be created by the abrupt termination of one shape next to another; by a line separating shape, pattern, or hue; or by a "wire" edge, caused by drying pigment that has puddled slightly along the edge of one shape against another.

When used exclusively in a painting, hard edges draw attention to each edge

Soft Edges

rather than to the shape, and so they can cause a painting to look flat and "painted by numbers." To increase a painting's effectiveness, mix hard edges with soft edges, lost and found edges, and so forth, thus creating variety. The edges should be planned in general detail before beginning a work.

Hard Edges

Architectural subjects are characterized by hard edges, that is, manufactured as opposed to natural forms. But even in this setting, hard edges should be balanced and offset by soft or lost and found edges.

GUIDELINE 8

Hard edges define one shape next to other shapes in a firm, solid manner.

GUIDELINE 9

Hard edges should be balanced with soft edges and lost and found edges.

GUIDELINE 10

Hard edges against a white or very light background maximize the contrast between objects and background shapes. Keep the background, foreground, and/or midground hard edges to a minimum so that the building or artifact (focal point) hard edges will have more drama.

GUIDELINE 11

Hard edges can be used effectively when limited to the edges of *major* sections, with those edges within each section either soft and/or lost and found.

BACKLIT EDGES

Locating the light source immediately behind objects causes them to be *backlit*, or silhouetted (if they are opaque). The edges will be sharp and have a sharp tone contrast. This is a feature of "plane change" accents, in which the surface immediately adjacent to, but facing away from, the light source will have a sharp tone contrast with the light, highlighted by a sharp or "white" edge.

GUIDELINE 12

If a light source is located behind an object, it will create a sharp contrast and hard edges.

Backlit Edges

FEATHERED EDGES

Feathered edges consist of lightened, lacy, or delicate edges caused by lightly brushing out pigment from the main application over another shape and/or tone or hue. Feathered edges are usually created in wet-on-dry and dry-on-dry applications. The pigment solution is brushed from the wet paint solution outward over the dry paper, mixing the pigment with the color beneath it, resulting in a feathery appearance. This is effective when a hard edge needs to be softened on a dry paper application.

IRREGULAR EDGES

Irregular edges are hard edges characterized by raggedness, roughness, and irregular patterns. Ideal for clouds, terrain, and vegetation, these edges are created as follows:

Sequence
- For wet-on-dry or dry-on-dry applications, apply the pigment solution over the previous wash (thoroughly dry).
- Using a stiff brush—such as a bristle brush or a damaged, shortened watercolor brush—work the pigment solution edges outward into the dry areas with irregular motions. The stiff bristles will impart an irregular pattern.

CURVED EDGES

Watercolor has a special ability to form *rounded* and *curved edges*. Because the pigment flows or spreads from one wet area into another, it is relatively easy to create a curved or rounded shape by applying the darker tone at the edge and causing it to bleed or merge into a lighter middle part of the shape, giving it a natural roundness. To create a sharper outline, use a lot of water to cause the color to spread out from the darker pool of pigment.

Curved Edges. Curved forms are achieved with blended or graded soft edges, strengthened in this example by the gradation of tone from light to dark shadow. The foreground grasses are interlocking shapes and edges, bordering on soft edges.

WIRE LINE EDGES

Wire line edges are created by puddling or pooling the pigment at the edge of a shape and allowing it to dry. The edge shape resembles a colored wire that is darker in tone than the same-color shape that it edges.

WHITE–DARK EDGES

An effective means of defining an edge and hinting at an overhead light source is as follows:

- Mask out a thin space at and within the edge of one shape where it is backdropped by a second shape.
- Using a wet-on-wet application, paint both shapes (foreground subject and background shape), and allow them to dry thoroughly.
- Rub off the masking fluid to reveal the white (or light) line-space, which now becomes the edge highlight between the two shapes.

To create a *dark edge* effect:

- After the preceding shape application has dried thoroughly, run a wet clear water stroke along the desired shadow edge. Make sure that the clear water application is a hard edge along the edge of the focal shape.
- Apply a single stroke of pigment along the hard edge of the focal shape (which

White-Dark Edges

is wet), and allow the paint to bleed away from that edge into the wet clear wash area. The edge of the focal shape should remain hard, with a softening effect occurring away from the focal edge.

SHADOW EDGES

Shadow edges are dark edges, with one edge that is defined by the object casting the shadow (hard) and the outer edge that is soft or fuzzy or blends in with the shape and material (texture) on which it is cast.

Pigment can be applied on dry paper with a clear wet wash stroke run alongside the pigment to cause it to bleed (on one side only). Another technique is to apply a wet pigment solution to wet paper, overlapping the dry paper at the edge of the shape casting the shadow. The shape edge will be sharp and hard, and the outward shadow edge will be soft. To avoid confusion, when prewetting the paper, do not apply the clear wet wash up to the actual shape edge, but leave a strip of dry paper between that edge and the beginning of the shadow so that a hard shape defining edge can be stroked.

GUIDELINE 13

Shadows act in one of two ways: They define the edge of the shape casting the shadows by high contrast of tones, or they conform their outer edges to the material, shape, and texture of the shape on which they are cast.

GUIDELINE 14

The more direct and bright the light source is, the sharper and harder the outer edge of the shadow on the backlit plane will be. Conversely, the more indirect and softer the light source is, the softer the outer shadow edge will be.

SCRAPED EDGES

One technique used by many artists to create hard edges is to *scrape* away freshly applied paint.

Sequence

- Apply a graded-tone wash to wet paper.
- Before the paint has a chance to dry, and using a sharp-edged tool, credit card, or plastic scraper, scrape away the paint.
- Pigment may accumulate at the edges of the scraped area because of the displacement of water from the area that was scraped. Therefore, avoid using cheap paper if you intend to scrape, scratch, and briskly blot.

GLAZED EDGES

To create subdued edges, glazing is highly effective. Layers of transparent diluted tone washes are applied over thoroughly dried previous washes, affording the painter a great deal of control over the final outcome. Each new wash application must be applied to a dry surface for maximum effectiveness.

Edges created by glazing are generally sharp and so are useful for cast shadows in interiors as well as on exterior surfaces.

Edges in which one shape, plane, or color meets another can usually be treated in one of two ways: with a defined edge formed by the abrupt ending of one shape and the beginning of another, resulting in

Interlocking Edges

a hard edge, or as an integrated edge in which shapes, patterns, and colors interlock, blend together, or are lost and found (a combination of hard and soft).

In urban settings, buildings and other artifacts create sharp or hard edges, compared with those created in natural settings. Yet even in this field of geometric shapes, edges interlock and blend into one another. If all edges were sharp and unbroken, much of the mystery and enticement of a graphic illustration would be lost to the viewer. Geometric sharp edges (in reality) can be effective as can softer representations of form, blending one plane into another without sharply defined edges.

LOST AND FOUND EDGES

Lost and found edges are created by the following methods:

- Playing peekaboo with one darker shape over a lighter-tone shape, allowing pieces of the underlying shape to peek through.
- Using hard and soft boundaries to break the line, by identifying a hard edge in one place and blurring it in other places.
- Allowing two wet colors to flow into each other on the paper. As they dry, extend parts of the merging colors into dry areas for a hard edge and allow other areas to remain soft.

Shapes

Shape is a design element in watercolor that acts in unison with other shapes, dominant and subordinate, to define a pattern or image on the paper. A shape is an abstract entity that has a compositional relationship with other shapes to communicate a particular design and graphic image.

POSITIVE AND NEGATIVE SHAPES

Positive and *negative* are terms that can be applied to both shapes or tones. The positive components of a painting are those shapes or patterns that dominate the image by means of design, color, or tone.

They are the shapes that are painted, whereas the negative shapes are those that are implied. Or positive shapes are those that can be recognized because of their dominance. Positive can refer to a tone that, regardless of the shape's location or hierarchy, is the dominant component. For example, painting the shadows and outlines of shapes in a dark tone and leaving the major shapes white or light can actually establish the background elements as the positive ones. The key is the dominance of the shape and/or tone. For practical purposes, a shape (rather than an ambiguous background tone) should be the dominant image.

Negative shapes are those that are present but are not directly defined. Rather, they are indirectly stated by means of darker backgrounds, edges, or mid-range colors. Negative shapes can be effective in landscape and urban forms when they are abstracted as foreground and/or background supports for a focal point or center of interest.

According to Couch (1987), positive shapes are those that are deliberate, planned as definite statements, whereas negative shapes are those that are formed by what is left.

SIMPLE COLOR SHAPES

In sketches or massing and color studies, an effective technique is to simplify color shapes using either local color or background highlights with light and shade:

- Local color is applied to simplified shapes without light and shade, thereby emphasizing shape, composition, and material color.
- Shapes are highlighted by painting the shadows and background components.
- Shapes can be either literal images or abstract translations.

Special Effects

TEXTURE

Texture refers generally to all "decorations" applied to the basic washes that make up the body of the painting. It can be calligraphy, dry brush effects, scrapes, spatters, dabbing, scrubbing, dragging, or blotting. In most cases, the brush or tool is dry (slightly damp) and/or loaded with pigment straight from the tube (palette).

Dry brush techniques for texture include

- Scrubbing the paper with a pigment-loaded dry stiff brush, producing grass and other short-stroke symbols.
- Dabbing the paper with a pigment-loaded dry stiff brush, producing a mottled, "clumpy" effect.
- Dragging the dry brush (one-inch flat) over the paper with slight twisting and jiggling movements, providing a wider pathlike effect, with lights and darks interspersed, similar to earth forms and their shadows. Dragging a stiff bristle brush in a straight line will result in wood grain textures and line patterns.

- Drawing calligraphic lines with a dry brush or a brush handle (into wet paint), producing weather lines for branches, vertical posts, or other thin architectural elements.

Both the wet-on-wet and wet-on-dry methods can produce interesting textures by means of the following techniques:

- Use a rough-surfaced paper.
- Apply washes to the paper until the brush dries up, moving from wet paper to dry paper for a ragged edge effect.
- Soften the edge of a wet color wash with a stroke of clear water, to cause the pigment to move into the lighter area.
- Apply a fully charged brush over an area treated with wax, mixing additional colors into the application while the wash is still wet.
- Quickly apply a fully loaded brush to dry paper, creating an effect ranging from intense, full-color coverage to speckles of white or previous wash.
- Apply a fully loaded wash of two dark rich colors, allowing them to mix on the paper. This can be achieved by adding a different pigment to each corner of a one-inch flat brush and applying the doubly loaded brush to a wet surface.
- After a wet-on-wet or a wet-on-dry application has nearly dried, run a razor blade, Exacto knife, or matt knife over the surface to expose the white paper underneath. This technique will work well if the scoring is made to a painted surface

that is not quite dry but will not absorb any more pigment in the paper. But if the colors have dried, brush clear water over the surface, and scrape out the texture.

TEMPERATURE

Temperature refers to the warmth, coolness, or neutrality of a color or painting. This is one of the fundamental features of watercolor (or any color application) and requires thought and practice to be used effectively. Lights, darks, shadows, and grays all have a temperature dominance. A painting should have an overall dominance of either cool or warm.

GUIDELINE 15

Warm colors are the colors of earth and fire (Couch 1987): red, orange, yellow, brown, and mixtures of them.

GUIDELINE 16

Cool colors are the colors of space and ice (Couch 1987): blue and some purples. Blue is the basic cool component.

GUIDELINE 17

Purple and green, in various mixtures, cross the line from cool to warm and warm to cool and form grays to be used to denote objects in space. Remember that grays should have a temperature.

GUIDELINE 18

Contrasting temperatures is an effective tool, for example, warm against cool, cool against warm. A cool shadow is a good contrast for a warm building.

GUIDELINE 19

Cool temperatures suggest recession, distance, and background, whereas warm temperatures suggest closeness and foreground.

WARM AND COOL CONTRASTS

Warm and cool contrasts provide subtle and important visual interests for planes, shadows, and other components of a painting. They are the temperature characteristic of a color, from cool blues to warm oranges. To achieve such contrasts, techniques include

- Placing warms against cools with hard or at least hard and soft edges.
- Glazing a lighter cool tone over a previously applied lighter warm tone, leaving openings and lost and founds.
- As in graded washes, blending a warm tone into a cool tone.
- Selecting either a warm or a cool tonal emphasis for the overall painting, using the other, less dominant temperature for contrasting highlights such as shadows and back lighting.

LOCAL COLORS

Painting in *local colors* (colors reflected from the shape itself, regardless of light and shade) establishes that color is more important than light and shade. Techniques useful in sketching include

- Painting masses (in silhouette) as the first step, producing stronger first washes. Use several colors blended by wet-on-wet or wet-on-dry methods.
- Selecting a midtone for the first wash in order to establish enough color yet not overpower the painting at the outset.
- Casting the shadows over the first wash after it has dried.

These techniques differ from the usual watercolor sequences in that the stronger medium- to darker-toned colors are applied first. A good exercise is to paint only the dark tones and all the shadows, emphasizing the local colors.

FLOW-THROUGHS

Flow-throughs are achieved by connecting one section area or shape to another by a wet merging of the two through color or tone. It is an effective way of connecting shapes through their edges and is useful for landforms, landscaping, and background "clutter" such as signs, building pieces, and crowded streets.

HARMONIOUS ADJACENT TONES

Balance in paintings can be maintained by *harmonizing,* or establishing tonal agreement among all the parts. It is important when three or more shapes interact and balance is needed among the dark, light, and midtones. To achieve such balance, use edges (hard and soft) to control the contrast among the tones, and grade the tone and intensity of a particular shape (usually the dark tone) to blend from light to dark, building up to a focal point within the dominant tone.

SECTION PAINTING

Section painting is painting whole areas or sections in a sequence to form complete natural units. This enables the painter to control the hard edges associated with a given shape, restricting them to the periphery of the section and not the middle. The danger of relying too much on this technique is that each section can stand apart from the others in an unbalanced manner if it is not united by color, tone, intensity, or connecting shapes.

For example, a background of trees surrounding a residential structure may be composed of numerous sections of various tree and brush forms. The composite of those sections constitutes a complete natural unit in the painting in the same manner that the residential structure constitutes a separate unit that could be painted in sections to comprise a second whole unit.

STAMPING

Often used in semi-abstract applications, *stamping* is the application of paint by pressing the paint to the paper with a flat hard or rigid surface such as cardboard, linoleum, or plastic. This technique can be used to create textures, with the degree determined by the stamping tool. For example, tree stamps can be constructed out of cardboard or erasures for stylized trees.

SCORING

Scoring is the application of calligraphy or hard-edged shapes using tools such as a razor blade (both edge and side), credit card, putty knife, stick, or brush handle. The line widths can be varied according to the width of the tool. Scoring and stamping are usually used together.

STENCILS

Stencils can be used to create shapes that can be lifted out of previous (dried) color applications. Negative stencils (using the actual cut-out shape as a mask) are also useful.

Sequence

- Cut a stencil from a thin sheet of material (plastic, paper, or whatever).

• Overlay the stencil on the previous wash (bone dry), and with a brush or sponge, rewet the area with clean water.
• Lift out the area by wiping the wet spot with a brush, sponge, tissue, or blotter.

Alternatively, stencils can be made with masking tape: Mask out the surrounding areas with the tape, exposing only the shape to be lifted out. The silhouetted shape can also be painted a darker tone rather than lifted out, a technique that works in the negative as well as the positive. When painting, brush away from the taped edge so that the edge of the image is not darkened by the accumulation of paint residue brushed under the lip of the tape, causing a wire edge. Using paper or plastic stencils requires caution; always paint from the stencil edge to the middle so that color does not seep under the edge of the paper or plastic. Finally, blot the area if it has been washed or lifted out.

Stencils. Stencils can be negative, constructed from tape or watercolor paper.

SPATTER

Spatter is a technique used to create texture and pattern. It is usually achieved by causing drops of pigment-laden water to fall on the predetermined shape. The designer can use masking tape and stencils to control the areas to be covered with spatter. The techniques include

- Using a brush (almost any size but large enough to carry an adequate charge of soluble pigment), flick or tap the brush to release the drops of paint. Experiment to determine the size and distribution of the drops. Remember that color always dries lighter than it is applied.
- Using a brush, roll, twist, and flick the brush handle to create a variety of textures and patterns.
- Using a toothbrush, run your finger or other tool over the brush hairs to release the drops of paint. Be sure to experiment in order to determine the direction of the spatter. A nylon brush with close bristles is easy to control with the thumb. First, wet the brush and then rub the wet brush into the pigment. Tap out any excess paint from the brush before placing it over the painting, because a toothbrush will not retain moisture in the way that a watercolor brush will. Once the excess

Spatter. In conjunction with negative stencils or masking shapes, spatter can create unusual and interesting effects. A toothbrush was used in this example to make the spatter.

has been removed, hold the toothbrush close to the paper, with the bristles down, and release the pigment by running a thumb or finger over the bristles.

These techniques are useful for realistic images and provide texture and detail such as gravel, rust, pock-marked surfaces, and granular images. Georg Shook and Gary Witt (1981) divide spattering into positive and negative effects: A positive effect is indicated by the addition of paint by means of spattering, and a negative effect is indicated by the removal of paint by spattering clear water on a freshly painted (wet) surface. A towel is used to blot up the excess.

LIFT-OUT

Lift-out is one of the most useful techniques in watercolor and can be used in all approaches. Lift-out is basically the removal of pigment, whether wet or dry, from a painting. The tools used include paintbrushes, sponges, tissues, blotters, scrapers, and knives. Remember the wetness factor; that is, the tool used to remove or lift out the pigment must be less wet than the painted surface is. The techniques include

Wet Lift-out

- Reducing the amount of paint after it is first applied, by wiping excess water from the brush and passing the brush over the applied paint (only if it is wet).

- Creating lighter highlights by stroking the wet paper to lift out paint where desired, using a brush, blotter, paper towel, and the like.

Dry Lift-out

- Adding a shape to a dry painting, by rewetting the desired area and lifting off the pigment with a brush, sponge, or tissue.
- Adding lines to a dry painting, by using a clean eraser.
- Adding a detailed shape on a dry painting when the background is darker than the intended image, by

  Rewetting an area large enough to take the image.

  Lifting out the area as described earlier.

  Letting the painting dry thoroughly (use a hair dryer for speed).

  Treating the surface with a quality eraser (plastic, pink pearl, or art gum).

  Drawing in the missing shape.

  Rewetting the area around and excluding the shape but including an overlap area beyond the lift-out (into the previous wash).

  Painting the background using the same color, in a wet-on-wet method.

Lift-out is particularly effective when painting light on shapes. By stroking a damp tool over a wetter surface, the resulting effect is light against dark with a soft edge.

PLANES OF LIGHT

Planes of light refer to two or more planes in differing light. A common example is the change in light on two building surfaces, one directly in line with the light and the other in shadow. Also referred to as the "plane-change accent" (Couch 1987), this phenomenon can be found in every urban and interior setting. Whether the light source(s) is direct or indirect, each plane will have a different tone and temperature (cool and warm) based on its original color, reflectivity from adjacent surface colors, and location relative to the light source.

One example is leaving white the plane most directly exposed to the light and, for the plane away from the source, merging a darker color with a second color from an adjacent surface, for reflectivity. If the surrounding ground is a hard surface colored by cool grays and blues, then the adjacent plane should have a cool aura. The same rule holds for the warmth of landscaped and earthen surfaces that cast a warm glow on adjacent planes.

GUIDELINE 20

In strong light, a strong contrast can be made between two (or more) planes by leaving the exposed plane white or very light and applying a darker tone to the unexposed plane.

GUIDELINE 21

All plane treatments use the following formula:

$$A = [\, LC\, (T)\, (t) + R\, (T)\, (t)\,] \times G$$

where

A = application
LC = local color
T = tone
t = temperature (warm or cool)
R = reflectivity from adjacent surfaces
G = gradation

Even though this formula should not be followed literally, it does provide a guideline to remind the designer of the components that constitute plane-change accents.

PLANE-CHANGE ACCENTS

The shadow of an object that immediately follows the shadow edge—the change from a lighted surface to a shadowed surface—usually is the core of the shadow, the darkest area, or the *plane-change accent.* The darkest shadow tone follows immediately after the change of planes, lightening as it draws away from the plane change, primarily because of the reflected light from adjacent surfaces.

GUIDELINE 22

The change in planes from light to shade produces a high-contrast shadow core immediately adjacent to the shadow edge.

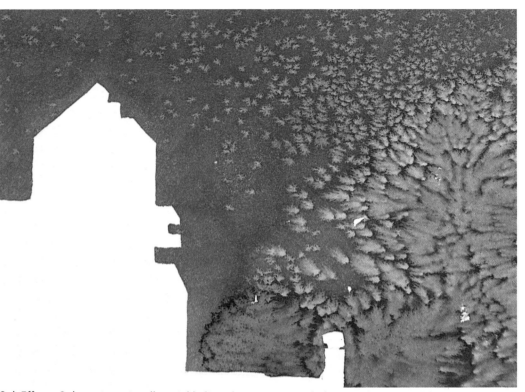

Salt Effects. Salt was intentionally sprinkled in a dense pattern at the lower right section of the diagram to illustrate its effects, ranging from single "stars" to almost a fountain or tree effect.

GUIDELINE 23

Reflected light from the ground and foliage is warm in temperature.

SHADOW CORE

Round shapes consist of curved planes with a different light condition at each interval of the plane. A good way to strengthen the depiction of curved planes is through a multifaceted shadow, one that has a dark tonal core at its center. All edges are soft on the curved plane. To create a *shadow core,*

- Wet the entire exposed surface with clear water.
- Apply the dark core shadow (at any place but the center of the object) with a single stroke. On a cylinder, the stroke may be

Star Bright. The salt pattern in this example was dispersed more evenly and not as densely as in the previous diagram. Experiment with different densities and patterns as well as paper wetnesses.

vertical, whereas on a sphere, the stroke should be a curved line.

- Grade the shadow from dark to midtone on the shadow side and from dark to light on the light-source side.
- Remember to add reflectivity at the bottom of the shadow to incorporate the adjacent surface.

SALT

Salt applied to a wet painting will absorb the pigment, leaving a white area in its place. Either table salt or kosher salt can be used, as they differ only in the size of their granules. To use salt in this way, use the following techniques:

- On wet pigmented paper, apply (toss, sprinkle, pour) salt to the desired area when the paper is more than damp, but is not soaking.
- Once the paint has thoroughly dried, it cannot be rewet and then salted; salting will work only on wet paintings.
- Brush off the excess salt.
- After the applied area has dried thoroughly, the area may be rewet and glazed.
- By raising, tilting, or twisting the board while the salt is drying, you can produce many unusual effects.

PLASTIC WRAP

To use plastic wrap to create white areas,

- Determine the shape(s) of the application area, although the wrap does not need to be cut in the exact shape desired.
- Apply plastic wrap to a wet painted area, pressing the wrap into the paint in the exact shape desired.
- Allow the paint to dry.
- Remove the plastic to reveal the shapes.

WAXED PAPER

Applications using waxed paper differ from those using wax, in that an image can be drawn on the wax paper over a painting. The image leaves a wax impression on the paper and resists pigment. This can be applied to dry white paper or dry paint applications and can be used to create background trees and calligraphy.

WAX

Paraffin or wax resists pigment and is therefore an effective masking tool for background and negative shapes. Use white wax crayons, wax sticks, or paraffin. Techniques using wax are the following:

- Determine the areas where the wax will be applied.
- On either white paper or a light tone (allowed to dry), apply the image with the wax instrument.
- Apply the paint.
- After the paint has dried, overlay the area with tracing paper or toweling, and lightly apply a hot iron to melt the wax and absorb it into the toweling. Do not press too hard or the wax will spread. Use as many clean layers of paper or toweling as is necessary to remove the wax.

CENTER OF INTEREST

The *center of interest* is the main area or point of interest and emphasis in a painting. The center is actually at the midpoint of a corner quadrant in a rectangle, formed by first dividing the rectangle into four equal parts by means of diagonal lines and then subdividing each quadrant into four sections. The intersection of each of the four quadrant diagonals is a center of interest, although it is never placed in the true center of the rectangle, but on one of the diagonals. The focus element can be an object such as a building, an artifact, a color, or a person. Many artists actually

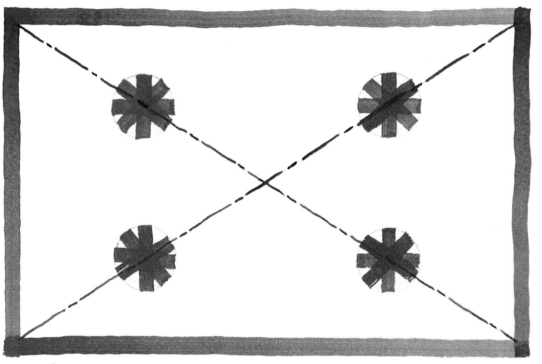

Center of Interest

begin their painting with the center of interest. Another general rule of thumb in selecting a center of interest is to locate it in a place where no two distances from the center to the edge of the paper are the same.

Another means of emphasizing the center of interest is to design a "cross" through the center point, by means of shapes and tones. An example is a design composed of a vertical building form intersected by a horizon of trees.

GUIDELINE 24

In traditional painting, the center of interest is rarely the center of the painting. It is at the center of one of the four quadrants of the paper.

GUIDELINE 25

The center of interest is where the most detail is placed, where the maximum value or tone is concentrated, and where the viewer's eye is encouraged to focus.

GUIDELINE 26

The center of interest should be at those locations where the distance from it to the edge of the paper is different for all four edges.

Center of Interest Sketch. The center of interest here is a barn located in the upper left-hand quadrant, supported by a substantial foreground in the other three quadrants.

GUIDELINE 27

The center of interest can be a shape, point, color, tone, texture, and/or pattern that the painter wishes the viewer to regard as the most important item in the painting.

MIXING COLORS ON PAPER

Using both wet-on-wet and wet-on-dry (direct) methods, the painter can mix colors right on the paper rather than on the palette. The results can be more intense and semiabstract in character. As a sketching technique, this is effective in that multiple layers of washes are not needed to produce variation. To mix colors on paper,

- Wet the paper thoroughly with clear water. With the direct method, apply the first wash with a very wet brush.
- With the wet-on-wet method, while the paper is still wet but the sheen has disappeared, apply two or more colors to the wet area, allowing them to mix with each other by applying each color next to or slightly overlapping the other colors. Avoid mixing the colors completely on the paper; the colors should spread into each other on the wet paper.
- With the wet-on-dry method, have a heavy charge of the first color in the brush, and after applying to the dry paper, charge the brush with the other color(s) along the edge-pool.
- When mixing colors on the paper, allow each color to show through; that is, do not overmix them. Create shadows by

placing a cool (blue, for example) against a warm (red) object and letting the cool and warm mix slightly, forming a soft edge.

- Remember that shadows can be made up of colors other than blues, browns, grays, and purples.

SHADOWS

Shadows are areas devoid of light, obstructed by other objects from the waves of the light source. In painting, shadow shapes, shadow edges, and shadow cores are useful in denoting objects in space. As a design tool, shadows serve as highlights, backdrops, or supports for focal objects, by contrasting them with other surrounding surfaces exposed to the same light source.

Shadow shapes are two-dimensional shapes that are usually in constant motion, changing their dimensions and proportions with every second that the moving light source (the sun) is exposed to the focal object. Even indoor shadows affected by fixed light sources (artificial) are influenced by moving daylight shadows.

Shadow edges are high-contrast interfaces between object and shadow, between light reflectivity and the absence of light. They help the designer define material, texture, tone (value), softness, or hardness.

Shadow cores are the darkest portions of the shadow, usually occurring at the change of planes between light and dark.

GUIDELINE 28

The shadows on light surfaces are light in tone.

GUIDELINE 29

The shadows on dark surfaces are dark in tone.

GUIDELINE 30

Shadows are graded in tone, from darker interiors to lighter edges or from darker plane-change edges to areas with a strong back light farther away from the plane change.

GUIDELINE 31

Shadows can be made up of many colors, influenced by local colors and reflectivity. Reflectivity changes the color of shadows by adding to the shadow reflected light (color) waves from other adjacent surfaces.

GUIDELINE 32

Shadows are composed of darker tones or values created by mixing any color with black, its opposite (complementary) color, or a darker staining pigment such as Winsor Green, Thalo Green, Alizarin Crimson, or opaques such as Ultramarine Blue.

HORIZON

The *horizon* should be placed either very high or very low in the painting. After adding background shapes such as mountains, trees, or buildings, the line created by the top of those background shapes should be above or below the mid-vertical point of the painting.

GUIDELINE 33

The horizon is an illusion in painting and should be placed where it will have the most dramatic effect on the image to be communicated.

DRY LIFT-OFF

For a dry lift-off, use the following techniques:

- Allow the painted area to dry thoroughly.
- Using a bristle brush, load the area to be removed with clear water, twisting the brush during application.
- Let the water stand for a minute.

- With a blotter or tissue, absorb the excess water by dabbing the wetness, thereby drawing it up into the blotter and bringing pigment with it.
- Repeat this procedure until the area has been lifted off.

STRAIGHT EDGE

Straight lines can be achieved in one of two ways: using a ruling pen and a straight edge or using a ruler to guide the hand and brush. Ruling pens are discussed in Part 5, "Materials and Equipment." The second method is as follows:

- Hold the ruler in your nonpainting hand, and rest that hand on the paper, with the nonworking end of the ruler resting on a safe place on the paper.

- With the charged brush in your painting hand, rest the tip of your middle finger of your brush against the edge of the ruler and glide it softly toward you or along the ruler, creating a straight line.

References

Couch, Tony. 1987. *Watercolor: You Can Do It*. Cincinnati: North Light Books.

Guptill, Arthur. 1949. *Color Illustration and Rendering*. New York: Reinhold.

Reid, Charles. 1985. *Pulling Your Paintings Together*. New York: Watson-Guptill.

Shook, Georg, and Witt, Gary. 1981. *Sharp Focus Watercolor Painting*. New York: Watson-Guptill.

ELEMENTS OF THE CITYSCAPE

Preliminary Studies

The first real step between the research of a design problem and the act of design is the *diagram*, or a graphic illustration that explains by means of its parts and their relationship. Many designers and artists believe that if they cannot diagram a concept for a design in a simple, straight forward manner, they cannot proceed further because they do not understand the issues and/or the analysis of the data or the concept.

This part of the book will describe ways to use watercolor as a diagrammatic medium expressing ideas and information conceptually, loosely, and with chromatic content. The examples that follow have three purposes: first, to illustrate the model that watercolor provides as a design process, second, to explain data analysis and/ or design concepts clearly and concisely, and, third, to begin considering color at the early stages of design.

Diagrams

Diagraming an idea is not unlike diagraming a sentence; that is, it usually requires a subject (the focal point), an object (the receiver of the action), and a verb (the action). Diagrams are charts composed of symbols that describe strategies for meeting some objective. Each diagram usually has one or more focal points, a supporting object (background, supporting use, and so forth), and an implied action (such as connecting one space to another with walkways or view corridors, or a focal space for festivals or a group activity).

The following figure depicts a diagram for the Missoula, Montana, Downtown Riverfront Corridor Design Competition, drawn with technical pens and India ink by architect James Pettinari. The symbols represent urban locations for various activities unified by a riverfront system and connected to the existing downtown form by penetrating circulation easements.

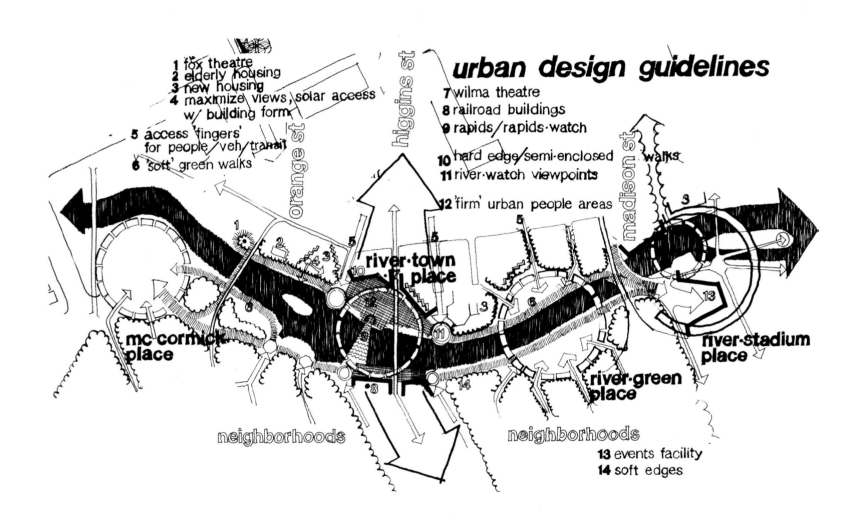

Missoula Diagram. This pen-and-ink diagram, drawn by Jim Pettinari in 1982, illustrates the conceptual delineation of a design without the specified building and open space forms.

Using watercolor to represent the same concept is relatively easy and, by means of color, portrays information with energy and excitement. The following examples will show how.

SKAGIT GATEWAY

Skagit Gateway is a 9″ x 9″ sketch diagram that is my first expression of an idea for a research center portico design. I consider it a diagram rather than a sketch because it represents broad relationships rather than specific design elements, yet uses three-dimensional forms to depict the portico.

The diagram was painted without any pencil guidelines or preconceived outline shapes. It is an experiment in form development patterns rather than mental visualizations. It is not a design as such but was one of eight three-dimensional sketch diagrams prepared for this project.

Skagit Gateway

The Center (11″ x 15″)

CENTER DESIGN

Center Design, a diagram composed of elevations, planes, and sections, was quickly developed to help free my mind from program details. It is another search for imagery rather than for form based solely on a technical program. The diagram is a graphic illustration that tries to identify an image according to its parts and their relationship. It is a *working* graphic, one that explores and tests idea-forms during the process of exploration. This represents nonverbal idea formulation. The color and tone help explore shape and pattern with masses of color (tone) rather than with calligraphy and the shades of gray to which calligraphy is limited.

Warm and vibrant or high key reds and oranges were used as focal areas, and blues and purples provided a soft darker background. White shapes were left for high contrast.

CREEK STREET

Creek Street portrays the relationship between an active salmon-spawning tidal creek functioning as a "street" and a collection of old buildings on pilings along this "street" in Ketchikan, Alaska: boardwalks, historic buildings, views of the creek and the surrounding terrain, and all the factors that influenced the redesign of this area.

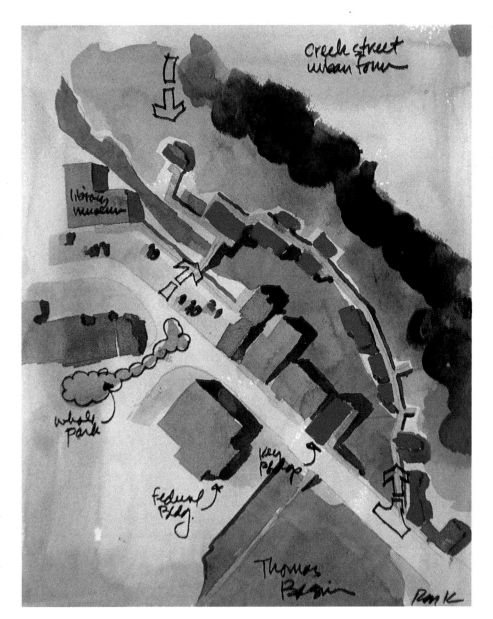

Creek Street Historic Form (8½" x 10"). The forms of the buildings, creek, and bluff all contribute to the uniqueness of the historic district. The diagram portrays these forms with the key buildings highlighted by the warmest colors.

Watercolor diagrams were used to represent through color and tone the existing conditions as well as what improvements could be made. They were drawn quickly using simple complementing colors and strong tonal contrasts for shadows. A one-quarter-inch flat and a one-quarter-inch stroke brush were used to paint the simple yet bold calligraphy. A one-inch flat brush was used for the larger shapes. The wet-on-dry method was applied to each diagram, allowing me to work quickly while not having to wait for pre-wet areas to dry. The results are similar in style to a Graphos pen application, characterized by wide sharp-edged calligraphy.

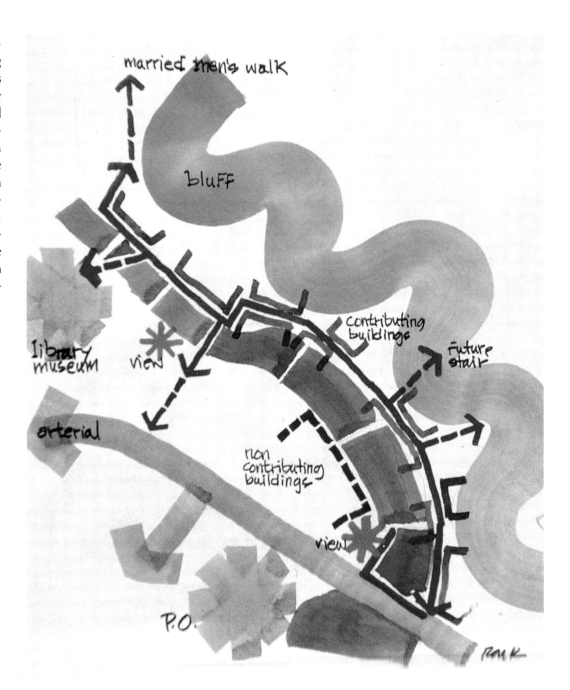

Creek Street Diagram (8½″ x 10″). Using flat brushes, from one-half to one inch in width, the elements of the diagram were quickly and colorfully illustrated.

HISTORIC WATERFRONT

Port Townsend Historic Waterfront is a ten-minute doodle on pencil-grade sketch paper, sized 8″ x 10″. Because I wanted to prepare a series of fast, 35-mm slide images, I used watercolor, with high-intensity colors such as Cadmium Red and Cadmium Orange as highlights. Green and blue depict the uplands and water, respectively. The background building form is painted in a subdued warm purple gray. The diagram represents built form and key activity areas. The application method was wet-on-dry, with the darker-toned water shape and red symbols applied last.

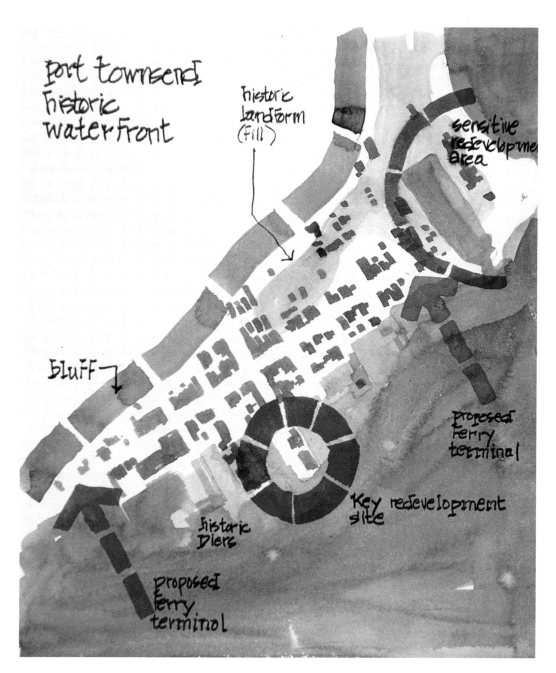

Port Townsend (8½″ x 10″)

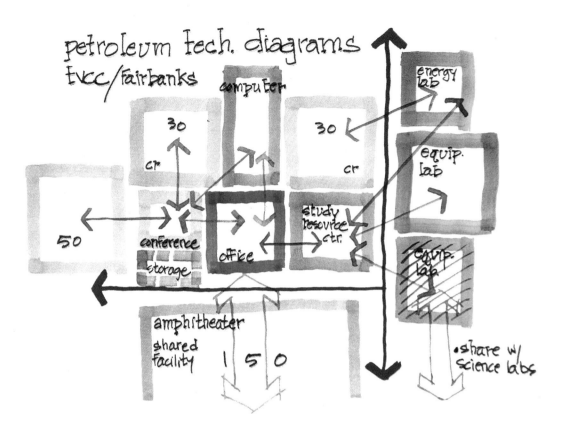

TVCC (8½″ x 10″)

SPACE DIAGRAMS

TVCC is a diagram that demonstrates the ability of watercolor to replace possible toxic markers to show basic technical program relationships. This diagram is 8″ x 10″, drawn on pencil-grade sketch paper (semitransparent) with a Pentel sign pen used for the lettering. A one-quarter-inch flat brush was used for the area symbols, and a one-quarter-inch stroke brush was used freehand for the arrows. Again, this sort of diagram is excellent for use in slide presentations, color copiers, and color photostats. The final image also reproduces well on black-and-white copiers as shades of gray and black.

YAKIMA URBAN PLACES

Yakima Urban Places is a diagram illustrating the existing and potential open spaces throughout downtown Yakima that exhibit potential with a sense of place, that is, have spaces defined by buildings, natural features, and/or urban activities that have special or unique qualities. I wanted a graphic that would be semi-abstract, exhibiting multiple enclosures without the accessories of cars, sidewalks, utilities, signs, and so forth.

Yakima Urban Places. This is an example of a large journal diagram, used to portray urban design concepts on a downtown scale. The diagram is 22″ x 30″ on 140-lb. cold-pressed Arches paper.

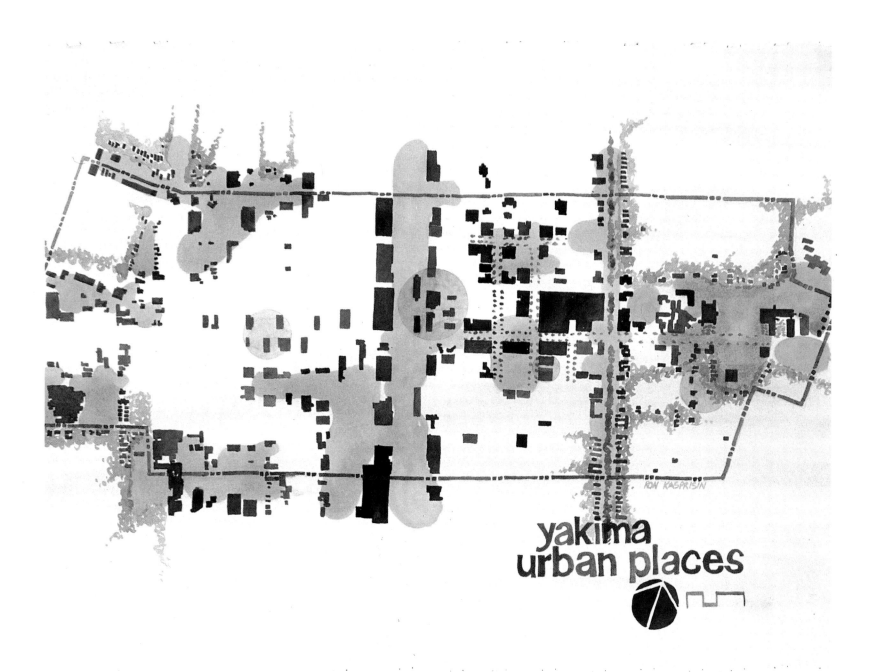

yakima
urban places

RON KASPRISIN

Construction of the Base Drawing

The base drawing was first roughed out on flimsy tracing paper and then transferred (outlined) to the watercolor paper using a light table. If a light table is not available, a daylit window will suffice; or a graphite transfer (a soft pencil coating applied on the reverse side of the flimsy, creating a carbon) can be used.

Palette and Brushes

The palette consisted of Cadmium Red, Aureolin Yellow, Cobalt Blue, French Ultramarine Blue, Viridian, and Rose Madder Genuine (Rose Madder, a synthetic, is a good substitute if diluted properly). I used a 2″ wash brush for underlayments and a no. 8 round and a ¼″ flat for detailed work.

Strategy

Because the "places" were the most important elements of the painting, a warm temperature was selected for the open space area, and cool contrasting temperatures for the buildings that defined the open space. Both together constitute the "place." Lettering was kept to a minimum in order to allow the semiabstract graphic to "read."

Sequence and Techniques

- The image was transferred to the watercolor paper in freehand using a light table.
- The paper was soaked in clear water,

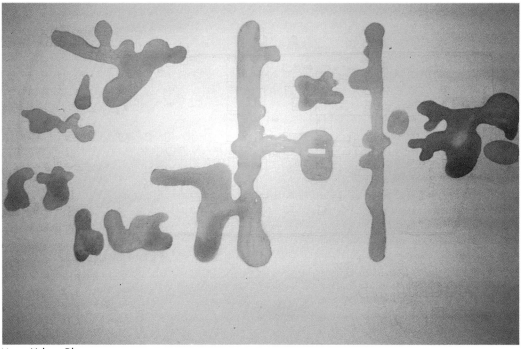

More Urban Places

mounted on a rigid board with staples, and allowed to dry and stretch.
- No masking fluid was used.
- A light-tone wash foundation was applied (wet on wet) using Aureolin Yellow and Cobalt Blue and a hint of Rose Madder Genuine.
- The urban places, drawn in intense light-tone to midtone orange colors, were washed in over unpainted building forms and vegetation after previous washes had dried thoroughly

- Next, the dark-tone blue buildings (Permanent Blue) were completed in a single application. Because the buildings are dark, there was no need to mask or paint around them—they simply covered the lighter orange wash.
- Trees, boundaries, and lettering were added last using wet on dry; Indian Red was used for the lettering so as to differentiate it from the Crimson Red boundary and the orange spatial shapes.

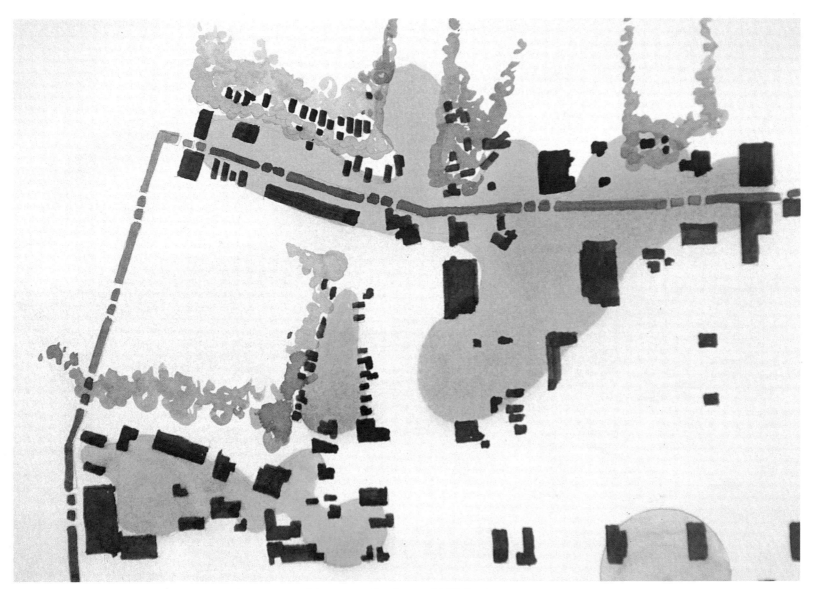

Summit Commons. This is a blowup of the northwest sector of downtown. The diagram highlights the open-space "places" in warm reds, the buildings active as "edges" in blues, and the tree stands in green stipple.

Sketch Studies

According to Tom Lynch, a sketch is "a brief interaction with a subject." And although "many sketches will never bring finished paintings . . . what is learned and observed in the process . . . is invaluable for the pleasure it brings, the experience the eye can get, and the experimentation [it brings] with subject and materials" (Rivers 1987, p. 57). The artist is required to work quickly, reducing the subject's complexity to a semi-abstract interpretation of the basic concepts, forms, shapes, and patterns that represents the underlying content or "essence" of the subject design.

Every designer should keep a hardcover sketchbook series, recording everything from five-minute doodles to one-hour sketches. For reference, many artists staple or tape a photograph of their subject alongside the painting. Sketches completed on other papers, from napkins (yes!) to smaller watercolor papers, also can be stapled or taped into the book. They will give the designer a chronological history of ideas, techniques, and advancement—a tool more valuable after one becomes experienced. The following are items to remember when selecting sketching sites:

Good value or tone contrasts (light and dark).

Interesting colors.

Distinctive shapes, patterns, and textures.

A focal point or center of interest

The time of day when you sketch is important. With the possible exception of winter months, the early morning and late afternoon light is best for high contrasts. Try to stay away from the midday sun as it minimizes the shadows and tends to flatten out colors because of its brightness. Also, during the warm months, the midday sun's heat causes washes to dry very quickly—perhaps too quickly for adequate control.

SKETCHING IN THE DESIGN PROCESS

Sketching using watercolors has two valuable lessons: First, it teaches the designers about the subject they are about to paint, helping them determine shape, pattern, tone contrasts, color temperatures, color and texture, and content. Second, it teaches them in model form the process of studying complex building and landscape design, by representing the design in basic forms, or even in abstract or at least semiabstract forms, in order to evaluate their relationships.

Sketching is communicating graphically in form and content: Sketch studies made prior to a final watercolor are the graphic "drafts" needed to explore structure, organization, and style before completing the final. It cannot be verbalized under any circumstances. Mental visualization only uses stored past images rather than fresh forms from a working sketch.

French Farm House One was completed

Abandoned Rectory (15″ x 22″)

on site in two phases. Phase 1 consisted of three small tone sketches that experimented with shape, massing, and tone. Phase 2 consisted of color temperature and tone sketches.

Phase 1's sketches enabled the designer to site the building, alter its orientation to the surrounding terrain, and determine direction and contrasts in lighting. After these studies, color was applied to a small sketch in order to experiment with various color temperatures and tones. The color sketches were made with a one-inch flat brush using the corners for calligraphy and small shapes as well as the flat portion for larger areas.

French Farmhouse One (6″ x 8″)

Farmhouse Kitchen (5″ x 7″)

French Farmhouse Color (3″ x 6″ each)

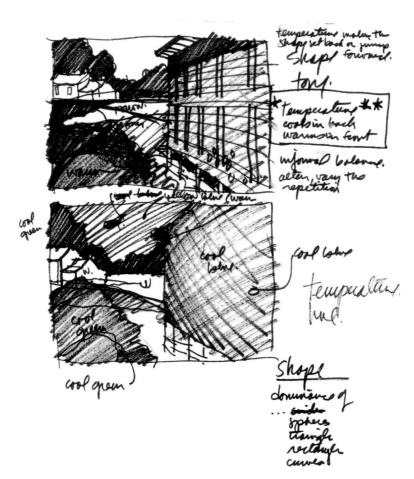

French Farmhouse Two (8" x 10")

French Farmhouse Two (22" x 30")

Farmhouse Field

French Farm House Two is a study of the same site but with the farmhouse relocated to another portion of the site. Two tone sketches were completed with a Pentel sign pen, and the colors, temperatures, and tones were decided during this phase.

The on-site final painting, 22″ x 30″, provided enough information for the studio completion of the watercolor design and artwork.

Window is another series of tone sketches or studies that were completed on site. Along with an information sketch—describing the colors, light source, direction of light, and other pertinent information—the designer was able to prepare and complete the final work in the studio. The issue in *Window* is the fast, informal exploratory nature of the sketch. Other more complete or finished sketches could be displayed here but I want to underscore the use of the sketch as a thought process that uses graphics as words—real graphic portrayals of what the designer "sees," not mentally visualizes.

Window

Pelican and *Beach* are examples of fast
sketches using watercolor with preliminary
tone sketches.

Pelican. A rough watercolor sketch was prepared on site (in the rain), and this more formal sketch
was completed indoors. I still consider this a sketch because it is a fast effort in the visualization
process, done more with imagery in mind rather than technical accuracy of painting methods.

Beach. This sketch was prepared on hot-pressed watercolor paper to practice using a magazine image as a guide.

Reference

Rivers, Valerie R. 1987. "Tom Lynch: Paris Sketchbook." *Amercian Artist* 51 (544): S7-S10.

The Landscape

Landforms

Landforms are an integral part of the foreground, midground, and background of most paintings and illustrations, and they serve to highlight or support the painting's subject.

This chapter describes a variety of landforms, ranging from aerial oblique rural and urban scales to specific building sites. Landforms discussed include mountains, bodies of water, and gently rolling hills. Each landform helps define the context or the setting of objects in space.

PREPARING AERIAL OBLIQUE LANDFORMS

Preparation

Aerial oblique views can be set up in one of three ways: (1) by freehand sketching from on-site locations or photographs, (2) by outlining a perspective from aerial oblique slides photographed from an airplane or high vantage point, or (3) by outlining a perspective from a slide photographed from a U.S. Geological Survey (USGS) two-dimensional map of the subject area.

Freehand sketching is a technique that can be used to analyze and think through a composition, shapes, patterns, and so on. Although initially it is the most difficult kind of sketch for many designers, it is the most instructive and rewarding in the long run.

Sequence

- Prepare a three-dimensional contour drawing or massing study of the subject area, indicating only enough detail to reflect surface texture and pattern from a distance; massing is the key.

- Make a new composition based on more detailed sketches of the area that are deemed interesting or supportive of the subject but that do not necessarily replicate exactly the natural scene. For example, if a series of rolling foothills has a monotonous form, it may be replaced with another landform (e.g., a river, or forest) that "fits" into the designer's conceptual idea of what he or she wants to communicate. This "right of authorship" is useful as a means of strengthening and emphasizing the main subject of the painting, whether it is a building, a city, or other sense of space.
- Use overlays of flimsy tracing paper to rework the sketch until the desired perspective and composition are achieved. Very few people arrive at a final freehand sketch image on the first effort; rather, it may take several attempts to achieve satisfaction.

Although freehand sketches are a desirable technique, they may not be technically accurate enough for some subjects; they may be beyond the designer's present skill level; or they may be difficult to make without a suitable vantage point.

Slide sketches are useful for portraying accurate views. Slides taken from an airplane or another high vantage point are projected onto a wall or screen (rigid) so that the image can be traced directly onto watercolor paper or tracing paper for further work. Once the outline images of the

aerial oblique have been transferred to tracing paper, together with any important reference points, the designer can then rough out any recommendations and changes. After an additional overlay or two, the final image should be massed out and ready to paint. The final image can be transferred to watercolor paper by means of a light table, a graphite underlayment, or a slide. The advantages of slides include the multiple images that can be photographed from the air, giving the designer a choice of view, and the flexibility in image size achieved by moving the projector closer to or farther away from the screen.

When an airplane or other high vantage point is not available, a useful technique is to make a slide from a USGS map.

Sequence

- Lay a USGS map of the project area out on a table or floor. Be sure to include enough of the surrounding area for a backdrop, particularly if there are features such as mountains or rivers that would add to the perspective.
- Using slide film, photograph the map at an oblique angle using a hand-held or tripod-mounted camera, with the appropriate lighting. The oblique angle will distort the two-dimensional USGS map enough to provide a horizontal "perspective." Use this basic perspective to exaggerate vanishing points until the right look is achieved.

- Sketch out the distorted plan (now in rough perspective) from the slide to whatever size is desired.
- "Raise" the vertical dimensions of the plan perspective and exaggerate the vertical scale for dramatic effect, by sketching the vertical landforms using as a guide the gross-scale contour lines on the USGS map. After a number of preliminary sketches, a three-dimensional aerial oblique sketch of a large scale area can be made with spectacular results. Do not hesitate to use your imagination—this is not a place for scaled measurements. Your eye is the best judge.
- Use a light table, slide, or large window (during daylight hours) to trace the image onto watercolor paper. The original sheet size of *Jacob's Pillow* (Kasprisin and Pettinari) is 43" x 53", a rolled piece of 125-lb cold-pressed watercolor paper. The image was transferred to it via a light table, working in sections according to the design graphics layout (plans, sections, sketches, and so on) until the entire sheet was filled with drawings.

PAINTING AERIAL OBLIQUE LANDFORMS

Painting aerial obliques should be approached as any other watercolor—as abstract shapes and patterns rather than as named objects, that is, buildings, cars, and so forth. Variations and combinations of wet-on-wet and wet-on-dry techniques are most effective.

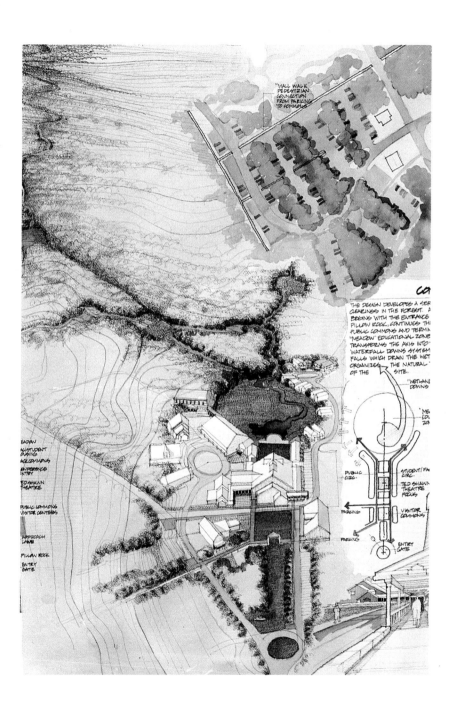

Sequence

- Prepare a pencil outline drawing.
- Lay down an initial color and temperature scheme with light and midtones.
- Establish distance by grading the tone, for example, from light background to medium-dark foreground. Recession (objects becoming less dominant in the background) is a basic component of territorial views. Establish the light tones first with quick washes, avoiding areas where white paper is to be left white (mask if necessary). Cooler colors and/or neutrals should be used for background masses.
- Masses should take precedence over detail, with detail limited to the focal point or edges and boundaries that define important shapes. Use multiple colors merged in a wet-on-wet fashion to provide a varietal underlayment that implies detail.
- Select a focal point or center pertaining to the subject to be emphasized (such as a building within the landscape or a portion of the landscape) and build the tone and intensity to that focus. In many territorial landform views, the focus may be extensive, for example, a connecting link such as a river valley or a sprawling urban area. The backdrop landform

Jacobs Pillow Aerial. This is a mixed-media aerial oblique, using India ink and technical pens over a watercolor base, applied to a pencil drawing.

Rural Landform (10″ x 10″)

should complement the focus, not compete with it.

• Build up the details step by step. Don't rush in and overwork the early stages, and don't try to save the painting at the last minute with your darks. Also, don't be impatient and add your darks too quickly, as they will be difficult—if not impossible—to lessen in tone. Carve out focal points by making the strongest possible contrasts between light and dark tones at the focal point, emphasizing light shapes with dark backgrounds, for example.

Rural Landform is an early illustration of mine, which was painted with a series of glazes. The color pattern was slowly built up by adding transparent washes to previously dried washes—essentially a wet-on-dry glazing technique. A pattern of a warm foreground and a cool background helped establish a recession effect of near to far. The initial washes were light cools, with the foreground's warm washes laid over the earlier cool ones to help color harmony.

Return to Juneau (15″ x 22″). This illustration was compiled from slides taken during a flight in southeast Alaska. The desire to detail the trees compromised the landform study.

Seattle Urban Design (20″ x 30″). This mixed-media illustration applied India ink with a technical pen over the watercolor to produce the dark contrasts.

ground landforms were kept subdued with light-toned blues and greens, whereas the extensive foreground was washed in midtones. The major artificial forms such as the downtown skyline and the freeway were left white to contrast them with the surrounding terrain. The background mountains were painted in a light tone, and the major elements, such as bodies of water and city neighborhoods, were given a midtone.

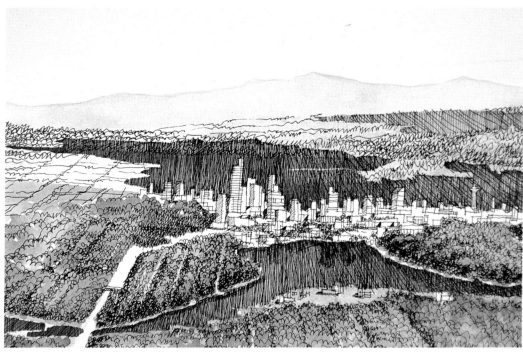

Seattle Urban Design (detail)

In *Seattle Urban Design,* on 20″ x 30″ watercolor board, light (white) tones and colored midtones were applied with watercolors, using both wet-on-wet and wet-on-dry methods. The midtones predominate because I wanted to emphasize the characteristic greenery of Seattle's neighborhoods. The dark tones were sketched in India ink after the previous washes had dried thoroughly. Landform and built-form edges were emphasized as a means of defining sections of the painting. The back-

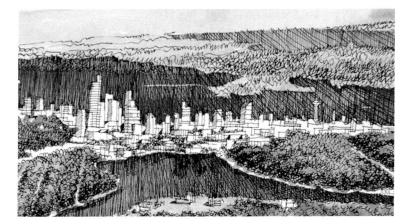

Seattle Urban Design (detail)

Seattle Study. The green rolling hills of Seattle were emphasized with medium-dark tones and a mixture of greens. The purples and blues of the downtown were contrasted against complements of yellows.

Seattle Study (detail)

Seattle Study is an earlier study for *Seattle Urban Design*. The darker midtones and darks were applied to the background, midground, and foreground, and a light tone was left immediately behind the downtown silhouette to contrast with the cityscape.

I decided early on to emphasize both the bodies of water surrounding the downtown and the downtown building forms themselves. Although I achieved this objective, the overall tone of the painting turned out to be darker than I had originally intended —particularly the tone of the background mountains and immediate foreground. Because the downtown shape is in the upper midground, the darker tones could have been closer to the midground area.

The initial washes were applied with a wet-on-wet method, and the darker final washes, with a wet-on-dry method. The dominant temperature is warm, although blues and greens predominate. Green can go either way in regard to temperature, and the Winsor Green stain in this painting was warmed with Raw Sienna and Alizarin Crimson. The downtown buildings were highlighted in dark-tone blues and purples to provide a subtle contrast to the surrounding landforms.

Seattle Study (detail)

Seattle Study (detail)

Seattle West is another aerial oblique study that experiments with the reflectivity of sky colors and adjacent bodies of water to create a secondary highlight. It also is a mixed-media illustration on 20″ x 30″ watercolor board, using pen and India ink to establish dark tones and edge highlights. The lesson here is the technique of using color reflections as a highlight to support a center of interest. A touch of Rose Madder Genuine was washed into the wet blue water to create the reflection.

Seattle West. This mixed-media, playful aerial experimented with reflective sky colors on major bodies of water. As in *Seattle Urban Design*, India ink was applied over the watercolor to establish dark tones and edges

Seattle West (detail)

Seattle West (detail)

Seattle West (detail). Alizarin Crimson was washed into the wet blue wash of Puget Sound and Lake Union to create a reflected light effect.

Mountains

Mountains are usually background or backdrop images and distant objects, reduced in color intensity. Tone (value) applications are usually light, painted in cools and neutrals, midtones, and dark tones where the landform is more dominant in the subject matter. The sky–mountain–midground relationship is critical, in that all three must work together as a backdrop rather than compete for attention. The edges between sky, mountains, and midground should flow together, not read as hard sectional lines.

The sky–mountain edge is achieved with a combination of hard and soft and lost and found edges. Clouds often obscure the mountain peaks, creating an opportunity for soft and lost edges. Mountains silhouetted against gray or blue skies work well with hard edges when the sun is low and backlights the mountain shapes. Lift-outs from the mountain shapes immediately following the application of a wash can establish mists, light striking the mountain, and variation in the tones of the rock masses among the alpine forests.

The mountain–midground edges are usually midtones and can be integrated by means of interlocking shapes and hard and soft and lost and found edges. Tree cover, rocks, and silhouettes provide opportunities to "dissolve" or lock in this edge con-

Mt. Baker Ridge

dition and make the mountains and midground flow together.

GUIDELINE 1

Mountain shapes can be painted in neutrals or warm or cool grays, light to midtones, and as masses with little or no detail. Rendering each tree or group of trees is neither necessary nor desired. The objective is to relate the shape and tone of these landforms as supporting shapes within the overall pattern.

The techniques for painting mountain forms are as follows:

- Plan and reserve the areas of white (paper) that will remain as white.
- Paint or sketch in the outline of the composition.
- For the wet-on-wet method, apply clear water to the shape, allow it to dry slightly (lose its sheen), and apply the pigment-charged brush, permitting the colors to blend in a way that emphasizes the mass yet provides a color variation hinting of forest, meadows, and tree massings without showing detail. Mix colors on the paper rather than on the palette for more variety in soft shapes and colors where this effect is desired.
- For the wet-on-dry method, start the wet-charged wash at the top or side of the mountain range, working down or across the paper, adding color in wet

Mt. Baker Ridge (detail)

areas and/or lifting out color and tone where desired. Variety in color and shape can be achieved by adding different colors to the wet edge, allowing them to merge without brush work. The bottom edge of the mountain, as it meets the midground, should be left to dry in interlocking shapes or should be kept wet in order to blend in quickly the midground colors. Obviously, if the midground is dark enough to cover the lighter mountain tone, the interlocking shapes will come from the midground.

Another approach to creating mountains with numerous shapes is to paint the darker areas first, thereby establishing the darkest tones. Clouds can then be added to a wet sky, with midtone shadows cast on the white areas. However, if the mountains are supporting shapes, remember that dark tones at or near the focal point need to be even darker.

Sky and Clouds

Sky and clouds are an essential part of any painting. They can serve as a simple backdrop; they can give direction to a viewer's eye; or they can act as a dynamic component in a composition in which movement and form in the background strengthen the subject matter.

Skies are usually soft, with fuzzy edges of clouds blending into light blue and then into deeper blue skies. Cloud shapes may have hard edges when the background sky is clear and deeper in tone, contrasting the cloud formations condensed together by means of cold air. A safe bet in portraying clouds is to use a mixture of soft and hard edges, defining some edges sharply while losing others to a blend of cloud and sky (Couch 1987, Szabo 1971).

GUIDELINE 2

Skies are usually painted first in the sequence, in order to set the mood and tone of light, which is reflected from objects on the ground. A dark sky cannot produce a bright vibrant field, nor can a bright sky produce a dark, sullen terrain effect.

CLEAR SKIES

Clear skies are depicted by means of graded washes, from dark to light (from dark outer space to the lighter atmosphere of earth). The graded tones can be composed of one or numerous colors, reflecting the subtle atmospheric conditions, the influence of the sun (or moon) as light sources, and the season of the year. The principal characteristics of clear skies are graded tone, transparency, and luminosity. To achieve the image of reflected light through transparency and luminosity, the paint should be applied in light to moderate amounts, and the multiple color washes should be graded and blended rather than completely overlaid. Methods that can be used for skies include wet-on-wet, wet-on-dry, and glazing.

To create a clear sky, try using a single-color graded wash, running it from the top of the sky (the darker tone) to the bottom of the sky (the lighter tone), by adding more clear water and less pigment as the wash is worked downward. Depending on the area to be covered, some artists try not to lift their brush from the paper when they begin to wash, moving from a fully charged dark tone to an almost dry light tone. On larger areas, for which multiple brush chargings are required, the ratio of clear water to pigment must be steadily increased at each charging. Practice in painting graded washes is important to achieve clear, clean, unblemished results.

Multiple-color graded washes are used to indicate a changing sky, an evening or morning sky, or a sky reflecting the near-earth colors. Both the wet-on-wet and the wet-on-dry methods work well for this effect.

Sequence

- Wet the paper thoroughly, waiting for the wet sheen to disappear.
- Apply the first light wash in the first color, fading from a stronger intensity to a weaker intensity.
- While the first color is still very wet, begin to blend in a darker tone with the second color and build up the second-color wash until it reaches the intensity and tone desired.
- Tilting the paper upright and at different angles will cause the dark and light colors

Monochromatic Clear Sky

to merge in soft irregular edges. Many patterns are possible as long as the washes are wet and mobile.

- Light tones are important to most background skies (there are exceptions when dark contrasting skies are desired).
- Apply the sixty-second rule from the start of the wash to the finish; that is. stop at sixty seconds and do not go back (Couch 1987).

Multiple-Color Clear Sky

HAZY, BROKEN SKIES

To create blue skies with haze or light broken clouds, use a wet-on-wet technique, quickly applying the lighter tone and color (e.g., Naples Yellow) followed by a blue wash (e.g., Permanent Blue). Roll and twist the brush over the wet paper, allowing the results to occur at random. Then quickly lift out any streaks or highlights with a brush or tool that is drier than the wash. Finally, leave the sky alone! If you decide that more definition is needed, permit the previous wash to dry before rewetting the surface for another wash.

Another version of this effect consists of combining the wet-on-wet and the wet-on-dry methods as follows:

- Wet the paper around the edge of the sky mass as well as in a small segregated area in the middle.
- As the sheen disappears, quickly apply the wash over the wet and dry surface, leaving the whites as they occur at random.
- Lift out a small section of wash in the center of the cloud mass.

This combination will produce a varied sky pattern.

Hazy Skies

BREAKING UP THE SKY MASS

To create interest and also to break up sky masses that might become monotonous, extend elements from the foreground and/or midground up into the sky. These can be anything from the background buildings, light poles, trees, statues, or whatever attracts the viewer's eye and can act as compositional aids. Leaving these extensions white against a midtone or dark-tone sky is effective when the extensions (building, flagpole) are connected to the focal subjects, as this connection then draws the viewer's eye down through the major segments of the painting (background, midground, and possibly foreground).

CLOUDY SKIES

Cloudy skies present an opportunity to incorporate shapes and changing tones into the overall composition of the painting.

Cold Crisp Winter Skies

- Apply a wash of Naples Yellow or its equivalent to a wet surface, covering at least the top half of the paper (the full sky area).
- Immediately (while the paper is still wet) add Rose Madder Genuine unmixed with Ultramarine Blue in a very light wash.
- Then tilt the board and allow the darker wash to blend gently with the first wash.
- After the first applications have thoroughly dried, using an old or stiff brush, add the light cloud cover wash as a light flat application that is one or two tone intervals darker than the first wash.
- At the edge of the second darker wash, feather the edge of the cloud wash to create a ragged edge. The work must be kept wet and fast, or blemishes can result (Bolton 1984).

Suggestions for Palette 1

Yellow Ochre

Permanent Blue

Winsor Yellow

Rose Madder

Suggestions for Palette 2

Sepia or Naples Yellow

Winsor Blue

Broken Skies

Winter Skies

Winter Skies (detail)

PARTLY CLOUDY SKIES

Partly cloudy skies are skies mixed with blues, white, and grays, in which the warmth or cool of the grays is determined by the reflectivity of the earth colors below.

The clouds should have direction and volume as well as mass. Common characteristics of partly cloudy day clouds include white on and near the top of the clouds and grays at and near the bottom. Such clouds are volumes, not planes, and should be treated as curved surfaces. Wind and pressure also affect the shape of clouds.

To paint party cloudy skies,

- Sketch and plan out the white parts of the cloud shapes.
- Wet the entire surface thoroughly, allowing the sheen to disappear.
- Apply the midtone grays in order to shape and give volume to the clouds.
- While the grays are still wet, apply the blues and then allow the blues and grays to mix edges on the paper.
- If a sharper edge is desired between the white and blue skies, do not wet the white shapes, as then the background blue will form a hard edge.
- Leave the painting alone, and do not try to patch or add as the painting dries. If you want to make changes, rewet the target areas after they have thoroughly dried, and add another wash. (Couch 1987, Szabo 1971).

Suggestions for Palette 1

Cobalt Blue

Burnt Sienna

Charcoal Gray

Suggestions for Palette 2

Winsor Blue

Warm Sepia

Charcoal Gray

Suggestions for Palette 3

Burnt Umber

Ultramarine Blue

Sepia

Partly Cloudy Skies

WET DARK SKIES

Wet Dark Skies usually have less white and more grays and dark grays. To paint wet dark skies,

- Wet the paper and apply a dark gray wash in an uneven manner, lifting out paint with a damp brush to suggest dull light coming through the clouds.
- While the wash is still wet, tilt the board steeply to encourage the wash to move, thereby giving the same direction and flow to the entire sky.

Suggestions for Palette 1

Cobalt Blue

Antwerp Blue

Charcoal Gray

Suggestions for Palette 2

Vandyke Brown

Ultramarine Blue

Charcoal Gray

Dark Skies

Treescapes

Treescapes in paintings are masses of trees that read as one object in the landscape rather than as one, two, ten, or twenty separate trees in a group. Seasons play a significant role in painting treescapes: They dictate overall color schemes; they determine the use of shapes and mass depending on foliage; and they act as a background for focal objects.

Treescapes have three main parts: the *distant mass,* which is usually soft in appearance and lacks definition; the *interior,* which includes the intermediate details highlighted by negative shapes; and the *edge,* which is a more definite form. Generally, the distant view is the darkest and the edge is the lightest in tone, although the tones can be rearranged for any desired effect. It is not uncommon for the distant view through a forest or stand of trees to be light, with the interior view a darker tone, owing to shading from other trees.

Distant Tree Masses

Distant Tree Masses (detail)

Distant tree masses can be created with a single wet-on-wet or wet-on-dry multiple-color application, allowing the colors to merge on the paper, yet not completely mix. The mass, tone, and color variation are the critical design elements. Proceed from light to dark, with wet-on-wet or wet-on-dry washes. Allow the first wash to dry thoroughly before adding dark tones, peekaboo dark interiors, dry brush shadows, and the like. Finish the calligraphy and dry

brush for single trees or branches in just enough detail to indicate a particular type of tree. Do not protrude branches into the sky beyond the edge of the tree mass, as they will attract undue attention.

Wet on wet, wet on dry, and glazing all are very effective for masses of trees. When the first wash is wet, apply additional colors in darker tones to establish variety in color and volume to the shape. Think shape and not detail.

Trees

TREE STRUCTURES AND SHAPES

The following guidelines are designed to help students and professionals paint realistic trees. It is not always necessary to portray each tree as an identifiable species (unless the species is important). Rather what is essential is that the image of trees be descriptive and accurate. Trees are among the most difficult landscape elements to draw and paint and so require practice and experimentation.

GUIDELINE 3

Trunks have one or more stalks, depending on the type of tree. The trunk is the thickest part of the tree and so is the primary visible element.

GUIDELINE 4

Limbs grow from the trunk and are the next largest element. They are extensions of the trunk, growing out from the trunk at a twenty- to thirty-degree angle. Limbs never leave the trunk directly opposite one another but are staggered.

GUIDELINE 5

Branches split off from the limbs and divide and separate from the tree in the same way as do limbs from the trunk. However, branches are lighter and less rigid than are limbs and are affected more by gravity than are limbs.

GUIDELINE 6

Straight lines are used to represent a tree's growth segments, whether they be trunk, limbs, or twigs. The structure should be composed of straight-line segments branching off at angles.

A rule of thumb is to point the branches outward in a 180-degree curve, with the 90-degree branches pointing upward and the 0- to 180-degree branches horizontal.

This fan shape can be useful in portraying branch development. Obviously, the branches can fall below the 180-degree horizontal lines, and the 90-degree vertical lines can be longer than the horizontals.

The actual lengths of branches vary, with the shortest branches usually located at the top of the tree and the longer branches at or near the horizontal mark. Below this mark, they become shorter again.

GUIDELINE 7

Twigs are extensions of branches and are the carriers of leaves. Light, mobile, and feathery, twigs also provide the edges and shape of the tree skeleton. Except for willows and a few other species, twigs can be painted as straight elements, thereby providing a consistent symbol.

Influences on Tree Development

Factors that influence the development of trees include

Soils

Climate

Wind direction

Light quantity and direction

Adjacent or nearby objects (trees, buildings, and so on)

This figure, redrawn from a diagram conceived by Arthur Guptill (1949), illustrates the basic skeletal or structural growth formations of trees and shrubs. These growth formations may be radial, tangential, unifying, alternating, or opposing.

GUIDELINE 8

Line representations of trunk, limbs, branches, and twigs range from thick, less thick, thinner, to thin lines.

TREES WITH FOLIAGE (DECIDUOUS)

Trees with foliage have shapes depicting full masses clustered around a vertical support system. Such trees are not symmetrical and should never be painted as such, even in an architecturally stylized manner. Instead, designers should adopt a few generic tree symbols with which they feel comfortable and then simplify their shapes. Trees are supporting elements in architectural paintings and focal objects in many landscape paintings. Their treatment will vary accordingly.

Shape and Pattern

- Paint the tree, not the leaves.
- Sketch the outline of the tree shapes, limiting the masses to a relative few, using the "hand" model—holding the thumb and the little finger out and the rest of the fingers together. This is a suitable structure around which to cluster the leaf masses (Couch 1987).

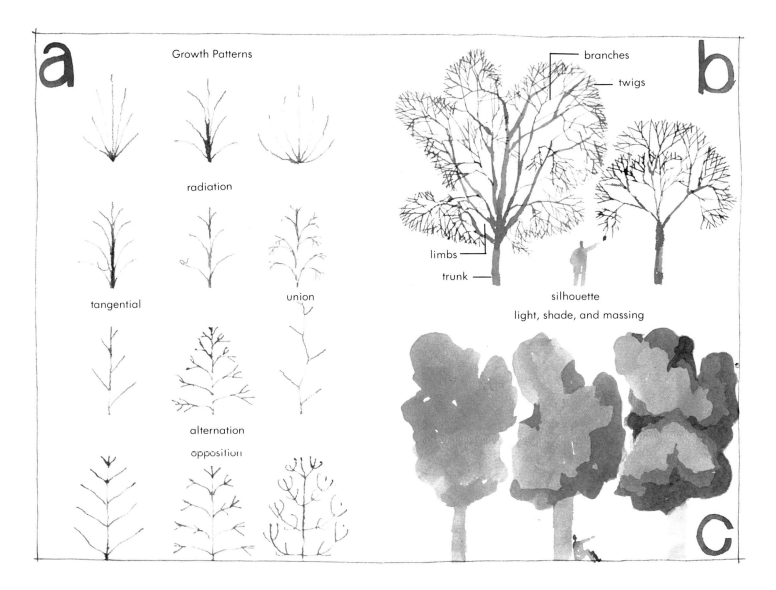

a

Growth Patterns

radiation

tangential   union

alternation

opposition

b

branches

twigs

limbs

trunk

silhouette

light, shade, and massing

c

Structure of Trees

Painting Trees with Foliage, Using the Hand

Painting More Trees, Using the Hand

Tone

- Use light tones for close-up shapes and dark tones for more distant shapes.
- Remember that each mass is a volume with a front, back, and sides, each reflecting light differently.
- Determine, based on the prevailing light, the tones (values) of each tree mass, with the lighter tones usually on top and on the surfaces facing the direction of the light. The undersides of the masses are in shade and thus are darker, as are masses in the distance or background.

Texture

- The edges of each mass should have frayed or rough edges, and the interior should be solid (with the exception of occasional peekaboo highlights).

Color

- Determine the seasonal influence on the painting scheme (bright colors for spring; mature, deeper colors for summer; browns and oranges for fall; and blues, grays, and starkness for winter).

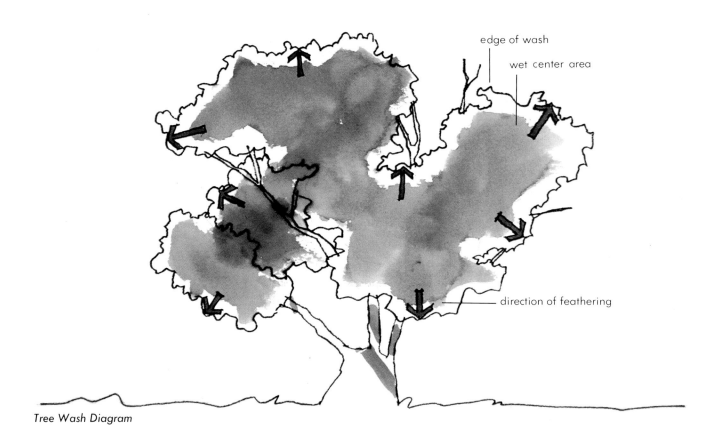

edge of wash

wet center area

direction of feathering

Tree Wash Diagram

- Determine the background effect desired for the painting, whether it should be regionally accurate or generic massing, or subdued or an integral part of the focal point.

  To paint trees with foliage,

- Paint the tree sectionally, one mass at a time.
- Wet the interior of each mass with clear water and leave the edges dry.

- Load a flat brush with several colors (each corner at least and also the middle if possible).
- Swirl, push, and twist the brush into the wet surface, minimizing the number of strokes so as not to "muddy" the colors. The colors should mix and merge by themselves on the paper.
- While everything is still wet, and with a damp-dry brush, drag out the paint to the dry edges to create a rough texture. Simply laying the brush flat on the paper and

rolling it can achieve the desired roughness.
- Paint the background masses a darker midtone so that hints of branches can be painted over when the wash dries.
- Restrict the branches to the interior of the tree form as much as possible, supporting, not competing, with the masses. The background masses should be thoroughly dry before overpainting them with branches (Couch 1987).

Thin, Lacy Trees

Trees such as aspen and young alder have thin trunks and lacy branches and foliage. An effective way to paint them is to use a palette knife with a filed edge (see Part 5). Use the knife to create delicate segmented trunks and branches by drawing the knife edge out of the main color application (the trunk) and gradually easing up on the pressure to fade out the branch (Szabo 1971).

Conifers

Cedar and other conifers have a structure different from that of deciduous trees, a less-dense mass, and a more skeletal form. Conifers in the distance are best painted using wet-on-wet and wet-on-dry techniques similar to those used for deciduous trees. In the foreground, where details are more apparent, wet-on-wet and dry brush techniques are appropriate. Conifers can be painted with either a pointed sable brush No. 6 (e.g., using a pointed stippling stroke) or a flat one-inch sable brush on its edge, in a calligraphic manner. Remember that the details should be illusionary, enough to communicate an overall image but not so much as to overwhelm the painting. Use multiple-colored dark-tone masses highlighted by treetop details emerging from the mass.

To paint conifers,

- Apply the dark trunk tone first, with a wet brush loaded with pigment. Move the brush (a flat sable is preferred) up the tree in a single stroke.
- While the trunk is still wet, load it with the branch colors, and work the brush from the trunk outward, letting the brush dry somewhat as it reaches the outer branches, resulting in a sharper hard edge. Be careful to depict the shape of the tree accurately, not symmetrically, and with variations in the tones (even the darks).

Painting Trees with a Sponge

Trees can be painted by mixing the paints on the paper with both a brush and a sponge. The sponge has an advantage in delivering additional texture and pattern by means of dabbing and stippling. The sponge picks up the colors and deposits them in a dense pattern.

Artists such as Georg Shook (1981) use synthetic, large-holed porous sponges for their textures, as natural sponges break apart when left moist. But although natural sponges are recommended over synthetics for most watercolor uses, the synthetics are stiffer and have more scratchiness for specialized effects. Experiment with both to determine which works best for you.

To paint trees with a sponge,

- Draw the image as desired.
- Apply with a brush an undertone of color, midtone on the scale depending on the desired effect. Use either the wet-on-wet or wet-on-dry method to apply this undertone, trying not to be too exact in the wash (brush stroke variations are acceptable, as a textured application will be dabbed over the undertone).
- Prepare one to three colors on the palette by mixing a small amount of water with each. This will allow the sponge to absorb enough paint and yet not be too watery. The texture is achieved by the imprint of the sponge, and so the imprint must be dry enough to have a "grain."
- Apply a small amount of each color to the sponge by touching the sponge to the palette. Then dab the sponge on the area with the undertone, and define the basic shapes.
- Establish shadows in the shapes by dabbing on darker colors (such as Prussian Blue and Vandyke Brown). Areas may be lightened with a clean damp sponge, dabbing up color where needed. Because dabbing with almost pure pigment will result in a darker-tone image, it is important to lighten the image, to shape it, and to show the reflecting light sources using a damp brush, sponge, or towel.
- This technique may be reworked either wet or dry, as the pigment is not greatly diluted. However, for the best results, wait until the first applications have dried thoroughly in order to judge the intensity (chroma) as well as the tone, color, and texture. A second application is then possible.
- A palette knife or small brush may be used to add branches in and protruding from the tree mass.

Painting Foliage with a Bamboo Brush

Both the sponge and brush are useful for detailed foliage work. But whereas the sponge technique is good for large masses, shrubbery, grasses, and the like, a bamboo brush may offer more control. In a technique used by Richard Bolton (1984), the hairs of the bamboo brush are splayed apart by jabbing it into the palette a couple of times.

To paint foliage with a bamboo brush,

- As a base, apply a wet-on-wet light-tone to midtone undercoat, capturing the lights and shadows.
- Beginning with the lighter colors, gradually dab the overall shapes on the paper, blending the darker tones into the lighter ones to create volume and shadows and deciding on the location of focal objects and tones. It is easier to use a bamboo brush to feather, as a means of creating a lacy effect for leaf clusters.
- In order to pick up lighter values or tones in branch or leaf highlights struck by the sun, a Naples Yellow gouache can be painted over the dark tones (once dried). Though not a transparent watercolor, the gouache—if used sparingly—can add an important sense of light and sun, but do not overuse it.

Another brush technique consists of cutting the hairs off of an old brush to one-quarter to three-eights of an inch out from the ferrule. The increased stiffness, combined with multiple strands, is useful for texture effects.

Painting Trees with a Sponge

Painting Foliage as Planes

The foliage of deciduous trees grows on planes. When painting such foliage, remember the following guidelines:

GUIDELINE 9

The overall foliage is a series of planes or contours in relief. Holes through the foliage normally break up the mass.

GUIDELINE 10

Light and shade shape the mass, defining bright foregrounds and darker midgrounds and backgrounds within the tree mass.

GUIDELINE 11

Interior branches and limbs are usually in shadow and are thus darker in tone. Branches behind other branches and limbs are also in shadow. Tree trunks and larger limbs often have shadows cast on them from other branches and limbs.

Painting Trees without Foliage

TREES WITHOUT FOLIAGE

The following techniques are used to paint deciduous trees without foliage:

- In one wet-on-wet or wet-on-dry application, paint the trunk from bottom to top, locating the warmer, lighter colors closer to the base of the trunk and the cooler, darker colors up the trunk in the more shaded zone. The warmer trunk base reflects the surrounding earth colors. Avoid painting any tree *brown*.

Trees in the distance may be all blue, purple, or warm grays. And avoid mixing reds into the color mix.
- While the initial wash is still wet or after the first wash has completely dried, shade the trunk of the tree as a volume, with a light and a dark side. Either the light side or the dark shade should be dominant; they should not divide the tree in half. Locate the core shadow near the plane change.
- To give a tree trunk roundness when the

trunk is to be left white (or very light), use a flat sable brush with color on one corner and clear water on the other. Run the brush up the trunk and allow the water and pigment to merge in a soft round effect.
- Add highlights such as darker blemishes, either when the previous wash is still wet enough to merge with a new color or after that wash has completely dried. For scrapings with a knife or razor blade, the surface should still be wet.

Painting Trees with Rounded Trunks

Symbolic Trees. Trees in design illustrations may be represented by symbols rather than full-flowing art forms. These examples were drawn with a ruling pen filled with watercolor wash. The trunks and limbs were formed with a scraping motion of the side of the pen, and the branches and twigs were constructed using pen strokes. Fine-pointed brushes and/or a palette knife are also effective.

Varied Symbolic Trees

As an example of trees with structure and style, refer to Richard Bolton (1984), an English watercolorist who has perfected background tree types that are well suited for architectural illustrations. Bolton uses Burnt Sienna and Ultramarine Blue as a base color for the tree, offset by Naples Yellow (but not mixed with it).

TREES AS SILHOUETTES

When trees are support objects and essential to the composition, seasonal description, and regional identity and yet are not required to show much detail, they can be used as silhouettes, common in many architectural renderings. To paint trees as silhouettes,

• Understand the structure and form of the tree, and avoid stylizing inaccurate shapes. Lightly sketch in the shapes.
• With a bamboo brush, a one-inch flat sable, or a larger round sable, paint the tree trunk in one motion, from the thick trunk to the tip of the main branches. Allow the paint to thin as it reaches the outer branches, and paint all of the main branch structure as fast as possible while the tree is still wet. The end of the branches can be softened with a small brush and clear water to reduce the stark hard edge.
• With a smaller brush, a No. 1 or 2 sable, or a palette knife, paint in the delicate, fine twigs at the outer edge of the main branches. Remember to lighten the tone of branches and twigs in the distance to contrast with the darker branches in the foreground. This is delicate work and should not be rushed. The payoff will be a lacy, transparent supportive effect.

Varied Symbolic Trees

To paint silhouetted trees with back-lighting, use the following steps:

- Determine the source and direction of the light.
- Either leave the sky white or apply a very light-toned wash and allow it to dry.
- Establish the shape to be made by the branches.
- Apply the lightest foliage with loose washes, covering the areas (general shapes) that are struck by the light source (use New Gamboge, Naples Yellow, or Winsor Yellow for the yellows). Allow the yellow washes to dry.
- Use the yellow base to mix with a blue, darkening it with a tinge of red or Burnt Umber, and apply the midtone color where appropriate (according to a tone sketch). The midtone may be darkened further for variation. Allow this to dry.
- Apply the darkest tone to the tree trunk before painting the dark leaf shapes. This will allow you to evaluate the light tones and midtones.
- Paint the limbs and branches into the interior of the tree, not on the outside.
- Finish the painting with the dark leaf shapes, making them slightly lighter than the trunk darks.

FOLIAGE AND BRUSH

Foliage, brush, and ground covers are dense, with shaded interiors that contain multiple shapes, all interlocking. They are difficult to illustrate, owing to the level of detail, but the following examples—using negative shapes, background painting, and glazing—will help simplify the task:

- Sketch in the overall patterns and shapes of the vegetation, highlighting the important ones. In complicated or very detailed illustrations, the pattern of the shapes is, in many ways, more important than the myriad of detailed shapes. The eye will first search for the overall pattern, as a frame of reference—and so the initial image is conveyed. The overall pattern may be the direction of the leaves or grasses, or the repetitive similarity of leaf forms against a chaotic background.
- Using wet-on-wet techniques, apply the light to light-medium tones using the lightest warm tone to establish a focal point for the viewer. The wash should be varied, mixing and merging colors on the paper. Color examples include Hooker's Green Light, Lemon Yellow; Cerulean Blue, and Ultramarine Blue; or Veridian Green, Permanent Blue, Sepia, Naples Yellow, and Ultramarine Blue.
- With the wet "fuzzy" background in place and dry, apply midtone colors (on the lighter side) in the background, shaping the leaves or pattern shapes that are in the foreground and are important. These foreground shapes are actually the color of the first fuzzy and varied wash in light and light-medium tones. This is referred to as silhouetting shapes by applying background.

- As the background wash is drying, add the darker tones in varying degrees to create depth and recession, hinting at like shapes in the interior of the foliage, brush, or ground cover. The darkest tones are reserved for dark shadows.
- By incrementally darkening the background tones, through glazing, and by hinting at the other shapes, the contrast between the more detailed foreground patterns and the darker, less detailed background should create an effective landscape element.

A similar effect can be achieved using the wet-on-wet method and glazing throughout each step. After allowing the background washes to dry thoroughly, rewet the target area and add another layer of color to the background, forming shapes out of the previous color. To establish hard edges for the shapes, move the wash out of the prewet target area onto a dry zone. In this manner, the wash can proceed from soft, blurred nonedges to hard, shape-defining edges.

LIGHT-TONE SILHOUETTES

An effective backdrop is formed by silhouettes painted with a light tone. An outline of trees or a small tree cluster can define space and provide scale and background without competing with the focal point. To paint light-tone silhouettes,

- Use the same color base for the sky, the

silhouetted tree outline, and the tree clusters and grass. Add different colors to the original base to differentiate between sky and earth.

- Change slightly the tone of all elements; that is, make the sky the lightest, the tree mass outline darker, the tree clusters darker still, and the earth (midground and foreground) the darkest.
- Although the same general stylized tree shape or outline should be used throughout, remember to vary them; that is, do not make them all the same size, height, and width.

TRUNK COLORS

Trunks are seldom if ever portrayed as brown (using reds, oranges, raw umber, and so on). Rather, trunk colors range from warm and cool neutrals to mossy greens and dark-textured blues and purples. Before selecting colors for tree trunks, determine your palette for sky and earth colors, as they should be reflected in the coloration of the tree structure.

TREE SHADOWS

Shadows cast by trees add depth and darker tones to illustrations. Even though a tree may be green, the surface that its shadow falls upon will be a different local color, which should be reflected in the color mixture of the shadow.

GUIDELINE 12

Deciduous tree shadows can be portrayed as elliptical shapes where they strike the ground surfaces.

GUIDELINE 13

The tree shadows of rounded masses are elliptical, with the y-axis dimension of the cast shadow narrower than the x-axis dimension.

GUIDELINE 14

The trunk shadow length is shorter than the height of the trunk because the foliage mass foreshortens the actual length.

GUIDELINE 15

Shadows cast on the ground by foliage should be portrayed as a series of elliptical shapes clustered together with occasional light openings. The edge of the shadow mass is irregular, characterized by rounded edges (from the elliptical shapes) (Guptill 1949).

GUIDELINE 16

Observe the response of shadows to the surface geometry; for example, shadows either climb up a curb or wall or drop down a curb into the street.

GUIDELINE 17

Surface textures affect tree shadows; for example, grass and weeds break up shadow shapes, whereas smooth surfaces keep them together.

GUIDELINE 18

Tree shadows that fall on darker surface materials are darker than is the same shadow on a lighter surface.

TREE LOCATIONS IN ILLUSTRATIONS

Locating trees in illustrations should follow the principle of variation; that is, the trees should not be the center dominant shapes; they should be asymmetrically placed; and they should be separate from the focal object, not "growing" out from rooftops or mimicking angles and other geometry of focal objects (Guptill 1949).

Determine the priority of trees within the landscape according to their size, location, color, and tone and their importance as focal subjects, supporting elements, or background.

Rocks and Boulders

Rocks and boulders are context items, props that indicate regional geomorphological site conditions. If painted properly, they will complement rather than detract from the focal subject. The following are a number of techniques for painting rocks and boulders:

SEQUENCE 1

• Sketch the silhouette of the rock(s), keeping the edges as sharp and angular as possible.
• Wet the interior of the rock shape with clear water, except at the edge or border (in order to establish a hard edge on dry paper).
• Add the colors to the wet surface, mixing them on either the surface or the palette. Use lighter tones to indicate the light source and also shapes, ground reflections, and variations in the surface of the rock itself.
• To create weeds and surface textures, scrape the base and profile of the rock with a razor blade, palette knife, or other sharp instrument when the washes are still wet. Use interlocking and lost and found techniques to merge the rock shapes with the ground, avoiding a straight-line base at all costs.

To create curved rocks, the dark tones must be bled into the curved form using a wet-on-wet method. For example, leave the top of the rock white (or light), and apply the dark tone on the side facing the viewer near the top. With a wet surface, apply the dark tone with a flat sable brush, allowing the dark to bleed upward toward the white top, thereby creating a soft, blurry, "curved" edge near the top.

Another way to create a curved form is to cast shadows from nearby vegetation or

Painting Rocks and Boulders

trees over the top of the rock and to wrap the shadow around the top of the rock, blending it into the wet dark tone applied earlier.

SEQUENCE 2

- Prepare a tone sketch with enough detail to establish massing, shape patterns, and light and dark tones.
- Using wet-on-wet techniques, paint each rock separately, applying the lighter and more intense highlight colors first and then quickly adding a darker tone to the first wet mixture, for shadows. Use modeling techniques to shade the rocks and blend the shadow with the curves struck by light. Some rock faces will be round, with soft, blurry edges, and others will be fractured, with sharp edges and contrasting planes, requiring abrupt changes between light and shade.
- Rocks, particularly light rocks, will pick up ground colors through reflection. As you bring each wash, whether light or dark, down to the ground plane, quickly add a hint of the earth colors, and blend, interlock, or lose and find the rock plane with the ground plane.
- Scrape cracks and blemishes into the rocks.
- If there are touches (tones, shapes, and the like) that still require attention, allow the rock(s) to dry completely. Then apply other wet-on-wet washes as desired, maintaining transparency and luminosity.

SEQUENCE 3

Zoltan Szabo (1971) is a master of wet-on-wet techniques. The following are guidelines inspired by his work:

- Without any preliminary sketch, define the rock shape in silhouette by painting a wet-on-wet application of several light-tone colors all mixed on the paper, that is, placed next to one another and allowed to merge on their own by means of the wet paper. Vary the warm and cool colors to reflect light and shade. Remember that the first wash should be light in tone yet varied in color.
- As the wash approaches the ground plane, and while the wash is still wet, apply midtone earth colors, immediately followed by dark-tone highlights for shadows.
- Before this ground wash dries, scrape some grass strokes out from the earth tones into and overlapping the rock shape.
- Spatter some drops of slightly diluted pigment over the rock shape, and with a dry stiff brush (flat bristle), dab at the drops to create mottling on the rock face. This spattering can be used to shape the face of the rock, hinting at fractures, crevices, and the like.
- A toothbrush spray can also be applied for a fine-dot pattern, imitating lichen, pock marks, and surface dirt.
- If any finished detailing is desired, allow everything to dry thoroughly before using a fine sable brush and a palette knife to paint in small flowers, weeds, and so on.

This technique does not require much glazing. Most of the effect is achieved in the first wash application by mixing and merging colors on the wet paper.

Another technique by Zoltan Szabo (1971) uses masking techniques and over-washes.

SEQUENCE 4

The following example is excellent for a sharp contrast between sun and shadow, and a great deal of intense light reflection from the rocks:

- Mask out the rocks completely, using masking fluid for the irregular edges and paper (brown wrapping paper) and tape for the large shapes.
- To apply texture to the background rocks, spatter as many layers as needed of almost pure pigment (Sepia and Cerulean Blue in this example). Use the spatter to create crevices and bold shapes in the background. Follow this with a dry stiff brush manipulation of the spatter to shape the rock crevices and cracks. Don't overdo it.
- Allow the splatter application to dry thoroughly.
- Apply a dark-tone wash over the entire spatter area, striving for a deep yet luminous wash. Use French Ultramarine, Cerulean Blue, Sepia, and Burnt Sienna,

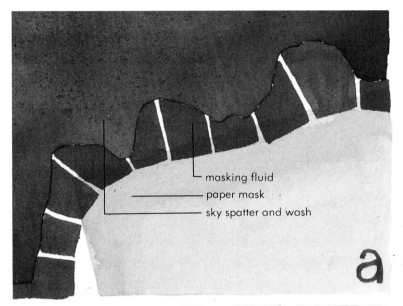

masking fluid
paper mask
sky spatter and wash

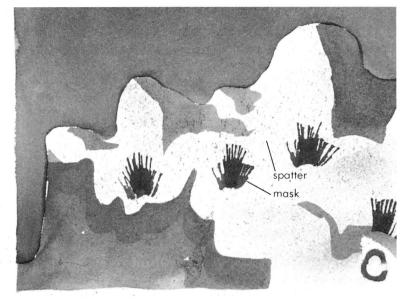

spatter
mask

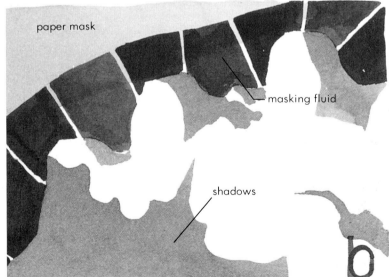

paper mask

masking fluid

shadows

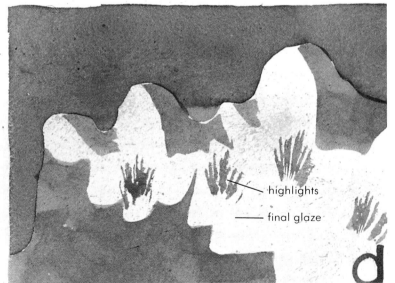

highlights
final glaze

Sequence Example

Demonstration

making sure to maintain the texture through the wash.

- A final touch for this wash, while it is still wet, is to lift out a small light highlight and to concentrate the darker tones in various places to hint at recession or depth.
- Remove the masking.
- Mask the background area painted earlier (make sure it is dry), and mask any other detail areas in the area to be washed.
- Paint the shadow shapes in the foreground with a wet, two-color wash, mixing them on the paper in a more uniformly consistent manner as a background wash without much shape definition. If you use Burnt Sienna and Cerulean Blue, notice that they will tend to separate a bit, giving a mottled effect. French Ultramarine can be used to establish depth and recession.
- Now apply spatter to both the sunlit area and the shaded areas, using a toothbrush or stiff bristle brush in several different color areas, with some of the mid- to dark-tone colors previously applied to other areas. Allow the spatters to dry thoroughly.
- The next step is very important. With the dark background and shadowed foreground, you will need to apply a light "glowing" wash over the sunlit area, the focal point of this painting. To do this, apply a layer of Naples Yellow or New Gamboge with Burnt Sienna as the shadow mix in a wet-on-wet technique. The Burnt Sienna is used as a wet-on-

wet overlay to shape the rocks with shadows. This application must be light yet dark enough to establish a strong contrast between the sunlit and shaded areas: a warm temperature against a cool background.

- After the paint has dried, if more lights are desired, use a wet bristle or other stiff brush to lift out light highlights. (Szabo 1971).

Artist John Blockely (1987) has developed some interesting ways of representing terrain, landforms, and rocks. Blockely mixes ink and watercolor and then applies the watercolor with either a pen and ink or brush. He dabs with his fingers, tissue, and other materials to produce a semiabstract texture and rock pattern. Some of his techniques for creating rocks and boulders include

- After masking out the rocks using a wet-on-wet approach, apply a variety of colors over the desired area.
- Dab (towel or rag), lift out (with dry brush), and shape other forms with slightly darker tones.
- Remove the masking fluid.
- Tint the previously masked boulders with light washes.
- Blot a recent wet application with a blotter, tissue, or rag wrapped around the finger.
- Use wet-on-wet washes in successive layers (after drying) to create a transparent, soft layering of color.

- Draw lines (calligraphy) into and over wet and dry washes with a crow quill pen, a ruling pen, or the tip of the brush handle, for direction, stratification, and a hint of detail in rocks and boulders.

In much of his work, Blockely uses a wet-on-wet, multicolor, merged base, with the different colors merging into one another at their edges. His paintings are in the midtones to dark tones, contrasted with whiter or light-toned focal points. Blockely emphasizes the terrain as major design forms. As does Szabo, Blockely often works from dark to light, the opposite of the more common light-to-dark sequence.

Flowers, Grasses, and Weeds

Flowers, grasses, and weeds are usually support elements in illustrations, forming the basis for the foreground and midground details.

FLOWERS

There are two approaches for painting flowers, either a soft wet application that hints at or highlights a spot of color surrounded by green and earth background colors and that uses a wet-on-wet method, or a dry brush application of fine detail using pigments mixed with very little water.

The following guidelines describe techniques of painting flowers in a landscape:

GUIDELINE 19
Leave a small amount of white surrounding the bright flowers to maximize contrast between the flowers and the background colors and shapes.

GUIDELINE 20
After painting in the more intense colors for the flowers and the less intense leaf background, use darker tones to define the shapes in the loose first washes.

GRASSES AND WEEDS

Grasses and weeds can be created by means of interlocking shapes, lost and found edges, and a combination of hard and soft edges. For most applications, grasses and weeds can be represented as one large shape without the detail of individual blades or stalks. When detail is desired, multiple color underlayments in wet-on-wet and the use of masking fluids provide interest and variety when combined with a larger covering or background washes. Simplify techniques by hinting at detail.

Dry-brush techniques with bristle, bamboo, or cut and modified brushes are effective but meticulous and time consuming. For dry-brush techniques, the underlayment is critical to set tone, temperature, and color. Stipple, scraping into wet un-

Painting Grasses. An interlocking pattern of shapes was used for these wind-blown grasses, coupled with wet-on-wet mergings of different colors.

derlayment, and calligraphy all are applicable as the final detailed touch. Stipple can be applied with a toothbrush or paint brush. Scraping can be done with a fingernail, credit card, palette knife, or brush tip. Calligraphy can be done with a ruling pen, crow quill, fine-pointed round brush, or pencil. The distance that the viewer is from the grassy shape will determine the type and detail of application.

Painting Grasses and Weeds. Glazing over previously dried wash applications with increasingly darker tones helped produce these foreground grasses and weeds. In certain applications, the jagged edge of each tone shape can be omitted to create a more manicured yet varied lawn coloration.

Painting Grass Shapes. To achieve this effect, an underlayer of light yellow was applied and allowed to dry thoroughly. Masking fluid was then used to create grass shapes in a varied pattern. A multiple-color graded wash from light yellow to dark umber with streaks of merged blue was applied over the washed shapes. When the masking fluid was removed, additional darker-tone grass shapes were added in a positive and negative fashion, providing depth and recession.

References

Blockely, John. 1987. *Watercolor Interpretations*. Cincinnati: North Light Books.

Bolton, Richard. 1984. *Weathered Texture Workshop.* New York: Watson-Guptill.

Couch, Tony. 1987. *Watercolor: You Can Do It.* Cincinnati: North Light Books.

Guptill, Arthur L. 1949. *Color in Sketching and Illustration.* New York: Reinhold.

Shook, Georg. 1981. *Sharp Focus Watercolor Painting.* New York: Watson-Guptill.

Szabo, Zoltan. 1971. *Landscape Painting in Watercolor.* New York: Watson-Guptill.

Building Materials

Building materials offer designers a unique challenge, which combines the selection of surface texture, tone, and color with the concern for expressing shape, mass, pattern, and detail.

In graphic communication, building materials can be viewed from two frames of reference: as specific building blocks as defined by each unit of materials in the building, and as the colors, temperatures, and patterns supporting the building as a whole.

Watercolor gives the designer the opportunity to represent specific materials fast and effectively. This chapter describes techniques using watercolor washes and watercolor, colored pencil, and pen and ink combinations. The wet-on-wet and wet-on-dry methods are the most versatile.

Brick

Brick surfaces are characterized by their varied coloration, from the differences inherent in the firing of each brick, and by the calligraphy effect made by the bricks' mortar joints, which forms horizontal and vertical patterns. Mastering the ways of illustrating these two characteristics opens up a wide variety of applications for brick surfaces. Tools useful in portraying brick surfaces include

watercolor and brushes

ruling pens, crow quills, and technical pens

colored pencils

DISTANCE EFFECTS WITH WET WASHES

For brick surfaces in a distant background, a wet-on-wet or wet-on-dry wash can produce effective and consistent yet differentiated surface patterns. With each method, use either a graded and/or multiple-color wash, or merged colors added to the wet paper.

Sequence

- Apply a light-tone basic color for consistency, allowing it to dry thoroughly.
- Using a wet-on-wet method, add one or two additional colors for variation, allowing them to mix and merge on the paper without total dilution. Use trans-

Distant Brick Masses

Brick Townhouses. These brick townhouse shapes were masked and painted with a wet-on-wet wash of Cadmium Red, Rose Madden, Alizarin, and Cobalt Blue. Light highlights were lifted out with a damp brush while the wash was still wet.

parent primaries to mix colors, if possible, unless an opaque effect is desired.

- Immediately after application, lift out a few light spots with a brush drier than the surface wash, to achieve a reflected light effect and to add variation in the wash.

EFFECTS WITH A RULING PEN

For brick surfaces in the mid- and foregrounds, where some detail is observable, use calligraphy to highlight mortar patterns.

Sequence

- Using a ruling pen, load watercolor into the pen opening or "jaws" with an eyedropper or by dipping the pen into the wash. Be careful not to overload the pen,

causing the paint to spill out onto the painting (if it does, simply blot it up with tissue or a blotter while it is still wet). Test the flow on a used piece of watercolor paper.

- With a straight edge as a guide (or free-

hand), use the ruling pen to draw mortar lines on the first wash. In most cases, the horizontal lines will be all that are needed.

- For the tones for the mortar, use a ruling pen for tones darker than the base wash.

Portal

EFFECTS WITH COLORED PENCIL

For mortar joints that are lighter than the brick surface, use a colored pencil with a hard sharp point. Suggested colors include white, beiges, light greens, and blues. Stroke the horizontal (and possibly vertical) lines onto the base wash either freehand or with the aid of a straight edge. The base wash should be thoroughly dry before doing this.

Portal (detail)

Brick and Colored Pencil

CLOSE-UP EFFECTS

For close-up views of more detailed mortar joints, try the following technique:

- For the mortar color, apply a light-tone wet-on-wet or wet-on-dry wash to the entire brick area.
- After the first wash has dried thoroughly, apply each brick course in a darker tone using a flat sable brush of the appropriate size, varying each brick or brick course coloration using wet-on-wet or wet-on-dry techniques. This application may be useful in interior design and for close-up brick views that are backdrops for other architectural elements such as door and window openings and trim details.

Brick Coursing

Stonework

Stonework is a pattern usually composed of irregular shapes set in a common field. Its characteristics include (1) variations in color from stone to stone and within each stone; (2) irregular mortar patterns; and (3) rectangular mortar patterns resulting from larger stone units, as opposed to the horizontal band created by the traditionally narrower brick unit.

The following examples of stone surfaces demonstrate treatments for close-up distance views. The tools required are watercolor and brushes, and colored pencils.

EXAMPLE 1

To paint a stone surface in the distance, abstract the pattern using a stipple technique, applying several colors with similar tones over a light dry background wash. The size of the brush will vary with the size of the area.

EXAMPLE 2

Another useful technique is applying a background wash of variegated colors mixed on the paper, allowing them to dry, and overdrawing the wash with calligraphy for the joints, using a colored pencil (similar to the technique for brick). For straight-line work, both colored pencils and ruling pens work well.

Winsor stone effects were applied in a nearly dry-on-dry process, with each stone glazed over with very little water solution.

Stone (variation 1)

Stonework emphasizes the individual stones more than brickwork. An effective technique is to vary the colors over the entire field or pattern, by slightly varying the color (not the tone) of each stone application.

The tone can also be varied, for example, from lighter at the top of a wall to a darker tone near the ground plane. Such subtle variations can create rich luminous surfaces. Light highlights can be lifted out from the washes either right after a wet application or after the wash has dried thoroughly, using a wet stiff brush.

Finally, close-up illustrations can be shadowed to reflect the light source and to highlight the individual units. A colored pencil or very light brush stroke can achieve this effect.

Stone (variation 2)

Concrete

Concrete is a poured material and is characterized by its mass rather than its units. Its surface is light in tone (value), usually from light to light midtone on the nine-interval tone scale. Concrete has a smooth surface with occasional aggregate pockets (dark) or blemishes. It is white to gray in color, with the grays varying from a warm to a cool temperature.

Concrete's responses to light give it definition, based on its surface treatment:

- Smooth concrete reflects light, making the surface appear white, bright, or sometimes glossy.
- Rough concrete absorbs or diffuses light, thereby appearing flat, more midtone with darker patches.
- Ribbed or textured concrete creates shadow patterns containing a mixture of interesting darks contrasted with midtone grays and white highlights.

A concrete wall reflects light in a varied, not a uniform, pattern across its surface. The smoother the surface is, the more colors it will reflect from adjacent materials. Various techniques can be used to depict concrete.

SMOOTH SURFACES

• Apply wet-on-wet and wet-on-dry graded-tint washes and diluted neutral colors ranging from white (paper) to lighter midtones, using the white paper as light concrete wherever desirable.

• Spatter fine-grained medium-dark tones to represent pock marks in the surface. Apply the principle of variation to achieve realistic results.

Smooth Surfaces. The smooth surface is in effect a white, unblemished, nonpainted surface, highlighted with joints and a very light-toned coloration.

NEARLY SMOOTH TO ROUGH SURFACES

- Using a wet-on-wet method, apply a midtone neutral gray (warm or cool).
- Before it dries, lift out lighter highlights with a damp brush or blotter.
- Add surface markings with a small sable brush, or use spatter with a toothbrush or bristle brush.

Ribbed, Textured Surfaces. Masking fluid was used to create the light-accentuated ribs, with a warm overwash applied next. Glazing for the shadows was added as the overwash was drying to provide depth for the ribs and recession for the background surface.

Nearly Smooth to Rough Surfaces. The techniques used consisted of a light-toned wet-on-wet merging of warm colors followed by careful spattering and dabbing of the wet paint into desirable patterns.

RIBBED, TEXTURED SURFACES

- Apply a wet-on-wet or wet-on-dry light-tone wash as a base, varying it for interest using warm or cool neutral grays.
- Apply masking fluid for the top of the ribbed forms.
- Apply darker-tone grays along the shadow side of the ribs, wetting the edges with clear water to soften the outward shadow edge.
- For more distant effects, use a ruling pen loaded with a warm or cool neutral watercolor charge, or a colored pencil. If the base wash is warm, apply cool rib shadows, and if the wash is cool, apply a warm shadow pattern.

Reflections

REFLECTIONS ON SMOOTH SURFACES

Smooth concrete sidewalks or walls reflect images in the same way that water does. In the figure, the landscaping is reflected on the surface of the walkway, an effect achieved by using a lighter tone for the flowers that contains a tint of the same local vegetation coloring.

Stucco

Stucco is a smooth-appearing unblemished surface characterized by a uniform tone and joint lines. Weathered stucco may have soft-edged streaks originating from the joints and flashing.

Stucco is most easily represented by flat clear washes, highlighted by colored pencil or ruling pen joints and shadow edges.

The most important highlight feature of stucco surfaces is the uniform light response. Stucco planes can be portrayed as consistent in light reflection (showing little variation across the plane). Contrasting one complete plane against others with changes in tones is an excellent way to portray stucco. Stucco also absorbs more light than do concrete surfaces with a similar—that is, extensive—surface texture.

Metal

Metal components that are often depicted include the metal panels for roof and wall installations, structural components, and finished elements such as handrails, lighting fixtures, and hardware.

Metal finishes are generally smooth with very little texture. They are painted, corrosive, or glossy. In most cases the finishes have a reflective quality, transmitting light waves reflected from other nearby surfaces (or the light itself, such as a bright sky or the sun).

Techniques for representing metal surfaces include

- Flat clear washes using wet-on-wet or wet-on-dry methods.
- Graded washes using wet-on-wet or wet-on-dry methods.
- Flat clear and graded washes with lift-out techniques indicating light reflections, changes in light direction, or changes in the geometry of metal surfaces that influence light reflections.
- Glazing, for use in interiors in which

multiple light sources cast multiple overlapping shadows and reflections, in exterior use on hazy days or in dim light in which subtlety is desired in the reflections and shadows.

Metal surfaces also change in tone and chroma or intensity. The use of darker and more intense colors on metal surfaces causes significant changes in tone and chroma from one plane to adjacent planes, depending on the natural and artificial light sources. These changes create much of the effect of color on metal and are hardly ever viewed in reality as flat color planes uniform in tone and chroma.

The plane changes on metal surfaces are due to multiple lighting sources, with the contrast between brightly lit planes and planes in shadow revealing subtle mixtures of neighboring colors. Brightly lit planes have almost a pure local color, very intense; shadowed planes consist of the base color mixed with adjacent colors (reflectivity) darkened in tone with blues, blacks, or greens.

Glass

Glass is a hard smooth material that is transparent, translucent, or reflective. All glass has some properties of reflectivity. *Transparent* glass is clear and less reflective

and reveals more of a building's interior elements. *Translucent* glass may be hazy or frosted, allowing light to enter but not enough to reveal interior elements other than amorphous shapes. *Reflective* glass is designed to reflect most of the light waves striking the surface.

TRANSPARENT GLASS

Transparent glass does not have a color surface; yet because of its dual transparent and reflective qualities, it has distinct color characteristics:

- With adequate lighting, the colors of interior objects become visible from the exterior.
- Without light, the interiors exposed by transparent glass are dark tones and contrasts to exterior surface materials.
- When the exterior light sources are at the proper angle, transparent glass can reflect white light, thereby creating another color aspect.
- Sky and cloud colors are often reflected in transparent glass, thus masking or at least modifying interior colors, giving rise to the "blue" misconception regarding window treatments.

When using watercolors to represent transparent glass, build up the transparency in order to combine the surface reflectivity of the glass, the tint (if any) of the glass itself, and the interior planes of the building interior to form the image.

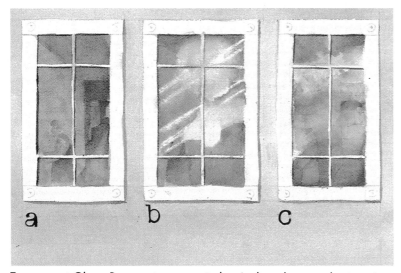

Transparent Glass. Because transparent glass is clear, be sure also to paint inside the space, which is altered by interior lighting or by views through the interior space and outside again.

More Reflective Glass. Multiple-color washes were merged using a wet-on-wet method, allowed to dry, and then highlighted with a colored pencil and additional glazings for cloud reflections.

GUIDELINE 1

Unless the interiors are brightly lit, transparent glass on the building side facing the light source will be highly reflective of exterior patterns, including those in the sky.

GUIDELINE 2

Be sure to paint background shapes and colors behind transparent glass surfaces, using appropriate lighting sources and indicating depth or recession of interior planes.

TRANSLUCENT GLASS

Translucent glass is generally nonreflective, light toned, and soft, owing to the dispersion of light through the glass. Translucent glass softens shapes that are formed by images on the other side of the glass.

REFLECTIVE GLASS

Reflective glass shows all of the surrounding environment. Reflective glass is essentially a mirrored surface, available in a range of colors, which adds local color to the reflected colors.

GUIDELINE 3

Combine the local color of reflective glass with the color reflected in the glass from nearby objects.

GUIDELINE 4

Images reflected in the glass are often distorted by the concavity or convexity of the glass panels.

Reflective Glass. After a graded wash was applied to the (masked) tower and then allowed to dry thoroughly, a light-colored pencil was used to delineate the window patterns.

Reflections that are light in tone can be applied as an unbroken mass over the entire building facade, with a darker-toned curtain wall or window frames applied over the first (dry) applications.

Reflections

Reflections bend or throw back the light images they receive from nearby sources. Reflective surfaces vary from water to smooth concrete sidewalks to smooth lacquered tabletops. Reflections follow basic rules of geometry. Although designers may alter these rules to suit their needs, they are important as an accurate base, particularly in realistic painting.

GUIDELINE 6
A reflection is a mirror image, altered only by the characteristics of the surface on which it is reflected.

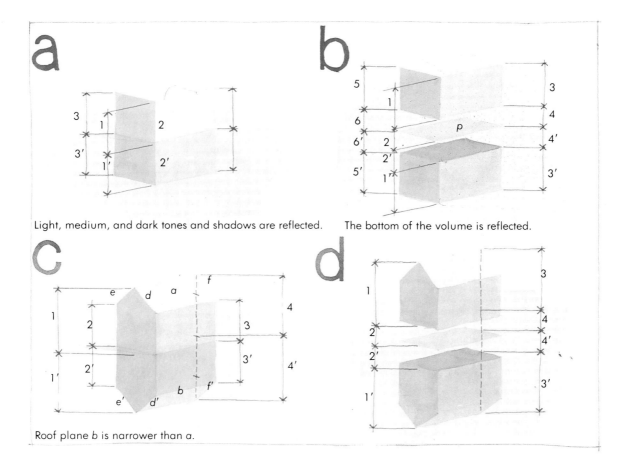

Light, medium, and dark tones and shadows are reflected.

The bottom of the volume is reflected.

Roof plane b is narrower than a.

The figure shows two volumes projected over a reflective surface. This example is based on a diagram by Arthur Guptill (1949) and denotes the basic rules of reflection as they apply to simple geometric volumes.

Reflection Diagram. The rectangular volume in sketch (a) is reflected in the mirrored surface, with its dimensions inverted exactly. Lines 1' and 1, 2' and 2, and 3' and 3 all are equal. In sketch (b), the same volume is raised a certain distance above the mirrored surface. The reflected image is lowered in the reflection by the exact same distance, thereby giving the reflected volume the same dimensions as the "floating" volume. If 2 and 2', 4 and 4', and 6 and 6' are the same measurements, then 1 and 1', 3 and 3', and 5 and 5' all are equal as well. Note that the bottom of the solid is reflected in the mirrored surface.

In sketches (c) and (d), rectangular solids with triangular prisms have the same reflective properties as do sketches (a) and (b), respectively, except that the angular roof planes are foreshortened in the reflection, causing b and c to be shorter in width than a, and d' and f' to be

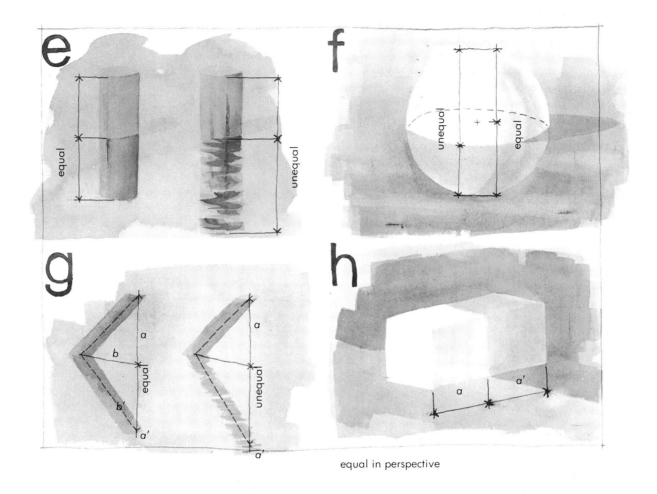

equal in perspective

shorter than *d* and *f* respectively. In sketch (e), the cylinder on the left is reflected equally in the calm surface, and its counterpart on the right casts a longer reflection, owing to the breaking of the surface.

Sketch (f) portrays a sphere in which the combined upper image and its reflections form a perfect sphere. Note that the reflection and the upper volumes are not equal based on the viewer's eye level.

Sketch (g) illustrates reflected angles with the same reflection distortion as in sketch (e). Sketch (h) is a vertical reflection of a cube, demonstrating that the laws of perspective apply as if the wall were not present; that is, lengths *a* and *a'* are equal only in perspective.

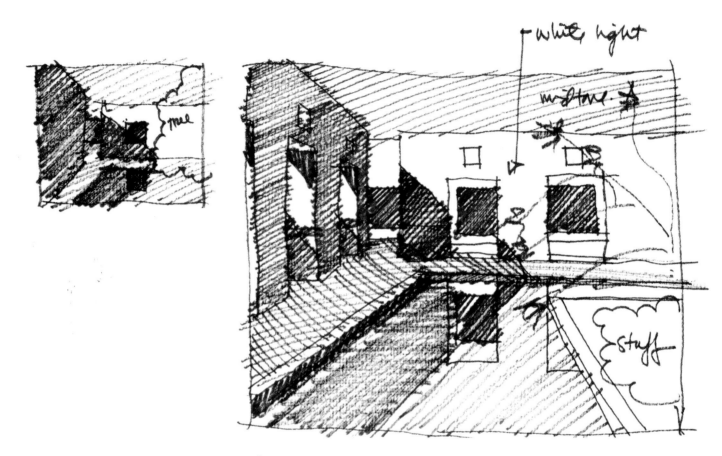

Reflection Tones

GUIDELINE 7
A geometric volume reflects its own image as an inverted identical image.

GUIDELINE 8
Each vertical line should be equally distant from its intersection with the horizontal baseline of that plane, in both the original object and its reflected image.

GUIDELINE 9
Both the object and its shadow—light and shade—are reflected.

GUIDELINE 10
The undersides of objects above the reflective plane are reflected on that plane.

GUIDELINE 11
The tones of reflections are darker than those of the object being reflected, owing to the addition of the reflective surface's local color.

GUIDELINE 12
An image's dimensions are distorted by the reflective surface. That is, a smooth

surface reflects a true inverted image, whereas a rough surface reflects a broken and distorted image.

GUIDELINE 13

The reflections of slanted objects are inverted images with the same angle, but their length varies according to the condition of the reflective surface.

GUIDELINE 14

A sphere's reflection should be measured from its center. A sphere's diameter, cut through the reflective surface, is an elliptical shape foreshortening the actual height of the reflection.

GUIDELINE 15

All reflections measured in the x or z plane are equal in perspective.

Reflection Pool

Reference

Guptill, Arthur L. 1949. *Color in Sketching and Illustrations*. New York: Reinhold.

Distorted Reflections

Buildings and Urban Forms

This chapter presents examples of buildings and urban forms that I illustrated in watercolor and mixed media. The examples range from presentation drawings to artworks. We shall discuss the objectives of each work, my overall approach and process, and any special techniques. Many examples are the various study sketches used in preparing the final work and, as such, should be viewed as guidelines for developing a personal style. As I stated earlier, I am interested in a speedy portrayal of ideas and concepts and so intentionally choose a loose style. Others may want more detail and precision.

Spokane Aerial Oblique

DESCRIPTION

The subject for this painting is the downtown Spokane core area situated on the Spokane River, site of the 1974 World's Fair. The complexities of the downtown offer the painter challenges of design, tonal and color emphasis, and detail (how much and how little?).

OBJECTIVE

The objective was to represent the key architectural characteristics of the downtown and how they relate to one another without becoming too preoccupied with detail.

CONSTRUCTION OF THE BASE DRAWING

The base drawing was assembled from an 8″ x 10″ aerial photograph in the following manner:

• A slide was made of the original photograph, which I took in my studio.

• Using the slide, I enlarged the image to the size I wanted and, using a Pentel marker, drew a massing sketch (see *Spokane Massing Sketch*).

• I then made a second sketch, using a tracing paper overlay, to correct any errors and to incorporate any features that I may have overlooked in the initial tracing (see *Spokane Overlay Sketch*).

• I made the final sketch overlay, the *Tone Sketch,* by using a Pentel sign pen and tracing paper to block out areas of importance and emphasis. I also used this sketch to develop urban design concepts in and around the central business district.

• Note that this sketch is a working sketch and does not need to be of presentation quality.

• Finally, I transferred the drawing to an imperial-size sheet of 140-lb Arches cold-pressed watercolor paper using a light table. If a light table is not available, during daylight hours, a window is suitable: Tape the watercolor paper over the tracing on the window. Applying graphite to the back of the sketch and tracing the sketch onto the watercolor paper is also effective, but it is easy to make graphite smudges on the watercolor paper, so be careful.

PALETTE

My palette consisted of Aureolin Yellow, Rose Madder Genuine, and Viridian as the base primaries and Winsor Blue, Alizarin Crimson, and Cadmium Red for highlights and darks.

STRATEGY

The *Spokane Aerial Oblique* is a complicated subject, composed of multiple buildings, a river–greenway system, and urban background clutter.

The focus of the painting became the core area of the downtown, represented by a number of key buildings connected by a pedestrian skywalk system and by the riverfront park, site of the Spokane World's Fair. In order to simplify the many components, I selected as the major shapes the dominant buildings, the riverfront, and the shadow of the core-area buildings.

Next, I determined the temperature of the components: I painted the key buildings and the riverfront in warm colors, contrasted by the cool blue-red shadows.

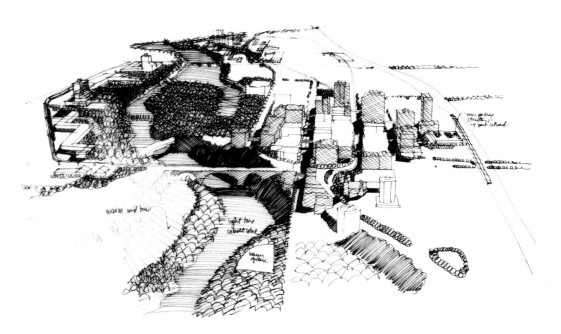

Spokane Massing Sketch. A massing study used also to assess tone (light and dark values).

Blue and orange are complementary or opposite colors and so provide a sharp yet pleasing contrast.

SEQUENCE AND TECHNIQUES

- I applied liquid masking to the roofs of key buildings to protect the desired white shapes.
- Then I applied a base wash of a warm gray to the entire sheet, providing a base for streets, unimportant buildings, and rooftops.
- I used glazing to define the general building shapes, using light tones of cool and warm grays and alternating them among the building shapes in a random pattern.
- Once I had defined the overall building pattern, I applied light warm tones of orange (Red Madder Genuine and Aureolin Yellow) to the key buildings.
- I roughed in with large washes the remaining background shapes and patterns, particularly the river–greenway area. When the base color application was complete, I glazed the key buildings again to sharpen their dominance.
- In the final stage, I darkened the river–greenway with an overwash of Winsor Green, Cadmium Red, and Aureolin Yellow. I then painted in the shadows of

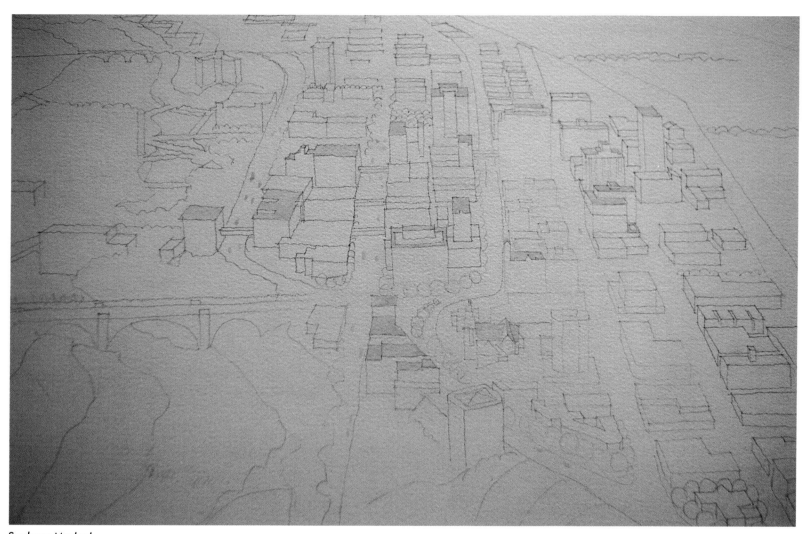

Spokane Masked

the core buildings and painted the street trees in greens, oranges, and yellows.
- I applied yellow and orange overwashes throughout the painting to increase its "glow" and to enrich the warm shapes.

- As shown in the final painting, I keyed the intense colors and mid- to dark tones into the focal area and relegated the weaker-intensity colors and light tones to the peripheral shapes.

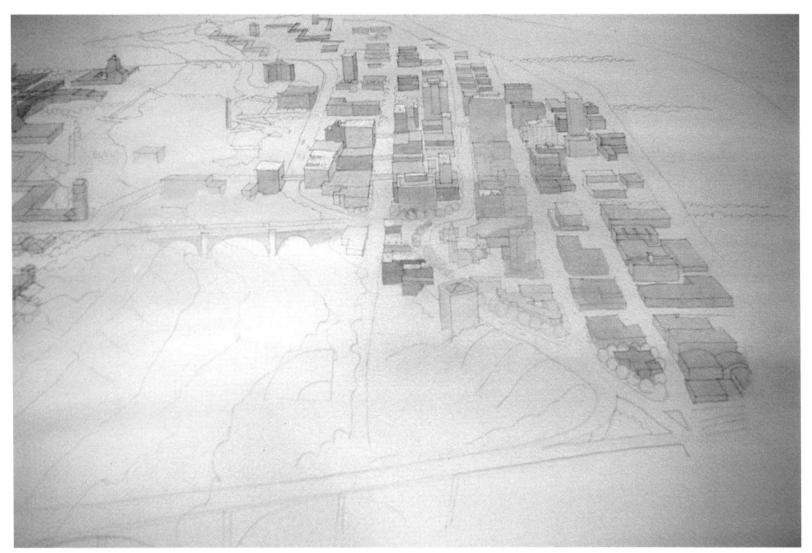

Initial Washes

Intermediate Washes

Spokane Aerial Oblique. The aerial oblique uses warm reds for the key buildings, highlighted by white rooftop shapes, thereby drawing the eye to the cluster of core area buildings.

Blowup of Core Area

Final Painting. The trees were painted in subtle mergings, protruding through the shadows to give direction and motion.

DESIGN

In many ways, the final painting of *Spokane* is a combination of a rendering and a semiabstract color statement of shapes and patterns. The watercolor design captured for the artist the key elements of downtown from the distant perspective of the view. Detail was not important. Massing, relationships of shapes, and the relationship of the core area to the river and far bank were considered the most important. Watercolor provided a rich, fluid medium in which to present the city and its key forms.

Downtown Yakima

DESCRIPTION

The two-dimensional "flatness" of a site plan often leaves much to be desired as a presentation exhibit. Pen and ink offer high-contrast patterns and sharp detail but are often limited to black-and-white contrast and a few shades of gray through cross-hatching. Color, on the other hand, can expand the two-dimensional image through temperature, chroma (intensity), and hue, providing contrast, warmth and coolness, and luminosity.

The retail core of Yakima, Washington, is composed of high-rise buildings, one- and two-story buildings, surface parking lots, and landscaping, all typical of medium-sized cities. To present this setting

and recommended design changes in an energetic fashion was an interesting challenge. I decided to highlight the key buildings in the warmest colors, lessening the warmth in relation to their importance (as I saw them).

OBJECTIVE

The objective was to portray the Downtown Yakima design changes in a unified pattern while emphasizing key architectural and urban design components.

STRATEGY

I used extensively both wet-on-wet and wet-on-dry methods throughout this illustration. Wet on wet was useful for the large washes, the larger building shapes, and where I wanted a consistent, unblemished wash. Wet-on-dry applications worked well in shadows, landscaping elements, and smaller building shapes.

SEQUENCE AND TECHNIQUES

- I used a light table to trace the image onto the watercolor paper.
- I soaked the paper in clear water, mounted it, and allowed it to dry and stretch.
- I used no masking fluid on this illustration.
- I applied two light-tone washes to the

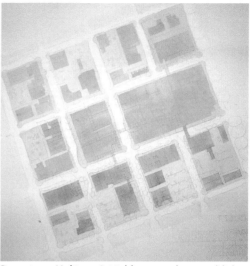

Downtown Yakima. Initial base washes establish temperature and color patterns.

entire surface area: an Aureolin Yellow wash followed by a wash of Cobalt Blue mixed with streaks of Rose Madder Genuine. These established a light neutral base for the road surfaces, with very slight variations in color.
- The next layer of wash was a light yellow application on each block, covering buildings, sidewalks, and so on.
- After this wash was dry, I glazed the buildings, overlaying two and three washes until the desired warmth and variation was achieved. I then intensified the key buildings using Rose Madder Genuine, Aureolin Yellow, and Crimson Red, all in separate applications until I

was satisfied with their luminosity, warmth, and prominence.

- Immediately before I glazed the key buildings, I gave each city block and its buildings a light green-gray wash to tone down the parking areas and low buildings.

- Details such as trees, the skywalks, and pedestrian arcade system I painted in mid- to dark tones. To draw some attention to the skywalks, I used a sharp knife blade to scrape away the light-exposed quadrant of each pyramidal-shaped section of the roof system.

- Finally, I added shadows of complementary blues to establish a sharp contrast among the buildings, pavement, and shadow.

- The surrounding city blocks I painted in cool to neutral colors to provide scale and setting in a noncompetitive manner.

Downtown Yakima. The final plan, high in key and warm dominance in temperature, focuses on key downtown buildings.

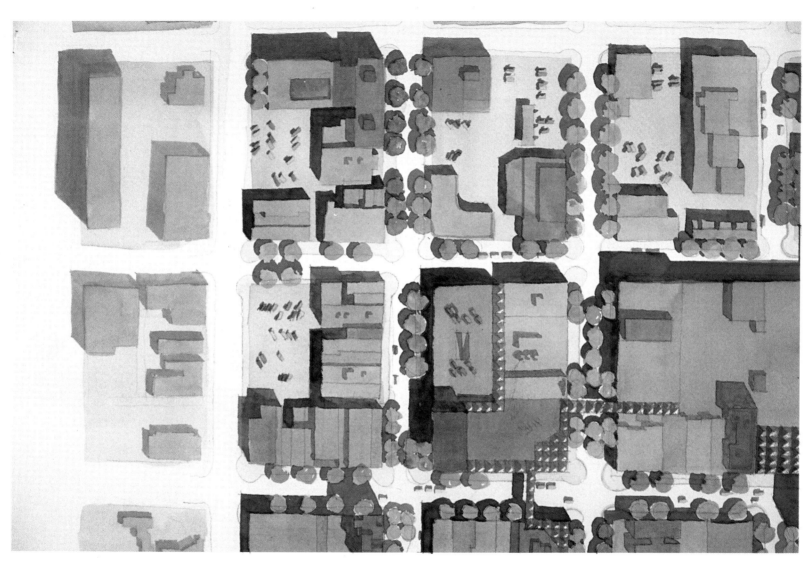

Retail Core Area

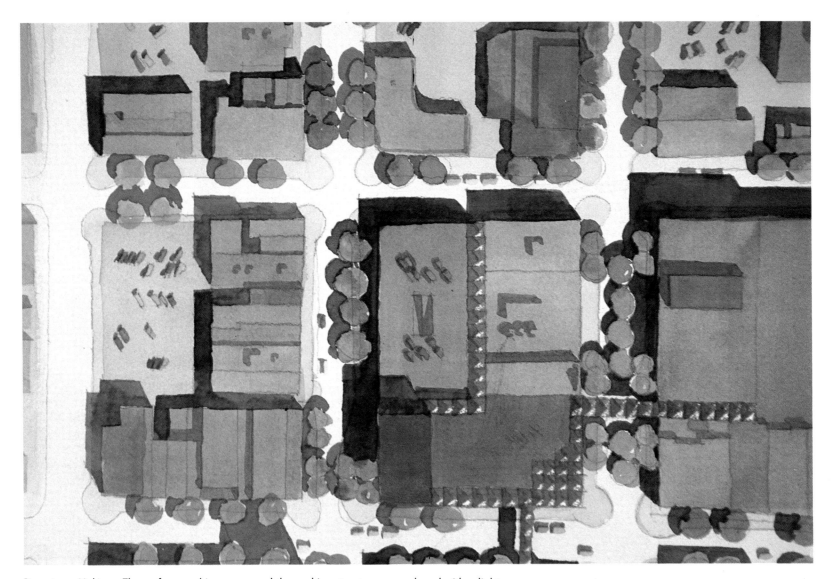

Downtown Yakima. The surface parking areas and the parking structure were glazed with a light Viridian wash to subtly recess their forms.

Riverwalk

DESCRIPTION

Riverwalk Waterfront Park is set against the lowland coastal hills of Washington State. The project serves as a visual gateway to the surrounding natural terrain and the Willapa River.

OBJECTIVE

The objective was to contrast the project and its geometry against the soft purple-gray background of the distant lowland hills.

STRATEGY

The project was designed as a colorful gateway to the riverfront. As such, the color relationship between the park structures and the natural background was considered important. Experiments in color ranged from near compatibles to complements, with the darker complements finally being selected.

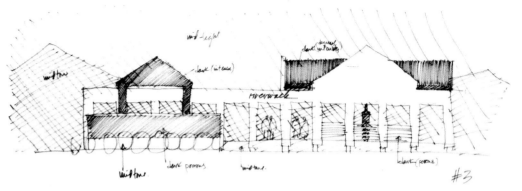

Riverwalk Tone One

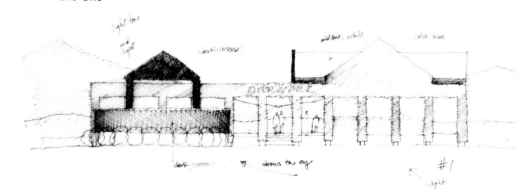

Riverwalk Tone Two

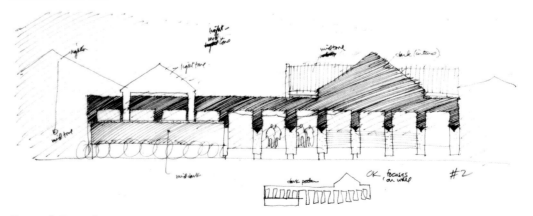

Riverwalk Tone Three

Riverwalk Masked

Riverwalk Unmasked

SEQUENCE AND TECHNIQUES

- I sketched the design freehand onto the watercolor paper using a light table.
- I soaked the watercolor paper in clear water, mounted it to the board, and allowed it to dry and stretch.
- I quickly prepared three tone sketches using tracing paper overlays and Pentel sign pens.
- I masked out the structure with tape and

masking fluid, and I roughed in the first cloud shapes with softened edges, using a wet-on-wet method.
- I formed the background terrain shape in the upper elevation using wet-on-dry washes of Viridian, Rose Madder Genuine, and Permanent Blue. When this first wash resulted in a darker, flatter effect than I wanted, I decided to alter the tonal arrangement of the painting, mak-

ing the background darker than originally planned and the structure entry wall lighter in tone.
- After the paint was thoroughly dry, I removed the tape and masking fluid.
- In the lower elevation, I painted the background lightly yet with an active sky pattern.
- I used Aureolin Yellow to glaze over each elevation sky to increase their brilliance.

Riverwalk Intermediate Stage

Shelter

Riverwalk (22" x 30")

Fort Lawton Historic District

DESCRIPTION

Fort Lawton is a historic district, the majority of whose buildings were scheduled for demolition by the city of Seattle. But the old military buildings—both as a collective form and as individual examples of architecture—were deemed salvageable by concerned citizens and professionals.

As a means of capturing the character of the historic buildings, I prepared this watercolor as part of a more expansive promotional document that was submitted to the Seattle City Council.

OBJECTIVE

The watercolor painting seeks to present the architectural character, scale, and detail of the historic Post Exchange and Gymnasium Building 733, constructed in 1905, in order to increase the public's appreciation of its architectural merits. The building is represented as an artifact that could be maintained as a vacant "prop," one unit in a collective historic district, or as a reusable space for the community's benefit.

STRATEGY

Two buildings became the focal point of the painting, one, the Post Exchange, more dominant than the other, the Band Barracks. The portico of the Post Ex-change building was selected as the center of interest and is located in the upper-left-hand quadrant, and the Band Barracks building has a subordinate yet central location.

The formality of the architecture was offset by a more informal landscape painted in a variety of subdued colors.

PALETTE

My palette consisted of Naples Yellow, Winsor Yellow, Viridian, French Ultramarine Blue, Permanent Blue, Rose Madder Genuine, and Indian Red.

SEQUENCE AND TECHNIQUES

- I masked out the building shapes with fluid (around all critical edges) and allowed it to dry.
- I washed in the sky color using a wet-on-wet method, which I carried into the foreground shape as well.
- While the sky was still wet—but after it had lost its sheen—I streaked Rose Madder Genuine into the wet blue wash.
- I applied the light tones and midtones to the buildings and foreground shapes. Once these early washes dried, I applied a series of glazes to all the shapes as a means of building up subtle light accents and plane changes. For example, multiple glazes within the window areas established depth in the interiors without creating too much contrast.

Barracks Buildings

- Shadow glazes were particularly important, as they helped define key architectural components.
- I added the dark tones last, using a combination of wet-on-wet and wet-on-dry methods, particularly for the vegetation. I used the dark backgrounds to pull out and define shapes in the vegetation and merged colors into the still-wet washes to provide variety of form without intricate detail.
- The darker washes on the grassed area in

Fort Lawton

the foreground used interlocking shapes, lost and found, and hard and soft edges.
- I painted the tree form, without foliage, with a half-inch flat brush, using predominantly warm grays.
- Last I painted reflections of local color from adjacent buildings on the concrete sidewalk surfaces, by using light-tone glazes of the building colors.

Gymnasium

Mercy Center

DESCRIPTION

The *Mercy Center* is an agricultural exhibition center and office complex located on a key downtown block in an eastern Washington city. The project consists of two mid-sized towers above an exhibition hall and retail plaza.

OBJECTIVE

The objective of the painting was to illustrate graphically the initial design concepts for the Mercy Center project and to show the relationship of the complex to the surrounding downtown and streets.

STRATEGY

The strategy for the painting was to draw attention to the temperature of the focal point and the tone of the surrounding cityscape. I selected a warm temperature and a light tone, respectively, to draw the viewer to the key buildings. The tone pattern included light tones for the surrounding background, foreground, and the outer edges of the midground; midtones for the landscaping elements throughout the painting; and dark tones for key shadows that highlight key building shapes. The three dominant vertical building shapes were deliberately kept warm so as to emphasize their importance.

PALETTE

Cobalt Blue

Naples Yellow

Aureolin Yellow

French Ultramarine Blue

Rose Madder Genuine

Cadmium Red

Viridian

SEQUENCE AND TECHNIQUES

- I transferred the image onto watercolor paper by using a light table. I developed the concept design images by means of multiple overlays on flimsy tracing paper.
- I applied a multiple-color wash to the sky shape using a wet-on-wet approach, with Cobalt Blue and Naples Yellow merging the two. I carried the yellow into the cityscape shapes with a graded wash until it "disappeared."

Mercy Center. The temperature dominance is warm, emphasizing the key downtown buildings.

Mercy Center. Light to midtone washes were used as an intermediate step.

- I applied a light-tone Cobalt Blue wash to all remaining landforms and cityscape shapes, to establish a base coolness.
- I layered all shapes except the three dominant vertical ones with warm and cool glazes to establish the midtone, weak-intensity background.

- I also layered the warm vertical shapes with at least three glazes, using Cadmium Red and Aureolin Yellow.
- Finally, I added the dark-tone shadows to establish contrast in both tone and temperature.

Mercy Center. Mt. Rainier has been "relocated" to add more drama to the composition.

Mercy Center. Even on the aerial oblique scale, the penetration of views into the building interiors was abstracted for additional depth of view.

Office Towers

DESCRIPTION

A composition (*Architecture,* January 1988) of three high-rise office towers provided an excellent subject for an experiment in cityscape painting.

OBJECTIVE

The objective of the painting was to highlight the primary tower in the midground area while incorporating two other towers in the background. The painting experiment explored techniques to represent facade details in a more semiabstract manner while retaining the scale and articulation of the facade designs.

STRATEGY

When planning this painting, I chose the rhythm and repetition of the window openings as an identifiable pattern to highlight. In order to experiment with this pattern in watercolor, I prepared a series of practice study sketches.

Pencil Study is a massing and tone sketch, exploring light tones, midtones, and dark tones. *Color Study One* is my first

Pencil Study. This sketch was completed on pencil-grade paper. It was a detailed graphic "thought" process to study form and detail.

experiment with watercolor in this series and explores color, temperature, and tone. *Abstracted Detail,* completed on pencil-grade sketch paper, investigates more abstract facade patterns. *Color Study Two,* on watercolor paper, tries to coordinate what I learned from the previous sketches regarding hue, temperature, and tone. I drew all of these sketches freehand in a spiral-bound watercolor sketchbook.

Abstracted Detail (8″ x 10″)

Color Study One (8″ x 10″)

Color Study Two (8″ x 10″)

SEQUENCE AND TECHNIQUES

- I used masking fluid and drafting tape to mask out the major shapes that protrude into the sky shape.
- Using a wet-on-wet method, I painted the sky shape with a monochromatic graded wash, carrying the wash into the foreground as a light tone.
- When the sky wash had thoroughly dried, I removed the masking.
- I applied warm, light-tone glazes to all of the major vertical shapes to establish a base hue.
- Based on the direction of the light, I glazed each medium to dark plane with enough pigment to create plane-change accents, lights, and mid-darks.
- With the base glazes established, I applied warm and cool grays, in the red and green hues, as wet-on-dry washes for façade elements (windows, mullion shadows, and the like).
- Last I added the darker highlights such as trees, vehicles, and shadows.

Sketch Study

Office Towers. A halo surrounds the top of the tower because of a back run that occurred under the drafting tape used to mask out the sky around the tower. Masking tape would have been a better seal. Also, a run from the green penthouse shape infiltrated the front facade area —not an unattractive effect—and so it was left in the painting.

Office Towers (22″ x 30″)

Second Tower

Market Fair

DESCRIPTION

Market Fair is an abstraction of a night scene portraying a lighted street framework and its accompanying signage.

OBJECTIVE

The objective of the painting was to communicate the contrast between the bright intense light of the signage and decorative lights and the dark of the silhouetted frame and the night.

STRATEGY

To carry out this objective, I had to establish the brightest or strongest intensity colors and protect them from the dark background wash. To do this, I laid the intense base colors first, followed by masking and then by the dark background washes.

PALETTE

Aureolin Yellow

Winsor Green

Cobalt Blue

French Ultramarine Blue

Cadmium Red

SEQUENCE AND TECHNIQUES

- I masked the small white highlights with fluid.
- I applied a base wash of Aureolin Yellow to the entire area of the painting and allowed it to dry.
- I used masking fluid to cover intense lights and lettering that I did not want to paint around.
- I applied a Cobalt Blue wash to the entire painting area and allowed it to dry.
- I used French Ultramarine Blue for the building framework and allowed it to dry.
- I applied a wash of Cadmium Red wet-on-dry, to Market Fair while the lights were still masked out and allowed it to dry thoroughly.
- I applied a final dark blue wash to the entire area, painting around "Princeton," and allowed it to dry thoroughly.
- I removed the masking fluid, thereby revealing the intended contrast of chroma between the lights and the background.

Market Fair (12" x 16")

Princeton. Masking and blue washes, before dark-tone overlay.

Picadilly

DESCRIPTION

I reconstructed *Picadilly* from my 1967 field notes taken in London. The challenge of the painting lay in the intimate coloration and chroma contrast of the advertising signs. It is an example of architecture as artform, as imagery seen only in the high contrast of the bright lights and the dark night. Conversely, during the day, the building was unsightly, poorly maintained, and unappealing to the trained and untrained eye.

OBJECTIVE

The objective of the painting was to capture the intensity of the colored lights against a dark background, while maintaining the complexity of the lights as an artform.

STRATEGY

I selected bright intense primary colors: Winsor Yellow, Winsor Green, Winsor Blue, Winsor Red, Grumbacher Red, and Alizarin Crimson. Note that they are staining pigments.

To deal with the intricate shapes, I had two options: first, to wash over all of the intense light-toned color shapes and to wash over the entire painting with dark tones, applying the intense colors last; and, second, to place the intense colors on the paper first, allowing them to dry, and then washing over everything with the dark washes. Because I wanted to vary the intensity and colors of the advertising shapes, I chose the second option, placing the intense colors first and then the darks.

PALETTE

Winsor Yellow

Winsor Green

Viridian

Winsor Blue

Winsor Red

Grumbacher Red

Alizarin Crimson

Picadilly (10″ x 17″)

SEQUENCE AND TECHNIQUES

- I masked out the desired white shapes with masking fluid.
- I applied the warm intense colors to the watercolor paper using a wet-on-wet approach and allowing the intense colors to merge together (not mix), thereby providing variation in the color pattern.
- After the previous washes had thoroughly dried, I applied masking fluid to the sign shapes.
- I applied the first large dark wash, using Winsor Blue as a base. I put on the wash wet-on-dry on the entire painting to achieve variation in the brush strokes.
- After the previous wash had dried, I applied a second variated wash to the building shape, providing a darker background, subtlely contrasting with the less dark sky and sharply contrasting with the signage colors.
- I applied the final dark washes to tertiary shapes such as dark cars and street elements.
- After all the washes had dried thoroughly, I removed the masking fluid.
- I strengthened the signage coloration with a No. 4 brush and by using graded monochromatic and graded multiple-color washes.

Mixed Media

Watercolor is an excellent match for India ink and quality sign pen markers using durable ink and provides a transparent and luminous contrast with the opaque black ink. This section illustrates examples of a mixture of pen and ink and watercolor.

Refreshing

Picadilly at Night

Jacob's Pillow

Jacob's Pillow is a competition illustration on a 43″ × 53″ 125-lb rolled sheet of watercolor paper. It was completed by me and Professor James Pettinari of the University of Oregon in a little under twelve hours. Once we established the design basics, we transferred the image onto the watercolor paper by means of a light table. We then fixed the paper to a rigid board, wet it, and left it overnight to dry and stretch.

We applied the watercolor just in large washes to define the background and key shapes. We then drew the details and design images in pen and ink over the dried previous washes. Next, we used glazes of watercolor and wet-on-dry applications to add highlights, shadows, brilliance, tone, and temperature. Most of the dark tones were created with pen-and-ink techniques.

Each image in this section is one segment of the overall painting, representing the site plan, aerial oblique and site diagram, and footprint image.

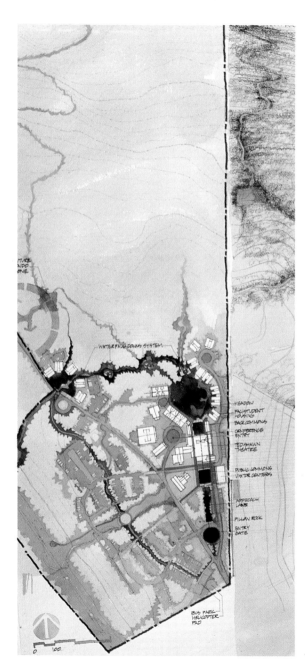

Jacob's Pillow (43″ x 53″ overall)

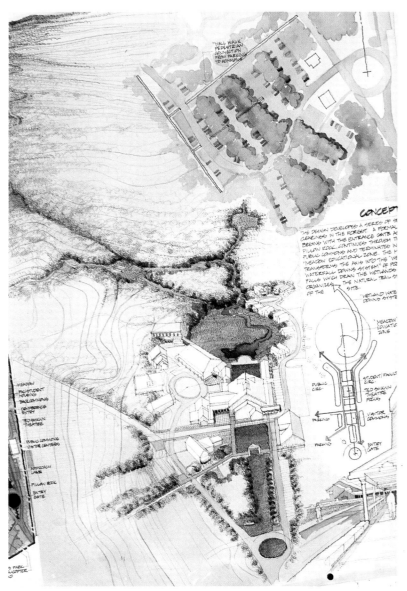

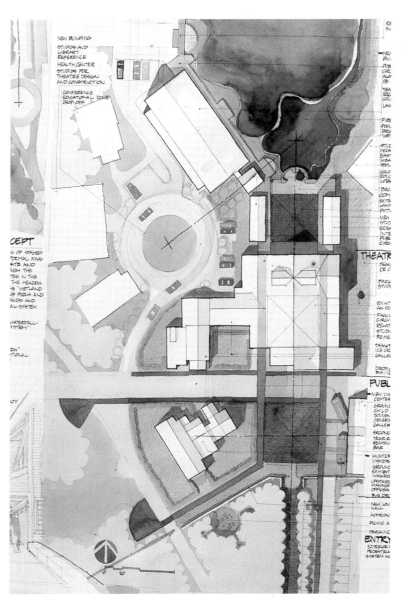

Mixed-Media Site Plan (43″ x 53″ overall). This was drawn with pen and ink on watercolor.

Site Plan

Haines Downtown Design

The small southeast Alaskan town of Haines provided an interesting backdrop for these fast mixed-media studies. I actually prepared some of these drawings on the Alaskan State ferry between Juneau and Haines, a four- and one-half-hour trip, using a small watercolor travel kit. I made the Haines drawings as follows:

- I drew design images on mylar with India ink.
- I made brownline diazzo prints from the mylars and mounted them on the illustration board with rubber cement.
- I applied watercolor washes to the background and building using wet-on-dry techniques and altering the color schemes for the Main Street buildings (three different color schemes were completed in this manner).
- I left the white board unpainted to highlight the highest building in town.
- I created the background contrast by adding dark greens to the tree line immediately behind the buildings.

Mixed-media techniques are useful for fast studies and for designers who want to use less-toxic color media, such as watercolor, without becoming involved with all of the overlapping relationships of tone using watercolor.

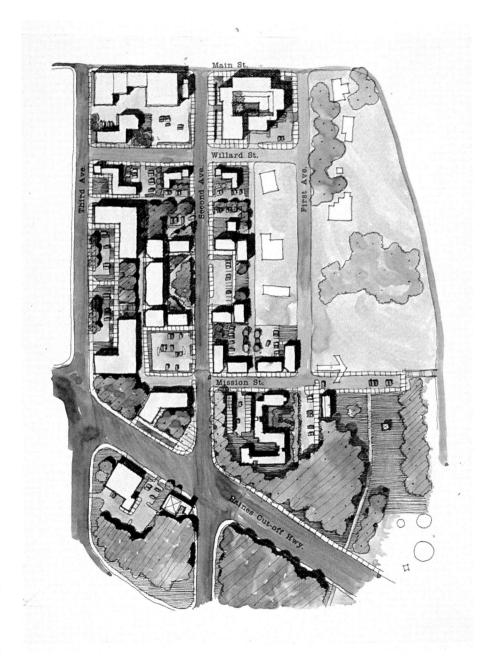

Haines Mixed Media (24″ x 30″)

Sketch Elevation (24″ x 30″)

Fast Color Studies for Building Facades. These were made in watercolor on brownline prints.

Color Study

MATERIALS AND EQUIPMENT

Pigments, Toxicity, Composition, and Permanence

Pigments

TYPES OF PIGMENTS

There are two common types of watercolor paints, generally referred to as *transparent* and *opaque*. Opaque pigments may also be called "opaque watercolors," "poster colors," "show-card colors," "mat colors," "body colors," "tempera," "gouache," "acrylics," or "new art powder colors." All have different characteristics, but all are soluble with water and all lack transparency.

Most painters prefer to select their own pigments. Pigments are available in many forms: small jars or bottles; cakes (or buttons) of numerous shapes and sizes; pans of glass, porcelain, or metal; sticks; papers coated with soluble pigments; jars of pigment in a powdered form known as new art powder and dry ground; and collapsible tubes. Of these, the cakes, pans, and tubes are the most common. Cake and pan colors are satisfactory if they are sufficiently soluble, and they are very convenient for outdoor sketching. They are most suitable for those occasional painters or designers who use only a little pigment at a time. A drawback is that they are often hard, requiring heavier brush pressure to release the paint. They may also become daubed or saturated with other hues. However, a wet cloth or rag drawn across the surface of the cakes usually removes other colors and residue.

Tube colors are moist, ensuring a fresh quantity of paint as needed. But over long periods of time, tube colors can harden. Care thus should be taken to keep the caps clean after use so that the tubes are not damaged by efforts to remove caps stuck on because of dried pigment at the tube mouth.

SIZES

Cakes, pans, and tubes are available in various sizes; most come in whole and half sizes. Ordering by mail can often be economical if sufficient quantities are purchased.

Toxicity

Over the last decade or more, there has been an increased awareness among professionals and educators regarding the potential hazards of artist materials used in the design process. *Toxicity* is one word that has concerned or confused many people who work with art materials, conjuring up visions ranging from the skull and cross bones of deadly chemicals to something more vague and unknown. Designers in particular should be increasingly aware and knowledgeable of the potential hazards present in the multitude of markers, inks, dyes, and other media used in their daily activities. Unfortunately, the demanding nature of creative work often leads to a neglect of the potential dangers of these workplace materials to artists and designers. Based on the information presented in this section, design professionals can develop a number of overall guidelines to assist their judgments in choosing materials to work with and in the manner the materials are utilized. The author would like to express his appreciation to Winsor & Newton and its Educational and Technical Services division for their information and review of the technical portions of this section.

DEFINITIONS

ASTM: American Society for Testing and Materials, a leader in establishing the *standard methodology for risk evaluation* presently used by major manufacturers in evaluating products for any potential adverse health effects that may be present in art materials.

ASTM D.4236: "Standard Practice for Labeling Art Materials for Chronic Health Hazards." This standard requires manufacturers to submit product formulations to an independent toxicologist who will then review them for potential chronic adverse health effects. Based on laboratory findings, the toxicologist may recommend warning and usage information. As a backup, a separate board of advisers reviews the toxicologist's work regarding the maintenance of proper standards.

ACMI: The Arts and Crafts Materials Institute. A body funded by manufacturers to promote the general health of the industry. ACMI has been in the forefront of developing the ASTM standard and is authorized to certify compliance with the standard via their certification bureau.

Toxicity: A toxic substance is a poison that causes illness or death when ingested or absorbed in small quantities. Toxicity can be divided into two categories for reference: (1) potentially toxic materials that can be handled safely as long as appropriate precautions are taken; and (2) high toxicity materials that should be avoided completely (Mayer 1985).

Chronic toxicity: A poison that adversely affects one's health over a long or extended time period is chronic in nature. Health hazards associated with chronic toxicity may not be experienced or become obvious for a long time and may be caused by persistent toxic effects that have developed from a single, prolonged, or repeated exposure to a toxic substance (ASTM D.4236).

Acute toxicity: A poison that adversely affects one's health immediately, or with a rapid onset following exposure, with obvious symptoms is acute in nature. It could be as simple as a rash appearing immediately after use or more violent than chronic toxicity symptoms including a fatal reaction. Warning labeling for acute toxicity is mandatory by federal regulations.

Labeling/certification: Manufacturers are authorized to display the Arts and Crafts Materials Institute's certification on their products following the institute's decision that the manufacturer has complied with the standards of ASTM D.4236. A new ACMI certified "health label," clearly and prominently designed, will replace the ACMI conformance label. *"No health labeling required"* is a phrase that appears with the ACMI conformance statement or seal if, within the terms of ASTM D.4236, the product does not warrant any specific warning information or special precautions. Certain manufacturers continue to use the ACMI "CP" or "AP" seals. Both these seals certify that products are nontoxic but are unsuitable for certain uses as they contain the phrase "nontoxic," which is illegal in many countries outside the United States. For this reason, most foreign manufacturers will use the health label seal described above. Since late 1988, during the transition period of label changes as described above, certain products will not have the ACMI conformance panel/seal. Individual manufacturer's technical information should be consulted for more information on health labeling. Finally, manufacturers are constantly refining the composition of their paints and the technical information regarding their potential hazards. Updated information can be obtained from manufacturers upon request.

If no ACMI seal or conformance panel is on a product, consult the following table for warning reference.

Artist Watercolors (WN) Warning Reference

Aureolin	H
Azure Cobalt	H
Cerulean Blue	H
Chrome Lemon	M
Chrome Orange	M
Chrome Yellow	M
Chrome Yellow Deep	M
Cobalt Blue	H
Cobalt Green	H
Cobalt Turquoise	H
Cobalt Violet	H
Cyanine Blue	H
Lemon Yellow	K
Manganese Blue	E
Permanent Mauve	D

Warning Reference
London Watercolors (WN)

Note: London brand is being replaced by modified and upgraded *Cottman*.

All Colors	A

Warnings

D Warning: Contains Soluble Manganese
E Warning: Contains Barium Manganate
H Warning: Contains Cobalt

K Warning: Contains Barium Chromate
M Warning: Contains Lead Chromate

Note: There are other warning references that apply to inks, dyes, and WN Artist Oil Colors that are not included in the list above but that may be referenced in Winsor & Newton's technical leaflet entitled "Health and Safety Information," L74 Issue #1 Effective 1/1/86 and subsequent updates. Write to Winsor & Newton, 11 Constitution Avenue, Piscathaway, N.J. 08854.

Bioavailability/solubility: Pigments are considered to be more hazardous to health if they are *soluble,* that is, capable of being dissolved or capable of being carried in solution, enabling the substance to be more easily introduced into the body.

The toxicity of heavy metal pigments (cadmium, lead, barium, etc.) is related to their *bioavailability* or the degree to which the toxic compound is available for absorption by the human body. The term *solubility* is often used to describe the level of bioavailability of a metallic compound within the pigment. Many potentially hazardous substances such as heavy metals are today *washed* to the point of being *insoluble* and therefore are not as readily available to the body as they would be in a soluble state. For example, cadmium (a metallic chemical element occurring in zinc ores) is not always listed as requiring hazardous labeling because it has been washed and made insoluble. Not all cadmiums, however, are insoluble.

POISON CENTERS

Local poison control centers are available in every state and in most communities. Their telephone numbers can be found in the Community Services section of most telephone directories.

SAFETY IN THE WORK PLACE

Assuming proper labeling of products' potential safety hazards by manufacturers, the final responsibility for safe use of products is with the user. When painting with watercolor, there are basic procedures and practices that if applied will greatly reduce or eliminate adverse health affects. These basic procedures and practices include the following:

- Do not eat, drink, or smoke while painting because paint substances can be transferred to the mouth from the hands.
- Wash hands thoroughly after painting.
- Keep brushes out of the mouth, especially avoid pointing the brush by wetting it with the mouth, as this can introduce paint residue directly into the body.
- Regardless of media, but particularly with those containing solvents, ventilate the workplace with adequate fresh air with a preferred exterior vented exhaust system.
- When working with mixed media containing solvents, *always without exception* put the caps or lids on containers or pens

immediately after use, particularly marker pens and other marker devices.

- If paint is transferred to the skin, wash it off thoroughly.
- Keep all professional paints, particularly those with chronic toxicity, out of the reach of children. The smaller body mass of children may not be as effective as adult bodies in dealing with toxic substances.
- When airbrushing, always use a NIOSH approved face mask or respirator fitted with the appropriate filters and/or cartridges.

OTHER MANUFACTURERS

Each manufacturer alters the ingredients of paints in efforts to improve and upgrade their painting characteristics. Therefore, while there are many similarities, the painter must also research each manufacturer for the important differences in product composition and potential safety and health hazards. The major manufacturers have labeling information and other guidelines for the use of their products.

Composition

Paint pigments are basically the same for watercolors, oils, and so forth. It is the material with which they are applied that creates a difference.

TERMS

Fugitive: Refers to colors that fade quickly.

Composition: The chemical makeup of pigments.

Permanence: Refers to the durability of a color after it is washed onto quality watercolor paper, framed in glass, exposed to ordinary daylight for a period of time (a number of years), and kept in a dry space. The framing should prevent the encroachment or introduction of "ordinary town atmosphere" (Winsor & Newton). Pigments likely to fade are considered semipermanent and borderline (Mayer 1985).

Lake: A pigment made by fixing a dye upon a base such as alumina hydrate for clear transparent lakes or blanc fixe for more body or opacity.

Gamboge: A gum resin derived from a tropical Asian tree and used as a transparent yellow pigment and a cathartic. It is not a true pigment color and is not reliable as a permanent color.

Stain: Refers to colors that adhere to paper and cannot be removed. Most colors are actually stains but some are far more persistent and so are labeled as stains.

Synthetics: Artificially manufactured pigments that characterize American and some European makes. The American synthetics are equal to or even superior to natural makes. Because of caution and exhaustive tests, only three synthetic organic pigments were universally adopted since 1950 (Mayer 1985).

COMPOSITION OF PIGMENTS

The following description of pigments was prepared by Winsor & Newton for use in the manufacture of their Artists' Oil, Water, Acrylic, and Alkyd Colors. The Color Index Name and Color Index Number of all pigments used in Winsor & Newton Artists' Water Colors, Artists' Oil Colors, Artists' Acrylic Colors, and Artists' Alkyd Colors is also provided. The Color Index is published by the Society of Dyers & Colourists, Dean House, Piccadilly, Bradford, Yorkshire. Copies can be found in the reference department of most major libraries.

Permanence

Winsor & Newton classifies its watercolors according to four levels of permanence: Class AA Extremely Permanent Colours, Class A Durable Colours, Class B Moderately Durable Colours, and Class C Fugitive Colours.

THE PERMANENCE OF ARTISTS' COLORS (WINSOR & NEWTON)

Class AA Extremely Permanent Colors
These are extremely stable colors under all ordinary painting conditions.

Class A Durable Colors
Durable colors are almost completely stable when used per se in full strength, and yet only as "Moderately Permanent" in thin washes, or glazes as the case may be, or in tints with the appropriate white; much also depends on the cumulative amount, and on the intensity and character of the daylight to which they are exposed. (Winsor & Newton, Notes).

While there is a sharp separation between "Extreme Permanent" Colors (Class AA) and other grades, there essentially is only an arbitrary separation for convenience between a "Durable" (Class A) and a "Moderately Durable" (Class B) or a "Moderately Durable" (Class B) and a "Fugitive" (Class C) Color (Winsor & Newton).

As a reference for artists, a four-category star system is used that generally aligns with the AA, A, B, and C category system used for the Artists' ranges.

**** = Extremely Permanent

*** = Durable

** = Moderately

* = Fugitive

CLASSIFICATIONS OF WINSOR & NEWTON'S ARTISTS' COLORS

Artists' Water Colors: Class AA

Extremely Permanent Colors

Azure Cobalt	Lamp Black
Blue Black	Lemon Yellow Hue
Burnt Sienna	Light Red
Burnt Umber	Oxide of Chromium
Cerulean Blue	Raw Sienna
Charcoal Gray	Raw Umber
Chinese White	Sepia
Cobalt Blue	Sepia, Warm
Cobalt Violet	Terre Verte
Davy's Gray	Venetian Red
Indian Red	Viridian
Ivory Black	Yellow Ochre

Class A Durable Colors

Alizarin Carmine	Manganese Blue
Alizarin Crimson	Naples Yellow
Antwerp Blue	Neutral Tint
Aureolin	Olive Green
Aurora Yellow	Payne's Gray
Bright Red	Permanent Blue
Brown Madder Alizarin	Permanent Magenta
	Permanent Mauve
Cadmium Lemon	Permanent Rose
Cadmium Orange	Prussian Blue
Cadmium Red Deep	Rose Dore
Cadmium Scarlet	Rose Madder Alizarin
Cadmium Yellow	Rose Madder Genuine
Cadmium Yellow Deep	Scarlet Lake
Cadmium Yellow Pale	Scarlet Vermillion
Chrome Orange	Ultramarine Ash Blue
Cobalt Green	Ultramarine Genuine (Lapis Lazuli)
Cobalt Turquoise	

Cyanine Blue	Vermillion			
French Ultramarine	Winsor Blue			
Gamboge, New	Winsor Emerald			
Hooker's Green Dark	Winsor Green			
	Winsor Red			
Indian Yellow	Winsor Violet			
Indigo	Winsor Yellow			

Class B Moderately Durable Colors

Chrome Deep	Purple Lake
Crimson Lake	Purple Madder Alizarin
Gamboge	
Hooker's Light	Sap Green
Prussian Green	Violet Carmine

Class C Fugitive Colors

Carmine	Mauve
Chrome Lemon	Rose Carthame
Chrome Yellow	Vandyke Brown

Painting Auxiliaries for Water Colours
Winsor & Newton Artist Materials (Catalogue)

Product Name	Main Purpose	Composition	General Properties	Influence on the Colour	To Be Thinned With	Packaging
Mediums (Water Colour)						
Aquapasto	A medium for giving an impasto effect to water based colours.	Gum Arabic/Silica	A translucent gel medium miscible with water.	Provides an impasto effect when mixed with water based colour.	Thinning not recommended, brushes can be cleaned in water. Use of a good quality brush not recommended as bristles can be damaged.	56 ml (No. 20) Tube
Art Masking Fluid	A liquid for masking areas of work to be protected when colour is applied in broad washes.	Rubber Latex/ Pigment	A material which when applied gives a water impervious film which can be easily removed by peeling or rubbing.		Thinning not recommended, brushes can be cleaned in water.	57 ml (No. 2) Bottle
Gum Arabic	One of the main binders in water colours.	Natural Gum/ Water/Preservative	A pale coloured gum solution.	Increases gloss and transparency of water colours.	Water	2 fl. oz Bottle

Painting Auxiliaries for Water Colours
Winsor & Newton Artist Materials (Catalogue)

Product Name	Main Purpose	Composition	General Properties	Influence on the Colour	To Be Thinned With	Packaging
Mediums (Water Colour)						
Gum Water	A binder of water colours.	Natural Gum/ Water/ Preservative/ Essential Oils	A pale coloured gum solution.	Increases gloss and transparency of water colours, with improved flow and wetting.	Water	2 fl. oz Bottle
Ox Gall Liquid	Wetting agent for adding to water colours. Improves the acceptance of water colours on paper.	Clarified Ox Gall	A pale coloured odourless liquid.	Increases the wetting and flow of water colours. Particularly useful for pale colours.	Water	25 ml (No. 1) Bottle
Prepared Size	Reduces the absorbency of paper, boards and light weight textiles.	Gelatine/Water Preservative	A soft gel which becomes liquid on warming.		Thinning not normally required. Clean brushes with warm water.	60 ml (No. 2) Pot
Raising Preparation	Provides an embossed foundation for illumination.	Pigmented highly bodied water colour paste.	A non-flowing paste which retains its form on drying and which becomes moist and tacky for accepting gilt when breathed upon.		Water can be added to reduce consistency.	14 ml (No. 0) Pot
Water Colour Medium	A water colour binder that improves the flow of water colours.	Acidified Gum/ Water	A pale coloured gum solution.	Improves the flow and wetting of water colours.	Water	57 ml (No. 2) Bottle
Water Matt Gold Size	Provides a flat foundation for illumination.	Pigmented hygroscopic gum solution.	A stiff paste which when applied becomes moist and tacky for accepting gilt when breathed upon.		Water	Whole Pans

Painting Auxiliaries for Water Colours
Winsor & Newton Artist Materials (Catalogue)

Product Name	Main Purpose	Composition	General Properties	Influence on the Colour	To Be Thinned With	Packaging
Varnishes (Water Colour)						
Fixative	Fixes pastel, crayon, pencil and chalk drawings.	Vinyl resin/ Methylated Spirit	Water white quick-drying liquid. Dries to a low sheen.	Protects pictures from smudging and dirt accumulation.	Thinning not recommended. Clean brushes with Methylated Spirit.	57 ml (No. 2) Bottle 150 ml (No. 5) Bottle 300 ml (No. 10) Bottle 500 ml (No. 20) Bottle 137 ml Aerosol 280 ml Aerosol
Modelling Varnish	Varnish for models painted with aqueous based colours. (Previously known as the Water Colour Varnish.)	Vinyl resin/ Alcohol and Glycol solvents	Water white quick-drying liquid. Dries to a semi-gloss film.	Protects models from smudging and dirt accumulation.	Methylated Spirit	57 ml (No. 2) Bottle

Pigments

WINSOR & NEWTON ARTISTS' WATERCOLORS

Color	Series	Product Information Codes
Alizarin Carmine	1	A (SL)
Alizarin Crimson	1	A (SL)
Antwerp Blue	1	A (SL)
Aureolin	4	A (SL)
Aurora Yellow	4	A (SL)
Azure Cobalt	3	AA (SL)
Blue Black	1	AA (SL)
Bright Red	1	A (SL)
Brown Madder Alizarin	1	A (SL)
Burnt Sienna	1	AA (SL)
Burnt Umber	1	AA (SL)
Cadmium Lemon	4	A (SL)
Cadmium Orange	4	A (SL)
Cadmium Red	4	A (SL)
Cadmium Red Deep	4	A (SL)
Cadmium Scarlet	4	A (SL)
Cadmium Yellow	4	A (SL)
Cadmium Yellow Deep	4	A (SL)
Cadmium Yellow Pale	4	A (SL)
Carmine	5	C
Cerulean Blue	3	AA (SL)
Charcoal Grey	1	AA (SL)
Chinese White	1	AA (SL)
Cobalt Blue	4	AA (SL)
Cobalt Green	4	A (SL)
Cobalt Turquoise	4	A (SL)
Cobalt Violet	4	AA (SL)
Crimson Lake	1	B
Cyanine Blue	1	A (SL)
Davy's Gray	1	AA (SL)
French Ultramarine	3	A (SL)
Gamboge Genuine	4	B
Hookers Green Dark	1	A (SL)
Hookers Green Light	1	B

Color	Series	Codes
Indian Red	1	AA (SL)
Indian Yellow	1	A (SL)
Indigo	1	A (SL)
Ivory Black	1	AA (SL)
Lamp Black	1	AA (SL)
Lemon Yellow Hue	3	AA (SL)
Light Red	1	AA (SL)
Manganese Blue	3	A (SL)
Mauve	1	C
Naples Yellow	1	A (SL)
Neutral Tint	1	A (SL)
New Gamboge	1	A (SL)
Olive Green	1	A (SL)
Oxide of Chromium	3	AA (SL)
Payne's Gray	1	A (SL)
Permanent Blue	1	A (SL)
Permanent Magenta	3	A (SL)
Permanent Mauve	3	A (SL)
Permanent Rose	3	A (SL)
Prussian Blue	1	A (SL)
Prussian Green	1	B
Purple Lake	1	B
Purple Madder Alizarin	1	B
Raw Sienna	1	AA (SL)
Raw Umber	1	AA (SL)
Rose Carthame	3	C
Rose Doré	4	A (SL)
Rose Madder Alizarin	1	A (SL)
Rose Madder Genuine	4	A (SL)
Sap Green	1	B
Scarlet Lake	1	A (SL)
Scarlet Vermillion	5	A (SL)
Sepia	1	AA (SL)
Terre Verte	1	AA (SL)
Ultramarine Ash Blue	5	A (SL)
Vandyke Brown	1	C
Venetian Red	1	AA (SL)
Vermillion	5	A (SL)
Violet Carmine	4	B
Viridian	3	AA (SL)
Warm Sepia	1	AA (SL)
Winsor Blue	1	A (SL)
Winsor Emerald	1	A (SL)

Color	Series	Product Information Codes
Winsor Green	1	A (SL)
Winsor Red	1	A (SL)
Winsor Violet	1	A (SL)
Winsor Yellow	1	A (SL)
Yellow Ochre	1	AA (SL)

AA Extremely Permanent Colors
A Durable Colors—generally sold as permanent
B Moderately Durable Colors
C Fugitive Colors
(SL) Selected List—colors with this designation may be mixed together without affecting their permanence

LONDON WATERCOLORS (STUDENTS' PIGMENTS)

The following thirty-five pigments are more economical alternatives for students and beginners:

Color	Product Information Code
Alizarin Crimson	B
Burnt Sienna	AA
Burnt Umber	AA
Cadmium Lemon	A
Cadmium Orange	A
Cadmium Red	B
Cadmium Red Deep	B
Cadmium Red Light	B
Cadmium Yellow	B
Cadmium Yellow Deep	A
Cadmium Yellow Light	A
Cerulean Blue	A
Chinese White	AA

Color	Product Information Code
Cobalt Blue	A
Cobalt Violet	B
French Ultramarine	A
Hookers Green Dark	B
Hookers Green Light	B
Indian Red	AA
Ivory Black	AA
Lamp Black	AA
Light Red	AA
Payne's Gray	A
Phthalo Blue	A
Prussian Blue	A
Raw Sienna	AA
Raw Umber	AA
Rose Madder	B
Sap Green	B
Sepia	AA
Terre Verte	A
Vandyke Brown	AA
Vermillion	B
Viridian	A
Yellow Ochre	AA

AA Extremely Permanent Colors
A Durable Colors—generally sold as permanent
B Moderately Durable Colors

ARTISTS' PIGMENTS—DRY GROUND

Dry-ground pigments are suitable for mixing with oil, alkyd, acrylic, or water. Be careful not to inhale the pigment dust or keep the dust in contact with the skin for long periods of time.

Color	Series	Product Information Codes
Alizarin Crimson (Crimson Lake)	1	A
Aureolin	3	A
Burnt Sienna	1	AA
Burnt Umber	1	AA
Cadmium Lemon	3	A
Cadmium Orange	3	A
Cadmium Red	3	A
Cadmium Red Deep	3	A
Cadmium Yellow Deep	3	A
Cadmium Yellow Pale	3	A
Carmine	—	C
Cerulean Blue	—	AA
Chinese White	1	AA
Cobalt Blue	3	AA
Cobalt Green	3	AA
Cobalt Violet Dark	—	AA
Flake White (Cremnitz White)	1	A
French Ultramarine	1	A
Indian Red	1	AA
Indian Yellow (Tartrazine Lake)	1	A
Ivory Black	1	AA
Lamp Black	1	AA
Lemon Yellow Deep	2	A
Light Red	1	AA
Manganese Blue	2	A
Mars Black	1	AA
Mars Yellow	1	AA
Oxide of Chromium	2	AA
Permanent Magenta (Quinacridone)	—	A
Permanent Mauve (Manganese Phosphate)	2	A
Permanent Red (Quinacridone)	3	A
Prussian Blue	1	A
Raw Sienna	1	AA
Raw Umber	1	AA
Rose Madder Genuine	—	A
Terre Verte	1	AA
Titanium White	1	AA
Ultramarine Dark (Permanent Blue)	1	A
Ultramarine Light (New Blue)	1	A
Vandyke Brown	1	C
Venetian Red	1	AA
Vermillion	—	A
Vermillion Scarlet	—	A
Viridian	3	AA
Winsor Blue	2	A
Winsor Green	2	A
Winsor Lemon (Azo)	1	A
Winsor Orange (Naphthol Carboxylic Acid)	—	A
Winsor Red (Anthanthrone)	—	A
Winsor Violet (Diaxazine)	—	A
Winsor Yellow (Azo)	1	A
Yellow Ochre	1	AA
Zinc White	1	AA

AA Extremely Permanent Colors
A Durable Colors—generally sold as permanent
B Moderately Durable Colors
C Fugitive Colors

NEW ART POWDER COLORS (WINSOR & NEWTON)

These powders are nontoxic substances mixed only with water to produce paint. They come in cans and are available in eighteen colors.

Color	Series
Brilliant Blue	2
Brilliant Green	1
Brilliant Orange	1
Brilliant Yellow	1
Burnt Sienna	1
Burnt Umber	1
Cobalt Blue	1
Crimson	2
Gamboge	1
Jet Black	1
Leaf Green	1
Lemon Yellow	1
Purple	2
Standard White	1
Turquoise	1
Vermillion	2
Viridian	1
Yellow Ochre	1

HORADAM WATERCOLORS

Horadam watercolors are made in West Germany by H. Schmincke and Company, which offers fifty-nine high-quality colors. The company has been in business since 1892 when Joseph Horadam invented the watercolors that bear his name.

Series 1

Brilliant Yellow Light	Opaque Green Light
Brown Ochre	Imitation
Burnt Sienna	Opaque White
Burnt Umber	Payne's Gray
English Red Deep	Permanent Green Light
English Red Light	Prussian Blue
Golden Ochre	Raw Sienna
Green Earth	Raw Umber

Indigo	Sepia Brown
Ivory Black	Vandyke Brown
Magenta	Vermillion Green Deep
Naples Yellow Reddish	Vermillion Green Light
Neutral Tint	Yellow Ochre
Olive Green	

Series 2

Brown Madder	Permanent Violet
Carmine	Permanent Yellow Light
Indian Yellow	Phthalo Blue
Madder Lake Deep	Phthalo Green
Madder Lake Light	Purple Violet
May Green	Sap Green 2
Mountain Blue	Scarlet Lake
Permanent Olive Green	Ultramarine Violet
Permanent Orange	Ultramarine Finest
Permanent Red 1	Viridian Glowing
Permanent Red 3	Viridian Matt
Permanent Rose	

Series 3

Cerulean Blue	Cadmium Yellow Deep
Cadmium Orange Deep	Cadmium Yellow Light
Cadmium Orange Light	Cobalt Blue Deep
Cadmium Red Deep	Cobalt Blue Light
Cadmium Red Light	

GRUMBACHER WATERCOLORS

Finest™ Professional Watercolors

Alizarin Crimson	III
Alizarin Crimson Golden	III
Brown Madder	III
Burnt Sienna	I
Burnt Umber	I
Cadmium Orange	I
Cadmium Red, Deep	I
Cadmium Red, Light	I
Cadmium Red, Medium	I
Cadmium Yellow, Deep	I
Cadmium Yellow, Lemon	I
Cadmium Yellow, Light	I
Cadmium Yellow, Medium	I
Cerulean Blue	I
Chinese White	I
Chromium Oxide Green	I
Cobalt Blue	I
Cobalt Violet	I
Davy's Gray	I
Emerald Green	II
English Red, Light	I
French Ultramarine Blue	I
Gamboge	II
Green Earth (Terre Verte)	I
Grumbacher Red (Naphthol Red AS-D)	II
Hooker's Green, Deep	II
Hooker's Green, Light	III
Indian Red	I
Indian Yellow	III
Indigo	I
Ivory Black	I
Lamp Black	I
Lemon Yellow (Hansa Yellow)	II
Manganese Blue	I
Naples Yellow (Hue)	I
Payne's Gray	I
Prussian Blue	I
Raw Sienna	I
Raw Umber	I
Rose Madder	III
Sap Green	I
Sepia Natural (Mineral)	I
Sepia, Warm (Mineral)	I
Thalo® Blue (Phthalocyanine Blue)	I
Thalo® Crimson (Quinacridone Crimson)	I
Thalo® Green (Phthalocyanine Green)	I
Thalo® Purple	III
Thalo® Red (Quinacridone Red)	I
Thalo® Yellow Green	II
Thio™ Violet (Thio Indigoid)	I

Finest™ Professional Watercolors

Ultramarine Blue (Permanent Blue)	I
Vandyke Brown	III
Vermillion, Deep	II
Vermillion, Light	II
Viridian (Vert Emeraude)	I
Yellow Ochre	I

Academy™ Watercolors

Alizarin Crimson	III
Burnt Sienna	I
Burnt Umber	I
Cadmium-Barium Red, Deep	I
Cadmium-Barium Red, Medium	I
Cadmium Orange	I
Cadmium Red, Light	III
Cadmium Yellow, Deep	III
Cadmium Yellow, Medium	III
Cadmium Yellow, Pale	II
Carmine	III
Cerulean Blue	I
Charcoal Gray	I
Chinese White	I
Chromium Oxide Green	I
Cobalt Blue	I
Davy's Gray	I
Emerald Green	II
Gamboge (Indian Yellow)	III
Geranium Lake	III
Golden Yellow	III
Green Earth (Terre Verte)	I
Grumbacher Red (Naphthol Red AS-D)	II
Hooker's Green, Deep	III
Hooker's Green, Light	III
Indian Red (Venetian Red)	I
Ivory Black	I
Lamp Black	I
Lemon Yellow (Hansa Yellow)	II
Light Red (English Red, Light)	I
Manganese Blue	I
Mauve	II

Naples Yellow Hue	III
Payne's Gray	I
Permanent Green, Light	II
Prussian Blue	I
Raw Sienna	I
Raw Umber	I
Rose Madder	III
Sap Green	I
Scarlet Lake	II
Sepia	I
Thalo® Blue (Phthalocyanine Blue)	I
Thalo® Crimson (Quinacridone Crimson)	I
Thalo® Green (Phthalocyanine Green)	I
Thalo® Red (Quinacridone Red)	I
Thalo® Yellow Green	II
Thio™ Violet (Thio Indigoid)	I
Turquoise	IV
Ultramarine Blue	I
Vandyke Brown	I
Vermillion	III
Violet (Thalo® Purple)	III
Viridian (Vert Emeraude)	I
Yellow Ochre	I

I—Excellent Lightfastness
II—Very Good Lightfastness
III—Moderate Lightfastness
IV—Fugitive

HOLBEIN WATERCOLORS

Holbein Watercolors are a Japanese product from Osaka and come in eighty-four colors of moist transparent watercolor.

Tube Colors
Holbein Artists' Watercolors (Extra Fine)

Series A—(50 colors)

Blue Grey	2
Burnt Sienna	3
Burnt Umber	3

Carmine	3
Chinese White	3
Cobalt Blue (T)	3
Compose Blue	1
Compose Green 1	1
Compose Green 2	1
Compose Green 3	2
Crimson Lake	2
Davy's Grey	2
Grey of Grey	2
Green Grey	Grey 2
Indian Red	3
Indigo	2
Ivory Black	3
Jaune Brilliant 1	2
Jaune Brilliant 2	2
Lamp Black	3
Lemon Yellow	2
Light Red	3
Naples Yellow	3
Neutral Tint	2
Olive Green	2
Payne's Grey	2
Peach Black	3
Peacock Blue	2
Permanent Green 1	2
Permanent Green 2	2
Permanent Green 3	2
Permanent Yellow Deep	2
Permanent Yellow Lemon	2
Permanent Yellow Light	2
Permanent Yellow Orange	2
Prussian Blue	2
Raw Sienna	3
Raw Umber	3
Rose Madder	3
Sepia	3
Terre Verte	3
Ultramarine Deep	3
Ultramarine Light	3
Vandyke Brown	2
Verditer Blue	2
Vermillion (T)	1

Violet Grey	1
Viridian (T)	3
Yellow Grey	3
Yellow Ochre	3

Series B—(13 colors)

Emerald Green	2
Hooker's Green	2
Manganese Blue	3
Mars Violet	2
Mineral Violet	2
Opera	1
Permanent Magenta	2
Permanent Red	2
Permanent Rose	2
Permanent Violet	2
Sap Green	2
Scarlet Lake	2
Turquoise Blue	2

Series C—(10 colors)

Cadmium Green Deep	3
Cadmium Green Pale	3
Cadmium Yellow Deep	3
Cadmium Yellow Lemon	3
Cadmium Yellow Light	3
Cadmium Yellow Orange	3
Cadmium Yellow Pale	3
Greenish Yellow	2
Indian Yellow	2
Viridian	3

Series D—(4 colors)

Aureolin	3
Cerulean Blue	3
Cobalt Blue	3
Cobalt Green	3

Series E—(5 colors)

Brown Madder	2
Cadmium Red Deep	3
Cadmium Red Light	3
Cadmium Red Orange	3
Cadmium Red Purple	3

Series F—(2 colors)

Cobalt Violet Light	3
Vermillion	3

Note: Each series refers to a price level, with Series A the most expensive and Series F the least expensive.

Artists' Cake Watercolors

Holbein offers twenty-four cake colors.

Series G—(24 colors)

Black	3
Burnt Sienna	3
Burnt Umber	3
Carmine	3
Cobalt Blue	3

Crimson	1
Hooker's Green	3
Jaune Brilliant	3
Lemon Yellow	3
Light Green	3
Magenta	3
Olive	3
Prussian Blue	3
Raw Umber	3
Sepia	3
Turquoise Blue	2
Ultramarine Light	3
Vermillion	
Violet	
Viridian	3
White	3
Yellow	3
Yellow Deep	3
Yellow Ochre	3

Durability or permanency ratings
3　Absolutely Permanent
2　Fairly Permanent
1　Not Permanent

Metallic Colors

Metallic colors are available in dry powders. Maimeri, an Italian manufacturer, produces six: silver, pale gold, rich gold, ducat gold, sequin gold, and copper.

Brushes

Composition of Brushes

Brushes are made up of brush hair (or synthetic fibers), a ferrule, and a handle.

Brush hairs are made from a variety of animal hairs, including Kolinsky red sable, goat, squirrel, ox, pony, camel, and hog (bristle). Synthetic fibers include nylon and other chemically produced fibers, sometimes mixed with natural hairs.

The ferrule is the metal tube fastening the brush unit to the handle. The ferrule is either seamless or seamed (soldered), and its size both determines the brush size and shapes it (round, oval, flat). The best ferrules are nickel-plated brass tubes (tapered, cylindrical, or seamless). The lesser-quality seamed ferrules can split if water and/or paint in the ferrule cause swelling.

Brush handles are most often made of seasoned hardwoods, woods that will not stretch or shrink, causing the ferrule to loosen. Handles are usually finished with enamel or varnish as a sealer.

The brush hairs are assembled from bundles premade in the exact amount needed to fill a ferrule. Shaping cups are used to mold the contour of the head or point of the brush. After the hairs are placed in the cup, it is tapped on a marble surface to bring all the hair tips into place at the outer surface of the head or point. High-quality brushes are tied with nylon at the root of the hair cluster before being inserted into the ferrule, and they then are trimmed at the butt end.

The brush is inserted tip first into the ferrule, measured for the correct exposed length (and proportion of hidden to exposed hairs), and cemented in place. Usually the exposed part of the brush is less than half the total brush length, giving it more spring. The ferrule is crimped at the brush end and the handle end to fasten it to the handle. If the ferrule ever loosens, use a nail and a small hammer to tap (not pound) indentations into the ferrule (without piercing it) to tighten it.

To make it easier to transport, the brush area is coated with a water-soluble gum arabic (a gum obtained from African acacias, used as a stabilizing emulsion).

Brush Classifications

Brushes can vary in width from one-eighth to two inches and are generally classified according to the following types:

- *Rounds*—brushes that are circular in cross section and come to a point at the tip.
- *Flats*—brushes that are rectangular in cross section, varying in width from ½″ to 2″.
- *Wash or Sky*—brushes that are rectangular in cross section, varying in width from ½″ to 2″.
- *Mop or Duster*—brushes with large thick heads extending 2″ from the ferrule. Oval shapes are also available, which form pointed tips when wet.
- *Aquarelle*—brushes that are flat and rectangular in cross section, varying in width from ½″ to 1″ and chiseled at an angle at the end of the handle, for scraping, burnishing, highlighting, and removing color.
- *Liner*—brushes that are used for calligraphy and line work and have a long fine point protruding from a round head.
- *Script*—brushes that are used in sign painting, are excellent for controlled lines, and are a long narrow round shape, available in many sizes.
- *Lettering*—brushes that are similar to script brushes in that they are a long narrow round shape, available in many sizes.
- *Fan*—brushes that are normally used for oils and acrylics, are shaped like a fan, and are useful for feathering dry or semidry washes.
- *One Stroke*—brushes that are wide and flat for fast broad washes. The Hake Series 1220 is available up to 6″ in width.
- *Bamboo*—brushes with bamboo handles and usually with round tips.
- *Travel*—brushes, usually round, that are small, compact, and collapsible, available in numerous configurations, and included in travel sets.
- *Hake*—brushes that are used in oriental paintings. They are flat, varying in width from ⅝″ to 6″. The wooden handles are attached with either metal ferrules or stitches.
- *Sumi*—brushes that have a core of stiff hairs surrounded by soft hairs. They are cone shaped, long, and pointed, and their sizes vary from ½″ x 2⅜″ to 1¼″ x 4¾″.
- *Calligraphy* (Japanese)—brushes with long round painted tips, varying in point diameter from ⅜″ to ⅝″.
- *Pipe* (Chinese)—brushes that are flat, similar to a hake brush but have a handle made up of small bamboo tubes, laid side by side.

Along with lasting durable pigments, brushes are an artist's most important tool. Today, many kinds of brushes are available, ranging from pure red sable to synthetics. Even though the cost of red sable brushes has risen substantially in recent years, there is no real substitute as yet for them. Artists should experiment, however, with the many substitutions on the market to determine their performance and durability. Each artist should own at least one sable. Many experienced painters use only a few key brushes, thus enabling them to purchase pure sable.

Brush Materials

SABLE BRUSHES

Quality sable brushes are made from Kolinsky red sable, a member of an Asiatic mink family. The brushes are made by hand and fastened with seamless nickel ferrules. The natural hairs are not the same diameter over their length but are thicker in the middle of the hair and thinner at the tip, providing a more versatile and flexible tip. The major manufacturers offer numerous grades of pure red sable brushes. Winsor & Newton produces seven different series of red sable brushes. Series 7 are round brushes ranging in length from 1½″ to ¼″, with size 14 the largest and size 000 the smallest. Series 8 are thinner brushes with longer points and come in sizes 4 through 000. Series 707 brushes are a less expensive alternative to Series 7 and are available in sizes 12 through 000. Series 33 brushes are red sable alternatives for students' use, in sizes 12 through 00. Other

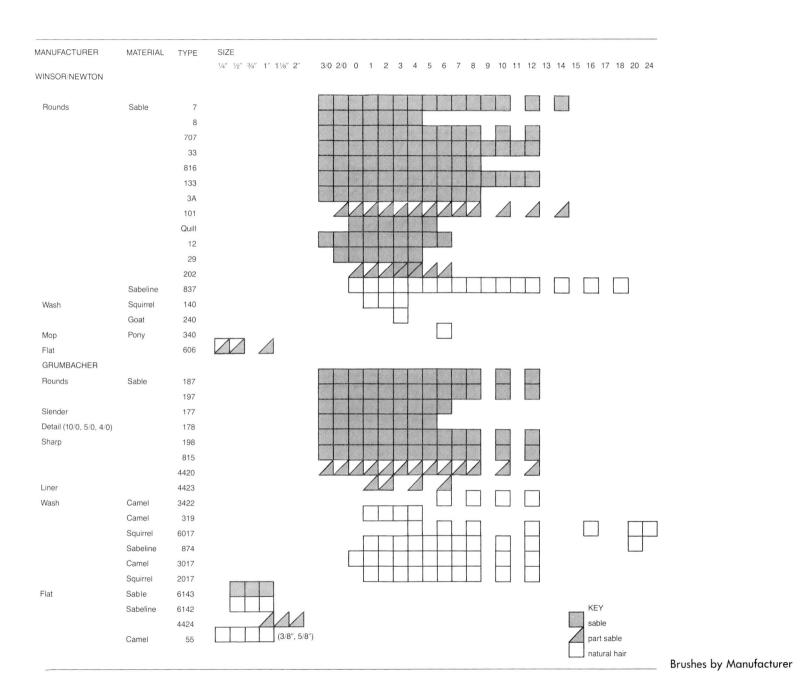

Brushes by Manufacturer

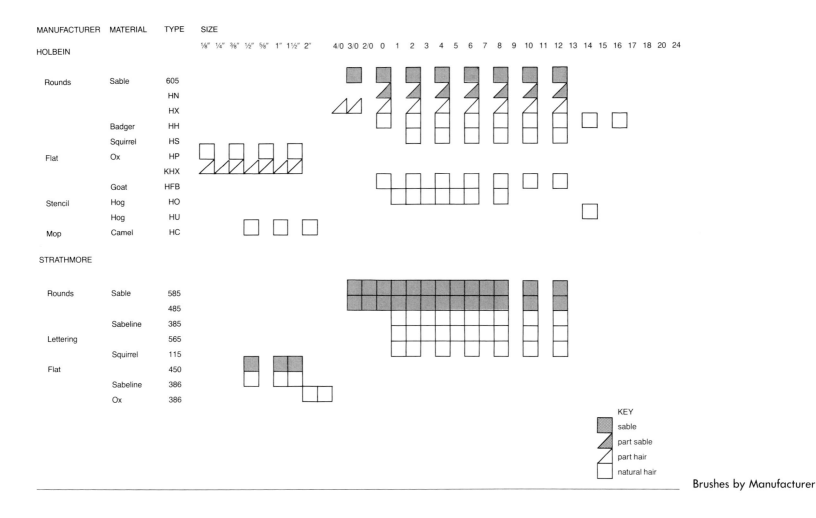

Brushes by Manufacturer

red sable Winsor & Newton round brushes include the thin and pointed Series 816 (8 to 000), Series 133 (12 to 000), and Series 3A (8 to 000); the fashion-design quill brushes (5 to 0); Series 12 (6 to 000) for fine delicate work; and Series 29 (4 to 00) for photographic spotting work.

Grumbacher also produces seven series of red sable brushes, ranging from sable rounds, Series 187, 197, 190, and 815, to flats and specialty brushes, such as Series 177 Graphic Arts and 178 Spot-rite for precision work.

NATURAL NONSABLE BRUSHES

Besides pure red sable hair, brushes can be made of squirrel hair (used in larger wash brushes), goat hair, combinations of pony and goat hairs, ox hair, badger hair, and camel hair. Many of these natural hairs are used in flat brushes, duster or mop brushes, and broader wash brushes. They are highly absorbent and do not have the "spring" or elasticity of sable hair brushes.

SYNTHETIC BRUSHES

Synthetic brushes can be economic alternatives to pure natural hair brushes. Each artist should experiment to determine his or her favorites. There are many available brands on the market.

The Winsor & Newton Series 101 "Sceptre" brushes and Grumbacher Sabeline Aquarelle and Sable Essence brushes are made with a combination of synthetic fibers and sable hair, called sabeline. These provide the bulk of my own brush supply and are available in sizes 14 through 000 in rounds and one inch to two inches in flats.

Nylon brushes in several sizes are available from Winsor & Newton, Holbein, Robert Simmons, and other manufacturers. Major distributors carry quality synthetics as well as sables from U.S. and European manufacturers. Consult your local directory.

Brush Care

The following guidelines are offered for the care of watercolor brushes, to prolong their life and to increase their effectiveness. These guidelines are based on interviews with artists and instructions from manufacturers (Winsor & Newton) and distributors (Daniel Smith, Inc.).

GUIDELINES FOR GENERAL CARE

- Never allow pigment to build up in the base of the hairs near the ferrule, as it cannot be removed once it hardens, and it will eventually ruin the brush. Therefore, always clean the brushes after each use.
- When resting the brush, do so in a place where the bristles or hairs are not pressing against any surface, so as to avoid damaging them.
- Charge brushes in water but never leave them in water.
- After cleaning the brush, wipe and shape it with your hand or a soft cloth.

- Dry all brushes thoroughly before storing them in closed containers. Otherwise they may develop mold and mildew. Moth damage is also possible if the container is left open—therefore, store thoroughly dry brushes in a tightly closed container.

GUIDELINES FOR CLEANING

- First rinse the brush in clear water.
- Lather up the brush by rubbing it on a cake of household soap (unscented), and continue to work up a lather by rubbing the brush in the palm of your hand. An alternative to using cake soap is to prepare a container of liquid soap and water, cool to lukewarm, and to dip the brush into the container to saturate the hairs (still use the palm of your hand to massage the lather into them). Avoid strong detergents.
- Dry brushes in a horizontal, not a vertical, position, so that water will not run down into the ferrule. Brushes can be placed on a paper towel, a brush holder, or a bamboo roll-up holder (which serves as a brush container when rolled up).

Chapter 14

Paper

Definitions and Terms

Acid free: Refers to paper that has a neutral pH below 7, usually between 6.5 and 7.0.

Buffering: The neutralizing of acid in the paper by adding an alkaline substance such as calcium carbonate or magnesium carbonate. A paper does not have to be buffered in order to have a neutral pH.

Cold pressed: Refers to mildly textured paper surfaces produced by pressing the paper through unheated rollers. Generally, it is the intermediate surface between rough and hot pressed.

Deckle edge: The natural fuzzy edges of handmade and mold-made sheets of paper, simulated in machine-made papers by "cut-

ting" them with a stream of water when still wet. Handmade papers have four deckle edges and mold-made and machine-made have two. The term *deckle* comes from the frame or board of the paper mold.

Fibers: Refers to the thread-like cellulose structures that form the paper.

Gampi: A vegetable fiber used in oriental papermaking that results in a strong, translucent sheet.

gm/m²: The European measure of weight for artists' paper. It compares the weights of different papers, each occupying one square meter of space, irrespective of the individual sheet dimensions.

Grain: Refers to the direction in which the sheet was made on the paper machine.

This may be important because the fibers of the sheet tend to run in one direction, occasionally causing problems in printing and binding. Handmade and mold-made papers have no grain direction.

Handmade: Refers to handmaking each sheet of paper by using a mold and deckle. It is a costly, time-consuming method that produces sheets without any grain direction.

High alpha: Refers to a nearly pure form of wood pulp. As a papermaking material, it has the same longevity as does any other cellulose, such as cotton and linen, because of its high purity.

Hot pressed: Smooth, glazed surfaces produced by pressing the paper through hot rollers after each sheet is formed.

Kozo: A tough vegetable fiber used by Asian papermakers. Makes strong absorbent sheets.

Laid: Refers to paper with a "chain" pattern running throughout the sheet. The pattern is determined by the mold used. Its counterpart is a wove sheet that has no chain pattern.

Machine-made: Refers to the method used to manufacture virtually all commercial papers. The machine is called a Fourdrinier machine. It makes a sheet very quickly, and the fibers point in a linear direction. Because it makes large quantities of paper quickly, this method does not offer much flexibility or variation.

Mold-made: Refers to an in-between process of papermaking, originally invented to simulate handmade paper by means of a rotating cylinder that slowly forms each sheet. This method is used to make Arches, Rives, many Fabriano papers, Dutch Etching, and other papers. No American company currently produces mold-made art papers.

pH: Refers to the amount of the hydrogen ion concentration of a water solution and substance, indicating acid or alkaline. A value of 7.0 is considered neutral.

Ply: Refers to the number of layers of paper, often laminated together to make heavier sheets, such as bristol boards and museum boards.

Rag: A term describing the nonwood products used in the manufacture of paper. Rag can be true rags, cotton linters, or other vegetable matter (hemp, linen, and so on). Rag papers can contain from twenty-five to one hundred percent of cotton fiber pulp. New cotton remnants from the garment industry are used in high-quality papers.

Rough: Refers to heavily textured surfaces produced by minimal pressing after sheet formation.

Sizing: The incorporation of gluelike materials in the sheet to control the amount of absorption of ink or paint. Sizing is a gelatin or cornstarch substance. Gelatin sizing can be applied with a brush and flows better when warm. Cornstarch is nontoxic and dissolves in cold water.

Sulfite: A term for pulp made from wood. It may have either a high acid or neutral content. A common misbelief is that sulfite sheets cannot be permanent.

Waterleaf: A paper with little or no sizing. It is very absorbent—a blotter is an obvious waterleaf paper.

Watermark: A design in the surface of the sheet created by sewing a thin wire to the mold during manufacturing, which makes the sheet thinner in that part so it is transparent.

Weight: Refers to either the European weight, grams per square meter (gm/m²), or the English weight, pounds per ream (lb/ream). The European method bases the weight of a paper on the weight of each sheet, measured in a square meter. The English method measures only the weight of the paper in a ream (five hundred sheets), regardless of its size.

Wove paper: Refers to paper that shows no fine lines running through the sheet when held up to light. This is a relatively modern invention. Until the eighteenth century, most paper was laid and showed "chain" patterns when held up to light. Most papers produced today are wove.

Source: Materials and Information for Artists, Vol.1/Reference Catalog 1988/1989, Issue No. 5, Daniel Smith, Inc.

Manufacturers

Most manufacturers and regional distributors furnish paper samples on request. The swatches in the packets are appoximately 4″ x 5″ or 3″ x 7″ and are an excellent way to test paper.

MANUFACTURERS BY NAME

Arches

Archival

Crescent (Board)

Fabriano

Gemini

Indian Village

Magnani

Morilla

Strathmore

Twinrocker

Waterform

Westport

Arches Watercolor Paper

Arches paper is one of the most popular watercolor papers on the market.

CHARACTERISTICS

- Made in France.
- Mold made, not machine made.
- Tub sized (i.e., "sized" or coated in a tub, by being dipped into a vat of animal gelatin).
- 100 percent rag.

SHEET SPECIFICATIONS

- 90 lb
  Cold pressed 22″ x 30″.
  Rough 22″ x 30″.
  Hot pressed 22″ x 30″.
- 140 lb (300 gm/m²).
  Cold pressed 22″ x 30″.
  Rough 22″ x 30″.
  Hot pressed 22″ x 30″.
- 260 lb
  Cold pressed 25½″ x 40″.
  Rough 25½″ x 40″.
- 300 lb (640 gm/m²).
  Cold pressed 22″ x 30″.
  Rough 22″ x 30″.
- 400 lb
  Cold pressed 22″ by 30″.
  Rough 22″ x 30″.
- 555 lb
  Cold pressed 22″ x 30″.
  Rough 22″ x 30″.
  12 sheets per carton, sold by the carton only.

Arches Watercolor Rolls

CHARACTERISTICS

- Made in France.
- 100 percent rag.
- Tub sized.

SHEET SPECIFICATIONS

- 140 lb (300 gm/m²).
  Cold pressed 43½ in. x 10 yds.
  Rough 43½ in. x 10 yds.
- 156 lb
  Cold pressed 51 in. x 10 yds.
  Rough 51 in. x 10 yds.
  Hot pressed 51 in. x 10 yds.

Arches Watercolor Blocks

CHARACTERISTICS

- Made in France.
- 25 sheets per block.

BLOCK SPECIFICATIONS

All block sizes come in cold-pressed, rough, and hot-pressed versions.

- 90 lb (cold pressed, rough).
  7″ x 10″.
  9″ x 12″.
  10″ x 14″.
  12″ x 16″.
  14″ x 20″.
  18″ x 24″.
- 140 lb (cold pressed, rough, hot pressed).
  7″ x 10″.
  9″ x 12″.
  10″ x 14″.
  12″ x 16″.
  14″ x 20″.
  18″ x 24″.

Arches Watercolor Boards

CHARACTERISTICS

- 90 lb paper mounted on board.
- 22″ x 30″.
- Cold pressed, rough, hot pressed.

Archival Student Watercolor Paper

CHARACTERISTICS

- 155 lb
- Cold pressed.
- 22″ x 30″.

Archette Watercolor Paper

CHARACTERISTICS

`
- 126 lb, 25 percent rag, neutral pH.
- 22″ x 30″.
- Cold pressed.

Fabriano Artistico

CHARACTERISTICS

- Made in Italy.
- 100 percent rag.
- Mold made, not machine made.

SHEET SPECIFICATIONS

- 90 lb (200 gm/m^2) cold pressed.
- 140 lb (300 gm/m^2).
  Cold pressed 22″ x 30″.
  Rough, cold pressed 22″ x 30″.
  Hot pressed 22″ x 30″.
- 300 lb (600 gm/m^2).
  Cold pressed 22″ x 30″.
  Rough, cold pressed 22″ x 30″.
  Hot pressed 22″ x 30″.

Fabriano Classico

CHARACTERISTICS

- 140 lb (300 gm/m^2).
  Cold pressed.
  27″ x 39″.
  Mold made, 50 pecent rag with 2 deckles.

Fabriano Esportazione

CHARACTERISTICS

- 147 lb (315 gm/m^2).
  Rough and cold pressed.
- 300 lb (600 gm/m^2).
  Rough and cold pressed.
- 100 percent rag, handmade, four deckles.

Indian Gray Watercolor Paper

CHARACTERISTICS

- Handmade
- 100 percent rag.
- Externally sized (relatively nonabsorbent when saturated with paint).
- 140 lb (320 gm/m^2).
- Rough 22″ x 30″.

Indian Burlap Paper

CHARACTERISTICS

- Handmade.

- Combination of cotton and jute.
- Externally sized.
- 140 lb (320 gm/m^2).
- Rough 22″ x 30″.

Magnani Acqueforti Watercolor Paper

CHARACTERISTICS

- Soft and absorbent.
- 100 percent rag, with neutral pH.
- 4 deckle edges.
- 140 lb (280 gm/m^2).
- Cold pressed.

Magnani Acquerello

CHARACTERISTICS

- Tub sized, hard.
- Mold made.
- 100 percent rag, with neutral pH.
- Cold pressed.
- 140 lb (280 gm/m^2), cold pressed, 22″ x 30″.
- 120 lb (280 gm/m^2), cold pressed, 19¾″ x 27½″.

Morilla 1059 Paper

CHARACTERISTICS

- Student-grade paper with small amount of rag.

Indian Village Watercolor Paper

CHARACTERISTICS

- Made in India.
- 100 percent cotton rag.
- Internally sized.
- Textures vary from sheet to sheet.
- Sheets do not lie flat as do machine-made papers.

SHEET SPECIFICATIONS
- 140 lb (330 gm/m²).
  Rough, cold pressed.
- 200 lb (400 gm/m²).
  Rough, cold pressed
- 300 lb (640 gm/m²).
  Rough, cold pressed.

Strathmore Watercolor Paper

(IMPERIAL) CHARACTERISTICS

- Made in Westfield, Mass.
- 100 percent cotton fibers.
- Machine made.

SHEET SPECIFICATIONS

- 72 lb (sheet, roll).
  Cold pressed.
  Rough, cold pressed.
  Hot pressed.
- 140 lb (sheet, block).
  Cold pressed.
  Rough, cold pressed.
  Hot pressed (sheet only).

(AQUARIUS II) CHARACTERISTICS

- Made in Westfield, Mass.
- Cotton and synthetic fiber combination.
- Machine made.

(AQUARIUS WATERCOLOR PAD)
CHARACTERISTICS

- Made in the United States.
- Rough (11¼″ x 15″, 15″ x 22¼″).
- 130 lb.
- Cotton and synthetic fiber combination.

(EXCALIBUR) CHARACTERISTICS

- Made in Westfield, Mass.
- 30 percent glass fibers and 70 percent cotton fibers.
- Rough surface.
- Machine made.

SHEET SPECIFICATIONS

- 80 lb (sheet).

(GEMINI) CHARACTERISTICS

- Made in Westfield, Mass.
- 100 percent cotton fibers.
- Machine made.

SHEET SPECIFICATIONS

- 140 lb (sheet, block).
  Cold pressed 22″ x 30″.
  Rough, cold pressed 22″ x 30″.
  Hot pressed (sheet only) 22″ x 30″.
- 300 lb (sheet).

  Cold pressed 22″ x 30″.
  Rough, cold pressed.
  Hot pressed.

MOLD-MADE CHARACTERISTICS

- Rough.
- 130 lb and 200 lb.
- Mold made with deckle edges.

Strathmore Watercolor Block

CHARACTERISTICS

- Made in the United States.
- 100 percent cotton.
- 25 sheets per block.
- Rough and cold pressed in 9″ x 12″, 11″ x 15″, and 15″ x 20″ blocks.

Twinrocker Feather Deckle Handmade Watercolor Paper

CHARACTERISTICS

- Exaggerated feather deckle.
- Circles and rectangles.
- 100 percent rag, neutral pH.
- Tub sized with animal gelatin, loft dried.
- Made in Indiana.

SHEET SPECIFICATIONS

- (All 400 gm/m²).
- Rough, cold pressed 10″ x 14″.
- Rough, cold pressed 16″ x 21″.

- Rough, cold pressed 20″ x 28″.
- Diameter, cold pressed 12″ and 18″.

Waterford Watercolor Paper

CHARACTERISTICS

- Made in Somerset, England, at St. Cuthberts Paper Mill.
- Internally and gelatine tub-sized paper.
- Cylinder mold-made paper with neutral pH.
- 100 percent long cotton fibers, acid-free rag.
- 4 deckle edges.

SHEET SPECIFICATIONS

- 90 lb (190 gm/m²).
  Cold pressed 22″ x 30″.
  Hot pressed 22″ x 30″.
  Rough 22″ x 30″.
- 140 lb (300 gm/m²).
  Cold pressed 22″ x 30″.
  Rough, cold pressed 22″ x 30″.
  Hot pressed 22″ x 30″.
- 260 lb (356 gm/m²).
  Cold pressed 22″ x 30″.
  Rough 22″ x 30″.
- 300 lb (638 gm/m²).
  Cold pressed 22″ x 30″.
  Rough, cold pressed 22″ x 30″.

Double elephant-sized sheets 26″ x 40″.
- 555 lb (638 gm/m²).
  Cold pressed 29½″ x 41″.
  Rough 29½″ x 41″.
- 1,114 lb (638 gm/m²).
  Cold pressed 40″ x 60″.

Westport Watercolor Paper

CHARACTERISTICS

- Made in Holland.
- Acid-free, mold made.
- 50 percent rag.
- Rough, smooth, 140 lb, 22″ x 30″.

Equipment

15

Easels

Easels are used for both studio and field-work. Because outdoor on-site painting is so important to the development of the designer's watercolor skills, an easel should be used that is mobile and lightweight.

In the field an easel (as opposed to a board on the lap) should be used for the following reasons:

- An easel permits the artist to move away from the painting to assess overall progress. If the artist remains too close to the work (as with a board on the lap), he or she may make mistakes in judgment re-

garding tone and intensity decisions. Working with a board (painting) on the lap also severely limits the artist's viewpoint and maneuverability.
- An easel is adjustable, thus permitting the artist to paint from either a horizontal or a vertical positioning of the work.
- An easel can accommodate water containers directly below the painting, permitting quick and easy access to water.

Easels are manufactured in woods (oak, beech, and so on) and metals. All fold up for storage. Some easels contain storage drawers for equipment, and others, such as the Mobil Easel, are designed to be turned,

tilted, and otherwise manipulated to assist in wet-wash techniques. Full-length and table easels are also available.

Manufacturers and/or distributors of watercolor easels are

Winsor & Newton

Eberhard Faber

Stanrite Aluminum Easels

Anco Wooden Easels

Holbein

Daniel Smith

M. A. B. E. F. Italian Wooden Easels

Art Boxes and Tins

Art boxes are not unlike fishing tackle boxes, designed to store many small items as well as larger and longer tools. There are many versions on the market, examples of which are

- Hardwood boxes (finished or unfinished) with a lift-out sectioned drawer.
- Aluminum (light and heavy gauge) boxes with mixing pans, suitable for carrying tubes, cakes, and pans.
- Black enameled boxes with a white interior.
- Small travel boxes (2″ x ¾″, 4″ x 2″, 2″ x 5″, 8¼″ x 4¼″) for pans.
- High-impact plastic multi-drawer boxes.

Saucers and Basins

Porcelain saucer sizes include small 2⅝″-, 3¾″-, and 3⅜″-diameter saucers with caps. They are available individually or in stackable "nests" (usually in sets of five).

CHINA BASINS

White porcelain basins, larger versions of the saucers, come with tight-fitting polyurethane lids. Sizes include 2¼″ deep x 6⁵⁄₁₆″ diameter, 2¼″ deep x 4½″ diameter, 2¹⁄₁₆″ deep x 3⅞″ diameter, and 2¹⁄₁₆″ deep x 2⅝″ diameter.

BRUSH WASHERS OR WATER WELLS

Brush washers or water wells are usually white porcelain containers, 5⅞″ to 6″ in diameter by 2″ to 2¼″ deep. The water well is divided into three compartments, one large—one-half the entire area—and two equal to one quarter of the area. Other wells may be rectangular with brush holders and come in porcelain and plastic, some with lids.

FLOWER WELLS

A flower well is a flower-shaped porcelain palette, usually with six cups clustered around a central cup. It has a total diameter of 5⅛″ to 7″, depending on the manufacturer.

Palettes

Watercolor palettes come in porcelain, plastic, and enameled metal. Enamel and porcelain surfaces are often preferred by artists over the plastic materials.

PLASTIC, PORCELAIN, AND ENAMEL PALETTES

Many variations of watercolor palettes are available from all the major manufacturers. The basic shapes include

- Fan palettes.

- Rectangular palettes with two or more larger mixing areas surrounded by pigment wells.
- Round palettes (10″ diameter) with two mixing areas in the center.

MIXING TRAYS

Mixing trays come in single-plastic-cup sizes (3⅝″ diameter is the most common) and in round and rectangular shapes with multiple mixing wells.

FOLDING PALETTES

Palettes that fold for easy travel are available in enameled metal and plastic. They are available with watercolor cakes, with partial cakes, or empty (for tube paints). I use an enamel metal folding palette in the studio as well as in the field.

BUTCHER TRAYS

The porcelain butcher tray is a traditional mixing tool for watercolorists. This simple tray is a basic, quality device that still has appeal. Even though chipping is a possibility for all enameled products, they still are durable and efficient.

MISCELLANEOUS PALETTES

White China or ceramic dinner plates make excellent inexpensive palettes.

Water Pails

Water pails are useful for indoor and outdoor watercolor painting. The handle permits the pail to be hung on a tripod directly below the painting when outdoors. They are available in plaster and metal, with plastic inserts available for the metal pails. Caution: Select only those pails that will not rust or contaminate the wash water in any way.

Masking Fluid

Masking fluid (also known as liquid mask, maskoid) is a rubber-cement-like substance that when dry, forms a temporary coating or mask on areas that the painter wants to paint over without painting on. The application can be with any instrument, such as brushes, pens, or even grass and twigs. If you use a brush select an old one that is no longer good for regular painting. Masking fluid is made from rubber latex and ammonia. It may be washed off with soap and water before it dries, but you must act quickly. If the fluid dries in the brush, clean the brush with rubber cement thinner followed by a soap wash. To remove the masking fluid from the paper, peel or rub off with dry clean fingers or a soft eraser (a kneaded eraser is preferred) or a ball or eraser made of rubber cement. Before applying the masking fluid to paper, experiment on a small piece if you have any doubt about the paper's strength. Soft

papers will not absorb fluid well, and images, such as from copy machines, will lift off from softer papers if masked over.

Many artists recommend that when painting in the field, the masking fluid be applied with a local instrument such as a twig or weed or other natural material. This adds a sense of connection between the place being painted and the painting.

Masking fluid is available with pigment (usually yellow) or colorless. A pigmented fluid is easier to see once applied to the paper.

GUM ARABIC

Gum arabic is the basic binding ingredient in transparent watercolor. It is primarily composed of natural gum, water, and preservatives. A small amount added to a watercolor thins it to a wash, enhancing its durability, luminosity, and transparency.

WATERCOLOR MEDIUM

Watercolor medium is a pale-colored gum solution composed of acidified gum and water that is added to watercolor to improve the flow of the solution. It is water soluble but should not be used with acid-sensitive pigments.

AQUAPASTO

Aquapasto is a transparent gel composed of gum arabic and silica that gives water-

color an impasto appearance, that is, as though it were thickly applied. The aquapasto does not require thinning, and brushes can be cleaned with water.

GUM WATER

Like gum arabic, gum water is a pale-colored solution of natural gums, water, and preservatives plus oils designed to increase the gloss, transparency, and flow of watercolors. It can be thinned with water.

OX GALL LIQUID

Ox gall liquid is a pale-colored, odorless liquid made from clarified ox gall (a fluid secreted by the liver and stored in the gallbladder). In its clarified state, it increases the flow and wetting of watercolors, acts as a surface-tension breaker, and can be thinned with water.

SIZING

Sizing is a gelatin compound that makes paper less absorbent. It is applied with a brush and is easier to spread if the container is heated in warm water for a few minutes. The brush strokes of the application will show through the transparent watercolor, a feature used to advantage by many artists.

WATERCOLOR DYES

Watercolor dyes are water soluble and suitable for camera-ready artwork, retouching, and coloring photographs. When used full strength, such dyes are brilliant in color and transparent when thinned with water. But they are not lightfast and should not be used for fine art work. Note that they are permanent and will not lift off when dry.

These dyes can be used with airbrushes, technical pens, crow quills, and ruling pens.

Winsor & Newton produces thirty-six watercolor dye colors, including six fluorescents. The black, white, gold, and silver all are made with pigments and are therefore more lightfast than are the other colors.

RULING PENS

A ruling pen is an important tool in the illustration of building materials and urban landscapes, owing to its flexible aperture. The pen enables the artist-designer to draw ultrathin lines or broad, one-eighth-inch strokes with watercolor. It is used for brick and stone masonry patterns as well as for shadow highlights when sharp crisp effects are desired.

A ruling pen consists of two metal parts connected by a threaded shank and control wheel. In its simplest form, it is a viselike device that permits a wide range of openings. The metal machined parts hold solutions such as ink and watercolor. The pen is loaded with an eyedropper or a well-charged paint brush. The pen may be used with a straight edge or freehand.

Working Surfaces

Rigid boards of various materials are used by watercolorists to hold watercolor paper in a way that reduces or eliminates its buckling. The materials used for rigid working surfaces include

Plywood

Masonite

Tile board

Plexiglass

Soft wood

For outdoor use and easy carrying, boards can be fitted on the back with a drawer handle, a sturdy rope, or a leather handle. The board should be cut so that it is one-quarter-inch larger on all sides than the standard paper sizes. This enables metal clips or tape to be used to attach the paper to the board.

If papers are to be stapled to the board (a common technique), it should be made of plywood. A quarter-inch thickness is light yet sturdy and will take gummed tape, staples, and paper tape (not desirable).

Blotters

Blotters, paper toweling, soft rags, and damp sponges are useful for blotting up excess solutions and drips and for lifting out washes for light highlights. Almost anything that is absorbent—that is, drier than the solution to be blotted—and that will not leave behind particle residue—for example, lint from rags—makes a useful blotter.

Sponges

Sponges are either natural or synthetic. The choice between the two types depends on the use and individual preference. Natural sponges have more elasticity than do the cellulose synthetics and last longer if maintained properly. If natural sponges are left moist, they will disintegrate.

Sponges vary according to pore size, ranging from large to very small pores. The most common natural sponge is the honeycomb.

Sponges are used for applying paint in larger wash techniques and for lifting out pigment already applied.

Three guidelines offered by Tony Couch (1987) summarize the characteristics of a sponge.

GUIDELINE 1
A sponge that is absolutely dry will not pick up any water from a painting's surface.

GUIDELINE 2
Conversely, a sponge that is saturated with water (thoroughly soaked) will not pick up any more water because it has no more room.

GUIDELINE 3

A damp sponge will pick up water because the small amount of water in the sponge will act as a capillary attraction, drawing water into the sponge's available pores. The uses for sponges include

- Wetting the paper with clear water in preparation for a wet-on-wet application of paint.
- Applying a wet pigment solution to the paper.
- Lifting out a wet solution from a solution already applied to the paper.
- Using the sponge as an intermediary between a water container and a palette or a palette and paper. A damp sponge will absorb excess water between the container and the palette as well as from the palette to the paper, giving the artist more control over the water in the brush than with the more traditional "flick-on-the-floor" method.

Painting Knives

Painting knives are used primarily to make fine, sharp-pointed images on paper, by pushing paint around or scratching lights into a wet painted surface. The painting knife's smooth surface does not retain water solutions well, and so it should be roughed up slightly with a file. Zolton Szabo (1974) uses a palette knife and scrapes the new lacquer finish off the blade with a razor blade or fine sandpaper. He

then soaks the blade in a vinegar (acid) solution for a few hours to remove the grease. Another method is to stick the blade into a lemon and leave it there for twenty-four hours.

Techniques using a painting knife include

- Putting paint onto the knife's tip from the palette and spreading the paint on the paper with the edges and flat tip of the knife.
- Once paint is applied to the paper, regardless of the method, using the flat part of the knife to spread the paint over the paper, by means of either a wet-on-wet or a wet-on-dry approach.
- Moving paint with the tip and edges of the knife into fine, detailed shapes, for example, grass, branches, and twigs.
- Scraping paint from a wet painted surface by scratching the wet paper with the sharp edge or point of the knife, to indicate, for example, grass weeds. This produces both darker and lighter impressions, depending on the paper's degree of wetness and the depth and width of the scratch.
- Using a dry-on-dry approach, mottling or spackling paint onto the dry paper for textured patterns.

Special Paper Effects

Plastic wrap and wax paper are used to create textures and patterns on wet surfaces. Some of these techniques were described by Barbara Nechis (1986):

Apply cut shapes of plastic wrap to freshly painted surfaces and press them down into the wet paint. After the watercolor paper has thoroughly dried, remove the wrap to reveal a textured pattern. This can be used to represent stonework and old marbled or heavily textured surfaces.

Waxed paper may be used as a stencil. The waxed paper is laid over the watercolor paper, and images are then drawn on it. The waxed paper imprints the image in wax on the watercolor paper underneath. Then when the watercolor wash is applied to the paper, a "ghost" image appears on the site of the wax imprint. This technique, when overwashed with a dark background tone, may be used to depict trees in the distance.

Wax Crayons or Candles

Wax crayons and candles are effective masking devices. The images are drawn onto the dry watercolor paper with the wax crayon or candle. Then after the paint has been applied and allowed to dry thoroughly, the wax is lifted off by placing a hot iron on a piece of flimsy tracing paper laid over the wax. The heat will melt the wax and make it stick to the flimsy paper.

Salt

Table salt and rock salt—fine and coarse grained, respectively—can be used to create textured effects. The salt is sprinkled onto a wet application and allowed to dry. The crystals soak up pigment, creating a white star-shaped image where the grain of salt rested. After the painting has dried thoroughly, the excess crystals are brushed off.

Straws

Some artists use drinking straws to move pigment around the paper, by blowing through the straw and directing the flow of the paint.

Toothbrushes

A toothbrush can be used to create spattering effects. When it is loaded with pigment, a thumbnail, credit card, or other stiff edge is used to flick the pigment from the brush onto the paper. The direction in which the brush is held is important. Remember to mask out those areas where the spattering effect is not desired.

TECHNICAL PENS

Technical pens are defined here as fine-pointed tips in holders that are available in thirteen tubular nib sizes. There are many brands on the market. Depending on the designer's use and habits, most of them are suitable for technical illustrations. Rough paper and freehand sketches will quickly wear out pen points. Tips are available in jewel tips and chrome-plated tips, with the jewel tips being the more durable (and expensive). I buy several brands because I am hard on all tips and so have to replace them often.

The Pelikan Graphos pen, still available through many art supply stores but unfortunately no longer manufactured, is one of the most versatile pen sets produced. The pen set is a nib system, with finely machined points available for fine line work or up to one-half-inch-wide solid, crisp-edged strokes. They are useful for watercolor as well as ink. I do not use the cartridge provided in the pen set, so as to avoid dried and clogging ink resulting from disuse. Instead, I use an eyedropper to place the needed amount of ink or color onto the nib itself. When that runs out (after a surprising number of lines are made), I refill it in the same way. This avoids dried solutions in the holding cartridge and nibs. To wash it, I simply swish the nib in clean water, remove it, and dry it.

Mounting Paper

Paper can be mounted in one of two ways: by clamping a loose, dry sheet of watercolor paper to a rigid board with metal clamps or by stretching a wet sheet of paper onto a rigid board by a number of methods, described next.

When stretching watercolor paper, it should be saturated, by soaking it in a bathtub for up to one-half hour. Remove the paper and lay it flat on the rigid board. Use either staples or gummed tape to fix the edges so that the paper will stretch tight as it dries. The paper should be mopped to remove excess water from the surface, enough to remove the high sheen. Staples should be spaced about one to two inches apart on all four sides.

Once it has dried, gummed tape may be removed from the paper and the board, by rewetting it and then carefully rubbing the wet tape off.

Dry stretching the paper is similar in that the dry paper is stapled or taped to the rigid board. The paper is then thoroughly wet with a large brush or sponge and allowed to dry and stretch. If the dry paper is painted on before it is wet, it will buckle.

The preferred method of stretching paper is the wet stretch, soaking or wetting both sides of the paper before it is fixed to the board. The artist can experiment to decide whether to soak it for one minute or thirty—both will work. Some artists believe that the longer soaking enables wet-on-wet washes to flow more smoothly.

Stretching frames are available at some art supply stores or can be made at home. Whichever you use, clamp the entire edge of the frame onto the watercolor paper, covering about one inch of paper on all four sides, and allow the paper to dry and stretch.

Staple Guns or Staplers

A staple gun or hand stapler strong enough to penetrate the mounting board is a handy tool in both the field and the studio.

Staples should be spaced around the outside edge of the paper approximately two inches apart. They may be removed with a pen knife or letter opener.

Metal Clamps

Metal clamps are devices used to hold the watercolor paper on the mounting board. They are available in many sizes and should be durable and capable of clamping over a sheet of plywood or plexiglass. They are excellent for fieldwork when using 140-lb or heavier paper. They can also be used to attach wash water containers to easels.

Dust Brushes

A dust brush is a hairbrush that is used to remove debris, such as eraser shavings and pencil graphite, from the surface of drawings. These brushes usually have wood bodies and horsehair bristles.

Matting Watercolors

Both for the presentation to clients and for the protection and preservation of the work itself, paintings should be encased in a glass or plexiglass facing. The air space between the transparent casing and the painting acts as protective insulation.

MATS

The mat is the border or outline around the painting. It is made of one or more layers of matboard placed over the painting, with an opening for the painting itself. The painting "floats" on or is affixed to a solid matboard in a manner not damaging to the watercolor paper.

MATBOARDS

For quality works and works presented to clients for long-term display, matboard should always be museum quality, acid free, and buffered. The most common matboard used is four ply ($\frac{1}{16}$″).

FRAME COMPONENTS

Mat window—The top of the overall frame; essentially a piece of matboard with the image area cut out.

Backing board—The bottom of the overall frame.

Mat—The mat window and the backing board connected by an acid-free gummed linen tape along one of the long edges. The connection or hinge is always attached along the longest edge, either the top or the side. This combined assemblage is referred to as the mat.

Margins—Experienced artists and framers recommend that the mat's top and side margins be the same in width but that the lower margin be wider by one-quarter to one-half inch. The rationale for this is that the eye will read the bottom edge as narrower if all margins are equal. Permit one-eighth to one-quarter inch of the mat to overlap the painting's image. Many artists then allow a mat margin of two to three inches around the painting, depending on its size. Always leave enough space at the bottom for a signature.

Mat burn—A brown discoloration of the watercolor paper resulting from inferior matboard and corner papers. If the original painting is on acid-free paper, the matboard should always be on museum-quality matboard. Ask for it when dealing with frame shops.

STANDARD HINGED MATS

The following steps describe the assemblage of a standard hinged mat and can be used for paintings with margins, deckled edges, and/or images that extend to the ends of the paper, that is, "bleed":

- The hinges should be made of handmade Japanese paper, which is thin, flexible, and made of long sturdy fibers. Use as few hinges as necessary to retain support.
- The hinge should always be weaker than the paper to which they are fastened. Then if stress is put on the hinge for any reason, the hinge will give way before the painting's paper.
- Use wheatpaste (cooked starch paste) to fasten the hinges. It is water soluble and can be removed later. In any case, do not use non-water-soluble pastes or glues or pastes that cannot be reversed (through wetting) after a reasonable time period. Do not use tape of any kind to attach paintings to hinges, as their glues over time will become non-water soluble and will require solvents to remove them.
- Construct the hinge out of a rectangular-shaped piece of Japanese paper with the edges torn, not cut, so that the feathered or ragged edge will have a higher structural or frictional value when fastened to the painting. The ragged edge should always be toward the painting. The edge facing the backing board need not be feathered. The reinforcing strip can also be cut.
- Long-fibered Japanese paper is feathered, or torn, by folding the paper along the line to be torn, placing a metal straight edge along the left and flat side of the fold, drawing a line of water on it with a size No. 000 to No. 2 brush, and, while wet, carefully tearing the paper by pulling it from the upper right-hand corner toward you, creating tension along the soaked edge and the straight edge.
- Prepare all of the hinges and reinforcing strips before working with the paste.
- Open the mat window and locate the painting's upper corners by positioning the painting where desired on the backing board (close the mat window to check for margin symmetry). Mark the upper corners lightly with pencil marks. Then pivot the painting with the axis along the top edge so that the painting is upside down but the top side and corners are still in place. Finally, weight down the painting and carefully erase the pencil marks.
- Before fastening on the hinges, place them on the backing board and the painting and lightly mark their corners with pencil, to determine their positions.
- Place the hinges on a blotter and apply the cooked starch paste to the entire surface.
- First attach the hinges to the back of the painting and then to the backing board, using the pencil lines as guides. As you do not want any of the hinges' creases or folds to show above the painting when it is in its correct position, make sure that the folds (before putting paste on them) are crisp and sharp.
- Now place the reinforcing strips over the hinges on the backing board (not on the painting) and cover them with a piece of mylar and a blotter. Weight them down and allow them to dry.
- After the paste has dried, place the painting in its correct position with the hinges at the top, close the mat window, and encase it in glass (see Weingrod 1987/1988).

CORNER MATS

Corner mats are useful for paintings that have margins. Their main advantage is that they do not require hinges or paste, and so the back of the painting is free of all adhesions. Their main drawback is the possible exposure of the corners through the mat window.

The corners are made of acid-free paper and should be large enough to hold the painting but not so large that they show through the mat window.

- Create four triangular corner "sleeves" by cutting four rectangles from the acid-free paper and folding each upper corner inward to the center of the bottom side.
- Locate the corners of the painting with pencil marks (as in the standard mat procedure), and remove the painting.
- Stick the four corner sleeves to the backing board with acid-free gummed linen, pressure-sensitive tape, or wheat paste, by applying the adhesive to the side of the corner sleeve with the folds. Place the corner sleeves (folds down) on the backing board, and burnish well; allow to dry or set.
- Insert the paper into the corners and close the mat window.

Premade mylar mounting corners are available in two sizes, ⅝″ and ⅞″, and have pressure-sensitive square tabs at the ends that adhere to the backing board.

SELECTING THE MAT

When selecting a mat, use the following guidelines: For light-value paintings, use a dark-value mat, and for darker paintings, use a lighter mat. The mat and painting should not compete. White or neutral-colored mats are always safe choices. White tends to open or make a painting larger, whereas a darker mat tends to frame or contain a lighter painting (Daniel Smith 1987/88).

LIQUITEX VALVE (TONE) FINDER

The Liquitex Value (Tone) Finder has nine scales, with two punched holes per scale to allow the designer to place the finder over a painting and evaluate its tone or value. It is available through

> Binney & Smith, Inc.
> Art Products Division
> 1100 Church Lane
> P.O. Box 431
> Easton, Pa. 18044–0431

(Liquitex is a registered trademark of Binney & Smith, Inc.)

References

Couch, Tony. 1987. *Watercolor: You Can Do It.* Cincinnati: North Light Books.

Nechis, Barbara. 1986. *Watercolor: The Creative Experience.* Cincinnati: North Light Books.

Smith, Daniel Inc. 1988/89. "Materials and Information for Artists," Volume 1: Reference Catalog. 1988/89, Issue No. 5.

Szabo, Zolton. 1971. *Landscape Painting in Watercolor.* New York: Watson-Guptill.

Weingrod, Carmi. 1987/1988. "Displaying Your Cut Work: Proper Ways of Matting." Daniel Smith, Inc. Full Catalog of Quality Artist Materials.

Manufacturers and Distributors

Winsor & Newton, Inc.
555 Winsor Drive
Secaucus, N.J. 07094
Canadian Distributor:
Anthes Universal Ltd.
341 Heart Lake Road So.
Brampton, Ontario L6W 3K8

Holbein (of Osaka, Japan)
c/o Artists' Mediums, Inc.
P.O. Box 756
Williston, Vt. 05495-0410

Grumbacher
Engelhard Drive
Cranbury, N.J. 08512
Canadian Distributor:
M. Grumbacher (Canada), Inc.
460 Finchdene Sq.
Scarborough, Ontario, Canada M1X 1C4

Sakura of America (Watercolors)
30470 Whipple Road
Union City, Calif. 94587

Da Vinci Paint Co., Inc.
11 Goodyear Street
Irvine, Calif. 92714

H. Schmincke & Co.
GmbH & Co. KG
Postfach 32 42
4006 Ekrath 1

Strathmore Paper Company
Westfield, Mass. 01085

Arches
Arjonari
Prioux S.A.
3, Rue Du Pomp De Lodi
Paris, France 75006

Aiko's
Art Materials Import
Japanese Papers, Dept. B
714 N. Wabash
Chicago, Ill. 60611

Waterford/Backingford Papers
G-P Inveresk Corporation
St. Cuthberts Paper Mill
Wells
Somerset BA5 1AG

Whatman Paper Limited
Maidstone
Kent, England

Twinrocker Handmade Papers (Organic)
Dept AA
P.O. Box 413
Brookston, Ind. 47293

The Morilla Co., Inc.
211 Bowers Street
Holyoke, Mass. 01040

Liquitex (Liquitex is a registered
trademark of Binney and Smith, Inc.)
c/o Binney and Smith, Inc.
Art Products Division
1100 Church Lane
P.O. Box 431
Easton, Pa. 18044-0431

Utrecht Manufacturing Corporation
33 35th Street
Brooklyn, N.Y. 11232

Sennelier Watercolors
Savoir Faire
Dept. AA
P.O. Box 2021
Sausalito, Calif. 94966

Marx Brush Mfg. Co., Inc.
403 Commercial Avenue
Palisades Park, N.J. 07650

Robert Simmons Inc. (Brushes)
45 West 18th St.
New York, N.Y. 10011

Isabey (Brushes)
Dept. AA
La Brosse et DuPont
3 Milltown Court
Union, N.J. 07083

Luco (Brushes)
Leo Unifelder Co.
420 S. Fulton Avenue
Mt. Vernon, N.Y. 10553

Yasutomo & Co. (Oriental Brushes)
235 Valley Drive
Brisbane, Calif. 94005

Fezandi & Sperrle (Dry Pigments)
Division of Tricon Colors Inc.
16 Leliarts Lane
Elmwood, N.J. 07407

Perma Colors Division (Dry Pigments)
1626 East Boulevard
Charlotte, N.C. 28203

Daniel Smith Inc. Art Supply
4130 1st Ave. S.
Seattle, Wash. 98134

New York Central Art Supply
Dept. AA98
62 Third Ave.

New York, NY 10003

Arthur Brown & Bro., Inc.
P.O. Box 7820
Maspeth, NY 11378

Art Supply Warehouse
360 Main Avenue
Norwalk, Conn. 06851

Pearl AA
308 Canal Street
New York, N.Y. 10013

Pro Arte
Box 1043
Big Timber, Mont. 59011

Tom Lynch
P.O. Box 1418A
Arlington Heights, Ill. 60006

Sax Arts & Crafts
P.O. Box 51710/Dept. A2
New Berlin, Wis. 53151

Crescent (Mats and Boards)
P.O. Box XD
100 W. Willow Road
Wheeling, Ill. 60090

Graphik Dimensions Ltd.
Dept. AA
41-23 Haight Street
Flushing, N.Y. 11355

American Frame Corporation
1340 Tomahawk Dr.
Maumee, Ohio 43537

Stu-Art (Frames)
2045 Grand Ave
Baldwin, N.Y. 11510